Circle of
Sawdust

Circle of Sawdust

A Circus Memoir of Mud, Myth, Mirth, Mayhem, and Magic

ROB MERMIN

With illustrations by
Karen E. Gersch

Rootstock Publishing

Published by Rootstock Publishing
an imprint of Ziggy Media LLC
Montpelier, Vermont 05602
info@rootstockpublishing.com
www.rootstockpublishing.com

Softcover ISBN: 978-1-57869-156-2
Library of Congress Number: 2023915479

Cover art: Big Top with Caravans (oil on canvas) by Eric Hesketh Hubbard (1892-1957), image courtesy of Laing Art Gallery, Newcastle-upon-Tyne, UK Tyne & Wear Archives & Museums / Bridgeman Images.

Book design by Mason Singer of Laughing Bear Design

Author photo by Melissa Mermin

For reprint permissions or to schedule an event with the author, contact Rob Mermin at robmermin@gmail.com.

*To the traditional circus folk I have
encountered, past and present,
as well as contemporary circus folk—and all
the idealistic young adventurers and dreamers!*

Contents

Prelude:
Circle of Sawdust

When the circus packs up its tent and travels in the middle of the night, the grassy lot leaves little trace that a circus had ever been there. The only sign is a faint circle of sawdust in the middle of the field where the ring had been. If you stand in that circle after the circus has moved on, you feel a shaft of energy that lingers for a few days and suffuses the air with smells of popcorn, sawdust, hot dogs, cotton candy, and the pungent scent of mud, manure, hay, and animal musk.

If you close your eyes, you can summon up faint sounds of children laughing; squeaky rubbery balloons; the excited after-show chatter of the audience wandering out into the night; the ringing hammer of sledge loosening heavy iron tent stakes; trucks being loaded with bleachers, poles, and canvas. It is the echo of the circus, come and gone.

If some youngster wanders out and happens to stand inside that magical circle of sawdust, who is to say they might not catch a whiff of wanderlust as the wind swirls around and plants a sense of adventure into their daydreams...

Introduction

WELL OVER FIFTY YEARS AGO, I RAN OFF TO JOIN THE CIRCUS. As a young lad, I had gotten it into my head that circus clowning was a way to travel and earn a living making children laugh.

This book tells the story of my adventures.

I have quoted throughout from nineteenth century memoirs written by circus proprietors, and from newspaper articles of the era, as well as entries from Ringling Bros. Route Books, the daily journals of their tours from one end of the country to the other. In a time before radio or television, the circus was America's main form of entertainment. Those old-time stories from towns across the country bear witness to my own experience. I can only laugh and marvel at the timeless nature of the culture and traditions of circus.

I recently discovered a short black-and-white home movie—from the early fifties, filmed at a backyard picnic. It's a perfect example of a clown act for the circus ring. No sound. Just visual comedy.

Setting: large grassy backyard of rural home.

Props: a picnic table, a large beach ball, one small rubber ball, a short ladder propped against one end of the table.

Players: children of various ages, the oldest perhaps six, the littlest, age two or three.

Action: The older kids stand in a line on top of the table. First kid, a girl, rolls the beach ball down the inclined ladder. As it bumps along the rungs, she jumps off the picnic table and runs around to get the ball and toss it up to the next kid in line on top the table, who rolls it down the ladder as the first kid runs around to climb up to the end of the line.

Several kids repeat this game nonstop, rolling the beachball, running back around, climbing up again, laughing, giggling.

The littlest one observes this fun from below. He holds a small rubber ball in two pudgy hands and decides he wants to play too. As the others jump down and run around fast and step back up to the table, he slowly and clumsily climbs, first up to the picnic bench almost his own height, then carefully edges up to the top of the table and gets in line.

Finally, it's his turn: he looks down to the ground—far below! He cautiously lets go of his little rubber ball to roll down the ladder. But instead of bouncing on each rung, the little rubber ball just falls to the grass through the first one. Plop!

Perplexed, the boy looks down for a moment and then, on hands and knees, laboriously climbs back down to the bench, one foot at a time, and then to the ground. Meanwhile, the others ignore him and keep running in a circle back up to the table, making three round trips by the time the little one gets down, picks up his ball, and slowly climbs back up to wait his turn again. This little comedy routine is repeated for ten minutes.

There are several reasons why this is an example of a classic clown routine. Let's say the picnic table and yard represent the circus ring. The camera is the audience. The children are the young circus performers with skills for jumping, climbing, running, cartwheeling, tossing, and catching balls—athletes, if you will. All except for the little one, the baby clown who just observes and then decides he wants to join the game.

We see his little brain thinking, as he waddles over to the picnic table: Why not, looks like fun, let's have a go at it. He is determined to meet the daunting challenge of climbing the table.

The comic timing comes in the pace of the action, the contrast and interplay between the characters, and the serious intention of the little guy. The rhythm is fast and joyous, set by the older kids, juxtaposed against the slow earnestness of the little clown amidst all the commotion. It's not unlike Buster Keaton standing stone-faced in the midst of a hurricane.

The main character is perplexed but undeterred by his failures. The more he tries to succeed, the funnier it gets each time the ball plops straight down after such a laborious effort. We know it's hopeless, amused by the clown's oblivion. We also appreciate the kindness of the other kids who let him play. They don't mock him; they leave him in his own world to figure things out. The little clown doesn't know he is being funny, doesn't realize we find humor in his very human attempts, over and over again, to solve the simple problem confronting him. He doesn't show frustration at all. He just perseveres at repeating the same mistake, having faith that surely one time it will work. We laugh: here he goes again!

At one point the older sister kindly takes the little ball away and hands him the beachball. It is bigger than he is but he manages to push it down the ladder—bump, bump, bump—and the girl hands him back the little rubber ball.

The other kids continue their play. The littlest boy stands at the back of the picnic table watching. Then, not wanting to just do what everybody else is doing, he once more waddles forward with his little ball, determined to play his own game. Plop goes the rubber ball straight down. He looks at the camera. The end.

It's a hilarious parody of the perplexity and naivete—and stubborn determination—of the human experience. The flickering film only shows a few minutes of my foolhardy attempts before my dad, the cameraman, cuts to the rest of our backyard family barbecue. My older sister Sheila was the sympathetic little girl.

Even now I smile at the persistence of the little solo clown among that group of normal kids. I cannot explain how I got the notion to run off and join the circus. But maybe that long ago game of roll-the-ball, my first true clown act, contains a clue to my character.

I grew up under the influence of classic adventure literature—stories of Robert Louis Stevenson, Mark Twain, Jules Verne, H.G. Wells, H.C. Anderson, Dumas, Dickens, Huck Finn, Robin Hood. These were tales of fate and hardship and travel and dreams of romance. They spoke to the childhood yearning—grownups called it daydreaming—to go somewhere else, do something different, see new things and—as grownups would say—make something of yourself.

For me, it meant stepping out on the path of adventure to overcome self-doubts and timidity, explore the world, and strive to be true to my own instincts and dreams. This all seemed like practical advice to a young idealistic mind. Finding a circus might be a way...

Growing up in New England in the 1950s, I read in *National Geographic* about traditional family-owned circuses still thriving in Europe, where clowns were respected as artists and large family dynasties passed on the circus culture for seven generations. I would run off to Europe to find a circus and apprentice myself to a famous clown to learn the trade.

★

The effect of a circus experience on a child's imagination can be profound. The year just before I took off to look for a circus, I was visiting the Italian family of my high school sweetheart, Jenny. Her grandfather, Poppy, was a slight gentleman in his eighties with white hair and white mustache, a gentle manner, and a thick old-world Italian accent. I was always happy to be invited over for spaghetti with meatballs the size of baseballs and converse with Poppy as he sat back, smoking his pipe.

After one of those dinners, as we waited for the homemade Italian pastries and pudding, Poppy looked over at me and asked what I was up to...any plans for the summer? I hesitated to say anything about flying over to Europe to join a circus, knowing how silly it would sound. But then he said: "Now, tell me, boy...do you have a dream?" He gestured with a hand spiraling up to his head, as if making some dream visible.

I blurted out, "Well, actually, I...um...I'm planning to run off and find a circus and be a clown...and learn to make children laugh. My dream is to someday have my own circus."

Poppy's eyes crinkled, "Mio Dio! Clown, eh?" He took on a distant look, chuckled and said: "I remember, when I was just a little bambino—maybe eight or nine years—a circo came to our village once every year. Fantastico! One clown...aiee! So funny!" He chuckled at the memory.

I asked, "Do you remember his act, what he did in the ring?"

He looked at me, still smiling, "Si, si...of course, why not?" (I remember thinking *Jeez, that's over seventy years ago...*) Poppy proceeded to describe the act, between fits of chuckles and animated gestures. You could tell he was reliving the moment fully.

He recounted how the clown entered the ring, tripping over his big flappy shoes, and started to climb a rope ladder to get to the trapeze, got halfway up the swaying ladder, but his big clown shoe got caught and wouldn't come loose, and he slipped and hung upside down by his ankle, caught in the rung, his bulky plaid jacket caught too—and then his hat got stuck over his face!

Poppy kept laughing at the image in his mind, and everyone at the table laughed together at his laughter, charmed at his child-like delight.

I asked if he remembered the name of the clown. No, he couldn't remember the name of the clown, nor the circus—but it didn't matter. I appreciated that an unnamed clown had made him laugh after seven decades. It appealed to my introvert personality: uncomplicated anonymity surpasses the burden of fame.

I was even more determined, now, to run off and find a European clown to apprentice with and learn how to make kids laugh for a living. I had no model for this path. The large extended Mermin clan—my father was one of ten children, dubbed The Mermin Decagon—were lawyers, doctors, teachers, psychologists, and other socially minded professionals. We loved the "original ten" for their intellectual wit, good-natured sense of humor, and political conscience.

What a marvelous circus dynasty they could have made! The Merminsky Troupe! I picture my innumerable Jewish aunts, uncles, cousins debating issues of nonprofit contracts while tossing juggling clubs in the ring, my favorite cousins boiling a kettle of borscht outside their caravan after their bareback horse act, my child psychologist brother Paul, with a wink, spouting Jungian symbology about the 'circle of sawdust,' while older sister Sheila, the music therapist, practices theme music on her keyboard and little sister Laura films all this jovial family commotion on video for viewing at the annual Mermin Decagon reunions.

In my imagination, my dad, Al—the respected director of a city housing authority—would have been in his element behind the cotton candy machine, kindly offering free samples to wide-eyed kids. My mom, Dottie, the schoolteacher, would—as she did in real life many years later for Circus Smirkus—host hordes of Russians, Mongolians, and other bleary-eyed circus artists just arrived from foreign lands, earning a reputation as "Mama Mermin" for her endless stacks of potato pancakes with sour cream and applesauce.

★

During the political traumas of 1968, I was in college, draft age, living outside Chicago. Friends marched in civil protests and inflamed political debate hung in the air like angry thunderclouds. I disliked the fervency of crowds. My radicalism was quieter. I wondered how I could best contribute artistically to the kind of world we envisioned.

What would a society feel like in which there was humor without malice, laughter without scorn, common sense in public discourse, decency in human relations, delight in sharing skills without aggressive competition?

Circus became a physical symbol for the community I envisioned and a vehicle for everything I loved doing in the arts. I'd studied mime, acrobatics, theater, and silent film. Circus incorporated all these forms of artistry, along with an intriguing lifestyle. Run off and join the circus? Heck, why not!

There is an epilogue to Poppy's story. Five years later—after my European circus adventures related in this book had begun—I was again home for a visit to attend the funeral of Poppy's wife. Nearing ninety, Poppy was frail, his face drawn from age and sorrow. At the reception later he saw me and asked quietly how I was, what had I been doing with my life.

He was so fragile; I didn't want to sound flippant and talk about myself. But I did say I was on a break from clowning in a European circus. He tilted his head, looked at me and seemed to awaken a bit. He put his hand on my shoulder tenderly and led me to a corner of the room. He started to tell me, at first without expression, as if from a long distance, about a clown he had seen when he was a boy, in Italy, in some small traveling circus.

I just listened, amazed, and moved. The clown came out, he said, and tripped on his flappy shoes as he tried to climb a rope ladder, but his shoe got caught and was hanging upside down... In a few moments his eyes crinkled, he started to gesture, and we both chuckled as he described, once again, the whole act of this beloved clown in Italy, whose name, no, he didn't know.

I thought to myself: This is it, this is the whole point, after all, of my dream. It's not about acquiring a famous name. It's about making a moment of delight for a child. It's a memory to be conjured seventy-five years later, like magic, even in the midst of deep pain and sorrow.

Here was a goal: to set out in search of apprenticeship under circus canvas. Here was the dream that followed: to make it in that world and ultimately pass on the legacy to young people by creating a new circus company that would bridge the traditional and the modern. I would find an unconventional lifestyle of renewable adventure!

When you set out on that path, you may not be looking for trouble—but it is sure to find you. Sure enough, while friends were stumbling through college or wallowing in the mud at Woodstock, I found myself getting bonked on the head by an unscrupulous camel in a traveling mud show in Wales...

– Rob Mermin
Montpelier, Vermont

Act I

Tales of Hoffman

Tales of Hoffman

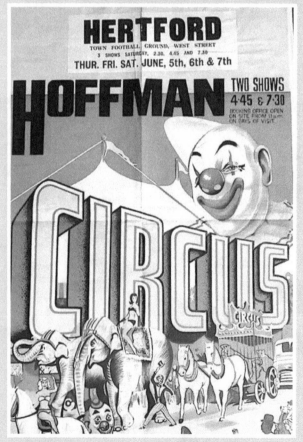

Top: Hoffman truck, circa 1960s, arriving on a muddy lot in Northern Wales.

Above: Rob known as "Tex" by the Hoffman gang, before tossed atop the camel, Achmed.

Left: Hoffman poster, 1969 taken from a store window while on tour in Wales.

Above: a portrait of the Hoffman gang, early 1970s, from left: Russell, Brian, Valerie, Geoffrey, Gerald, and Peter.

Left: Rob and pal, about to go for a swim between the matinee and evening shows.

The Pink Room

"It is with circus-going as it is with Sin. One sin is always followed by a long procession of others. He who goes to the Circus is Lost Forever."

–*Free Press & Times,*
Burlington, Vermont, July 27, 1883

We were standing on a hilltop in the village of Ludlow, near the border of England and Wales. Far below was a circus tent, comfortably sprouted in the cozy valley like a colorful mushroom.

"There she is," I said, in as unaffected a manner as I could muster.

My traveling companion, John B., nervously shifted his stance and glanced from me to the big top below. He knew I had packed baggy pants, big shoes, and a red rubber nose in my bag. He distinctly heard me say I would follow the wind right to this moment. "Gonna run off to join a circus," I had said months earlier. But when he decided to join me in my travels in the summer of 1969, he was totally unprepared for coming face to face with a circus.

John was from Ontario, Canada. We were acquaintances in college. At eighteen, he was a year younger and handsome in a

Robert Redford way, more fleshed out than my long Buster Keaton face and lean frame. He was the son of a diplomat, with genteel manners, a reserved and polished bearing, and a willing amiability and youthful inexperience that lent him a certain charm. Back at school when I compared his conservative style to my vagabond impulses, I wondered how fate might grin at such a pair. We needed to discuss a few things.

I recounted the contents of my money pouch and then presented to John a few ideas for our travel arrangements and budgeting procedures. I endorsed the virtues of frugal travel and encouraged the attitude of vagabonding, concluding that, for the sake of adventure if nothing else, we should endeavor to seek employment while on the road and not hesitate to offer our services for nightly lodging.

"Fine," he commented, "that's all well and good, but I don't think it's quite necessary to overdo it, now. It's a vacation, after all, and..."

"Vacation? We're not signing up for some tour group, now are we?"

"No, but still, I don't see..."

"Well, that's just it—you don't see. We're on a quest. We've got to do it right, with proper style. We'll hit the open road and follow the wind wherever it blows us. We'll let our wits keep apace with destiny's path. We'll..." I stopped waving my arms, seeing how my grandiloquence was wasted.

"Right," said he. "We'll get a Eurail Pass. They're fairly cheap, I hear."

"What! We can't do that, John!"

"Can too. Easy enough, Rob."

"But so can anybody!"

"So can we."

"Well, come on, John," I said. "What's the use of going to foreign shores if we go the way everyone goes? How would it read in a book? ...And they went to the ticket office to seek their fortune, and bought a Eurail Pass, second class.'" I looked at him. "Well?"

"Sounds okay to me," he said, shrugging his shoulders.

"Anyway, after the airfare I've only got $50 to last the whole summer."

John stopped what he was doing and regarded me for a moment. "That's the first straightforward thing you've said. So tell me, how do you propose we travel around?"

"Well," I answered slowly, "once we catch up with the circus, travel and expenses will be taken care of, I imagine."

Pause.

"What circus?" he asked, warily.

"Why, the one we're looking for."

There was another pause. We had begun having two separate conversations.

"Why..." he asked carefully, "are we looking for a circus?"

"Because that's the reason for this trip in the first place." He knew I wanted to work in a European circus someday, and experience that lifestyle.

Silence.

"Tell me, where do we find this circus of yours?"

I bit my lip, upset with myself for once again getting into this conversation. None of my friends or family took my quest seriously. Always in my young life I had to make a conscious decision to either be a quiet observer, which was the more familiar and comfortable part of my nature, or to engage in something greater than myself, which required a concerted effort. I took adventuring as a necessary but private activity. I was not used to the compromises a companion required.

I tried to be tactful and pretended to back off. "John. I don't know where it is yet; that's why we're going over to look for it." He looked very dubious. "Don't worry, these things have a way of taking care of themselves. We just need to take the first step, with good faith."

There was a long pause while John thought the matter over. He obviously concluded that first of all, I was impossible to argue with and secondly, this whole business about a circus was irrelevant since there was really no chance we would ever encounter one.

"Okay." He smiled, and we shook hands. "Let's just go and enjoy ourselves and see what happens."

★

So far in my life, it had been natural for me to go adventuring on my own, without the hindrance of discussion or debate with another person. At moments of "crossroad decisions," I tend to shift into philosophic mode: what's the greater metaphor here, is there a symbolic handle to hang on to?

I looked at John, packing his new clothes, wearing a nice cardigan pullover sweater over a white button-down collar shirt, brown loafers and white socks, his carefully combed hair. I looked at my old, worn-out canvas duffel bag packed with dirty sneakers, denim shirt and faded jeans. We were two sides of society, maybe really two sides of myself.

John represented the careful, no inordinate risk, well planned out, conventional worldview. My intention to find a circus represented an instinct that said there was another way to experience life, a belief we could hit the road without a detailed map, set out in good faith, react spontaneously to circumstances, and be inspired by a daydream.

To paraphrase, dictionary.com says it best: an adventure is an undertaking of uncertain outcome and involving risks. It doesn't require any special courage; it is more a presence of mind, being ready to step out of the conventional at any time. And it's keeping your wits about you when inevitably confronted with the unexpected. It would be interesting to see how John and I would each handle whatever came our way. I would learn just from observing how fate dealt our hands and how we played them.

For moral support I thought of Tom Sawyer. By gosh, I reckoned, no question as to his opinion in the matter—for him style was everything. And Huckleberry Finn was ready for any adventure the river floated his way. Robert Louis Stevenson's David Balfour was my age when his adventures began as "he closed the door on his father's house for the last time" and was Kidnapped. Nearly out of my teens, there was just time enough left for gathering stories of my youth to tell in old age.

In his old age, Hans Christian Andersen remarked wistfully, "I wish I were twenty again; then I'd take my inkpot on my back, two shirts and a pair of socks, put a quill at my side and go into the wide world."

★

John B. and I had first arrived in London and immediately set out on the road, thumbs out, heading north. As fate would have it, our first ride took us way up into the lush Shropshire countryside. Our gracious hosts insisted we stay the night at their impressive estate outside Wolverhampton.

I mentioned we were looking for a circus if they knew of any in the area. They were mildly amused.

We were given separate bedrooms. John B. in the Blue Room, my lot fell to the Pink Room, its plush carpet a cotton candy pink. The bathroom faucets had pink marble knobs and embroidered frilly pink lace topped the luxurious pale pink canopy bed—the whole room smelled pink. I dreamt that night of pink elephants.

The next morning, we were served a sumptuous English country breakfast of eggs, bangers and mash (sausage with mashed potatoes), toast, and fruit cocktail. We had it made! Before hitting the road again, we asked our hosts if there was anything we could do to repay their kindness. Oh, yes, was the reply.

After we spent the day tending the grounds—clipping hedges, raking around the duck pond—we were encouraged to stay on as caretakers. A perfect invitation! It was easy scurity for a couple of loose lads, and the appealing young maid added to the attraction. In short, it was an offer I knew we would dare not accept.

That night John and I had a conversation that went like this:

John, lounging on his blue canopy bed: "We could stay, maybe for a fortnight at the very least, until we get restless..."

"We could," I said.

John, hands behind his head, staring at the blue ceiling painted with faint blue clouds: "The food is quite marvelous, wouldn't you agree? Where would we ever find equivalent accommodations on the road?"

"We wouldn't," I replied.

"We could even stay half the summer, perhaps. It sure would be a good break from traveling," he said, sighing, ignoring that we had been on the road barely one day.

I grunted a response.

John turned to look at me, earnest: "You know, this Fate of yours may have dropped us here for a very good reason. Did you see that pretty maid smile at me? Perhaps we should stay the whole darn—"

"—What!? A whole summer in the Pink Room? Sorry, partner, I'm outta here."

We decided to wait for some kind of sign. It came on the third day when our wonderful hosts took us to a Shakespeare festival in nearby Ludlow. We watched "Romeo and Juliet" performed outdoors that night in the hilltop ruins of Ludlow Castle, silhouetted by a full moon.

After the performance we walked around the castle in a romantic reverie, basking in the blissful comfort of the warm summer night. In the moon shadow of the castle ruins, we looked down on the valley below and saw a sight that made me smile. It was a circus tent, sleeping in the field way down in the valley, like a turtle in the midst of a cluster of tiny toy trucks.

"There she is," I said. I smiled and looked at John, who stared in dismay.

It was only fitting to find the circus that night. It was a perfect piece of stage direction: Shakespeare up on the hill, playing for the romantics under open heavens, and the circus, down in the valley, playing for the masses, planted firmly in the earth—or mud, as we were to find out soon enough.

The Wildest Show on Earth

"Happy Jack Snellen, boss canvasman, was busily engaged in laying out the lot when he was approached by a typical Hoosier, who requested a position. 'You're hired,' responded Happy, laconically. 'What do I do?' asked the new employee. 'Is the work hard?' 'Not a bit of it,' responded Snellen, with a wink to one of his assistants. 'All you have to do is to help put up the tents in the morning and take them down at night.' The new recruit lasted just two days."

—Ringling Route Book,
Indianapolis, Indiana, May 11, 1892

They were finishing the tent set-up the next morning. The day was already hot and humid. Roustabouts carried sixteen-foot-long stringers—heavy wooden bleacher seats—stacked and balanced on their shoulders like seesaws. Rusty iron stakes, like thick needles, were pounded at an angle by twenty-pound sledgehammers. Ropes were flung over the stakes, pulled taut and knotted with a half hitch twist by calloused hands.

Trucks pulled onto the grassy field, finding their proper parking space as if they were commuters accustomed to coming there every day. Sporadic shouts and cussing in several languages punctuated the noise of the bale rings of the big canvas tent being ratcheted up the tall king poles, and caravans circled the tent like wagons on the western prairie, hunkering down for protection.

The rich smell of hay and dung of unlikely creatures in close quarters hovered like a redolent canopy over the circus lot, a whole animal kingdom of horses, camels, elephants, bears, dogs, lions, llamas, geese combined with sawdust, muck, mud, manure and musty canvas to create a pervasive aroma. The local cows across the field grazed innocuously, ignoring all the commotion.

Particles of ubiquitous sawdust settled from the spreading of the circus ring. Circus hands wearing thick work gloves pulled and pointed and carried and pounded, or glugged a warm beer, leaning for a moment on the newly erected shoulder-high wood fence encircling the grounds, proclaiming the territory conquered by the imperialist circus invaders, challenging the lazy English farmland, a step-right-up taste of an exotic world for the price of a ticket.

The Hoffman Brothers Circus—run by the Hoffman siblings, five brothers and a sister—was billed on the posters as "The Wildest Show on Earth!"

It was an archetype of the old one-ring traveling "mud show," a moniker from the old days, when rain mired the horse-drawn wagons in the soft, muddy lots. The Hoffman tent's sidewalls were brown with dried mud, a time-travel flashback to the small itinerant shows of a century ago.

It was just what I was looking for. I glanced at John, who refused to go inside the fence surrounding the circus yard. I went in. I approached a lean, bare chested sweaty individual wearing a cowboy hat who was busy hoisting bleacher seats from a truck. Waiting until he paused to wipe his brow, I said, "Could you point out the director, please? I'm looking for work."

The fellow regarded me for a moment, and then resumed hoisting bleachers. "You American?" he asked.

"That's right," I said, suddenly feeling exposed.

Wham! He tossed another bleacher onto a pile. "What can you do, cowboy?" he said grinning, without looking at me.

"Well, I, uh...the clowns. I just thought..." I had no chance to finish with my hope of apprenticing with the clowns and one day going into the ring...

Crash! A bleacher landed on the pile. Without breaking his working rhythm, the fellow asked, "Clown, eh? Can you talk?"

I looked at him, puzzled, then stammered, "Well, I...uh...sure. I mean..."

Crash! Another bleacher. What kind of question was that? I hadn't the foggiest notion of what he meant.

"Go see Charlie over there," he said, pointing vaguely behind him with his thumb, and he resumed his work, clearly through with me.

Charlie, a big bear of a fellow, shirtless, huge muscles gleaming with sweat, was straining to tighten a thick guy rope that seemed to hold up the whole big top. He tugged hard and tied it to a stake while I waited, suddenly feeling skinny. This is the strongest man I've ever seen, I thought.

When he noticed me, and I announced my intentions, Charlie, whose real name was Karl Brenner, asked me the same baffling question, with a thick German accent: "Yah, can you talk pretty good?"

"Well, sure," I said. *"Why?"*

Charlie grinned, brushing back his bushy blonde hair. "Vell, you know, over here the clowns, they talk. They don' do this in America, heh? Iz too big, the show. Here you vant to talk a good patter, always the patter, und make noise mit the public, yah?" He looked me over, still grinning. "So, you do this, hah? Okay, ve see how it goes mit you, eh? Come..."

Charlie took me back over to the fellow with the cowboy hat, who turned out to be one of the young Hoffman brothers. Charlie arranged the whole thing, his arm around me like a big brother. I would go in the ring that very afternoon with Charlie—*he* was the clown?—who had a partner, Little John, a midget who stood up to my waist and could tap-dance.

Before we parted Charlie said something I didn't appreciate at the time, "Stay close to me...I vatch out for you."

I hadn't forgotten my hapless fellow journeyman. John stood a distance away, looking out of place in his collegiate sports jacket. I told him the arrangements: I would go in as a clown, and he could sign on as part of the roustabout crew.

John put on a very sober countenance. He looked like he was trying to gather up some angry determination, but it only made him look like he had a stomach ache.

"John, it's a job."

"Oh, yeah? How much do we get?"

"Ten pounds."

He stopped for some silent figuring. "About $25 a day, eh?"

"No...a week."

"Each?"

"Ah, well...no...for both." I shrugged. "It's a trial run."

John looked exasperated. Our former hosts had dropped us off at the tent that morning, wishing us luck. Poor John had known I couldn't pass it up. Now he sighed, shaking his head, disgusted. He must have felt the inevitability of the situation as much as I did. I grinned as I shook his hand.

★

Before the matinee show that afternoon, I put on clown makeup borrowed from Charlie inside an old trailer. I peered into the cracked corner of a small mirror obscured by cloudy pockmarks. Lying on a bunk watching me was the resident of the place, a curly-haired youth from the tent crew in a dirty sleeveless undershirt, his sunken chest hairless, his skinny arms bulging with Popeye biceps.

Clothes were strewn around, trunks stuffed half under the bunk. A pinup poster graced the closet door, and his cigarette smoke mated with my makeup started my eyes itching. The smell of manure and hay complemented the scene.

It was my first circus dressing room. I felt strangely at home, despite the nonstop cockney comments from the bunk, discoursing on my waste of energy to paint a full face. "Regular" clowns just threw on a nose and a wig, dashed a line or two on the eyebrows and were ready to go in five minutes, he said. Just what kind of clown was I, anyway?

I took his advice and wore minimal makeup. When I finished, I glanced out the window and saw a sight that stopped me. John was

stationed across the yard, wearing a smeared workman's smock, arms limp by his side, and looking green in the face. I rushed out of the trailer.

"John? What the—" I stopped in midsentence, struck by his dazed countenance. His face was the color of ripe avocado.

"Rob," he groaned, too feeble to move from his position.

"John?"

"Rob, I can't do this. I've been at it for half an hour. I've gotta get out of here. Look at this. Just take a look, Rob, will you? Just look at this!"

On the ground in front of John lay a heavy tarp. In the middle, piled high, was a stack of what looked like raw dinosaur bones. I glanced at blood stains on his smock and the sledgehammer at his feet. Before I could ask what in the world he was doing, up strode the Hoffman brother with his cowboy hat tilted back on his head, wiping sweat off his face with a dirty kerchief.

"Say, Tex," he said to me in his mock cockney/cowboy drawl. "I see yer-all gittin' yer face painted up, eh?"

I would learn he had a curious fascination with the American West. The opening number of the show featured a ridiculous rodeo scene with him dressed like Roy Rogers, swinging a lariat above his trusty white steed, a horse who looked truly bored.

Having never been to North America, he expressed doubt to me that cowboys, and especially Indians, still existed.

Nevertheless, I was quickly dubbed "Tex," and John the Canadian became known as "Canadia," full names beside the point.

"Come on, now, Canadia," Hoffman said next, slapping John a good whack on the back. "This ain't no tea party. Stand back—this 'ere is 'ow you get the job done." He reached for the sledgehammer. "You've got to be sure..." he said, swinging the hammer behind him, "...not to come down in th' middle of the for'ead."

The hammer smashed down into the pile with a crunching splat. "Or th' bloody eyes'll pop out at ye!"

He wiped his hands on John's smock, snorted a few times, and looked from John to me and back to John. We were struck dumb.

"Right. The eyes, watch out for 'em," he said over his shoulder, already striding away.

Mute, we stared at the pile. "Dead cows' heads," John explained in a monotone. "So the bones can fit through the bars of the lions' cage."

"I'm leaving," he said, standing still as a statue.

Half of me wanted to leave with John right then and there, but it wasn't the stronger half.

"Come on, John, just a few days. We'll get you out of this job!"

"Rob, look at me." He opened his arms, displaying a bloody smock. Behind him, his sports jacket was neatly folded on a truck fender.

"Ok, I've got it." I was thinking fast. "We'll tell them we're a clown duo, and get you into the ring with me. What do you say?" The image of this conventional Canadian in a clown suit was as comical as the idea of him smashing dead cows' heads, but not as bloody.

He agreed to try it, and the Hoffmans didn't care. We had until the next day to work up an act. In the background circus music began a rendition of "There's No Business, Like Show Business," played on an asthmatic organ. Show time for me.

John only muttered, "So this comes under the heading of 'Adventure,' eh?"

Into the Ring

"The Great Forepaugh Circus today. Cool and comfortable weather. Beware of thieves and pickpockets."

—*Burlington Free Press,*
Vermont, July 26, 1883

The Hoffman Circus was a medium-sized tent operation, seating perhaps eight hundred customers. The canvas tent came in three sections, laced together on the ground at the midseams. The tent was attached to bale rings, which were hoisted up the two king poles and secured below. Inside was one ring with a painted ring curb about forty feet in diameter, and above the ring entrance was a sign painted with "The Wildest Show on Earth."

On one side of the performers' entrance was a low platform—a couple of sheets of plywood—for the band: a drummer and an organist. The musical director was a fellow known as Frankie the Face, who played drums. Frankie the Face had a large scar on the left side of his profile, from the eyebrow down to the chin. He was quite proud of this scar, and never tired of telling anyone the story of wrestling with the lion one day when he used to work the animals.

He would grin as he told the story, showing off a lack of several teeth on one side, supposedly where the lion had ripped open his jaw. No, he said, he wasn't an animal trainer. He just liked playing with the cats and got himself in trouble one day showing off for a local girl when he stumbled close to the lions' cage after too much booze.

His drumming was accompanied by Phyllis, who played a wheezy rendition of Hoffman's theme, "There's No Business, Like Show Business," on a small portable organ that seemed to have respiratory problems. Phyllis was pleasantly accommodating, a bit dowdy, middle-aged, sitting behind her instrument, absent-mindedly churning out old standards, mildly taking in the ring's action, as if she were a 1950s housewife listening to the radio as a pie baked in the oven.

★

Nervous, I stood backstage during the afternoon show, listening to the melodious chords of the organ, thinking the band could sure use some brass instruments. We clowns were about to go on, the first time for me in a circus ring. Charlie, the strongman with the German accent, now in costume looking less intimidating, prepared the props while Little John, standing there on his solid little legs like an immovable tree stump, explained the act to me.

He didn't have time to outline the whole thing. I was to stay with him and mimic the action. "Just follow me," he said, pushing me behind him, "and do what I do."

The acrobats finished their number and came dashing through the curtain. The fast music began, the curtain opened again, and into the ring we clowns ran. It must have looked properly silly: Charlie the big one, Little John the midget, and me, Tex, medium rare in the middle. It was a warm summer day outside and running into the ring for the first time, I was hit full in the face by the soon familiar warm redolence of an audience in a tent—the smell of popcorn, canvas, sawdust, the heat of the lights.

I relaxed right away. This wasn't the quiet tension of walking out onstage in a darkened theater. This was alive and buzzing.

Charlie ran into the ring first, carrying a large suitcase patched all over with stickers from every country imaginable. He shouted "Hellos" to the audience and announced he was leaving on vacation and commenced with shaking hands and saying farewells to people sitting close to the ring.

Little John and Tex enter next and stand by the curtain, watching Charlie from a distance.

Charlie shouts to the audience: "Vacation! South of France, to za Ree-vee—er-rah!" Little John starts cat-whistling. Tex wiggles his hips like a bikini-clad bather.

Charlie says: "Vell, I vait here for de bus. Come any minute." He sits down on the ring curb, puts the suitcase next to him, and pretends to fall asleep.

Little John comes closer and notices the bottom corner of the suitcase is leaking some liquid. (I think we used orange soda.) He goes over, tastes it with his finger, tiptoes back to Tex: "Yum! Tastes like whiskey! You go taste it."

Tex goes over, tastes it, and comes back: "Yup, whiskey!"

Little John goes over again, tastes, and shakes his head: "No, it's cognac!"

Tex, getting in the swing of things, joins him: "Nope. Gin!"

Little John: "Uh, uh...more like rum!" Little John takes out a cup, fills it with a sample, takes it to people in the audience. He lets them taste it, continues the debate with them, smacking his lips, sipping the sample. Tex does the same, making toasts with audience members, getting "tipsy."

Suddenly Charlie leaps up, grabs his suitcase: "Ah, here come de bus!" As he runs out of the ring, through the audience, the suitcase falls open and a little white shaggy dog jumps out, shakes himself, and chases after Tex and Little John, biting and hanging on to the bottom of Tex's baggy pants. They run out of the ring, the audience hooting with glee.

★

Such was my debut in the ring, with a very old vaudeville gag that I didn't know at the time. The pup was a surprise to me as well as the audience. I don't know why, but I had a moment that felt akin to embarrassment—maybe because I was taken in as much as the audience? My immediate thought was: *I'm glad my mom isn't watching this.*

The gag wasn't high art, but it was comic tradition, nonetheless. I also understood now why I had been asked if I could 'talk.' Most European clowns did in the ring.

John, feeling better, met me behind the curtain. He looked at me with a stuck-on grin, as if to say: Now it's your turn to play the fool, Tex.

I looked back and said, "Well...we'll think of something for our own act," adding, with a pause for effect, "partner."

★

After a few more clown entrances, running around with quick ring gags, the first half of the matinee was over. The second half was to be an easy one for us. Just two more entrances with big Charlie and Little John, one being a simple animal walk-around. I was standing in the backyard, behind the performers' entrance, shooting the breeze with John and Charlie and some ring hands, feeling partly like an old trouper and partly like a kid playing hooky from school. The French family had just finished their juggling act in the ring, and the horses were entering.

Suddenly one of the Hoffman brothers backstage looked around, spied me, and shouted for me to get ready with the horse hurdles and to "move it" if I knew what was good for my health. My reveries abruptly shattered, I was left a wreck of befuddled anxiety. I didn't even have time to ask what a horse hurdle looked like!

I was shoved through the curtain and saw horses thundering around the ring. Over the noise of the crowd, the racing horses, and the asthmatic organ, someone shouted in my ear and pointed to a stack of eight hurdles, painted wooden poles about six feet in length, with inverted 'V' legs on each end, about eighteen inches high.

I was told—yelled at—to grab the stack in my arms, wait for the signal from the Hoffman who stood in the middle of the ring with his whip, and then dash out and place the hurdles, one at a time, half-way around the ring at a distance of exactly two-and-a-half feet apart, angled inward, and timing it so I'm doing all this as the horses are running around the other side of the ring. "Finish before they reach the first of the hurdles, so they won't break stride. And be sure to get out of there fast!"

I started to protest the advisability of having a novice be responsible for this essential task, pointing out that I would learn how to do it at the next rehearsal and meanwhile I would gladly observe carefully as my instructor did it just now, and I turned—but 'he' had disappeared.

I was about to do the same before anyone noticed me, and then someone did notice me—it was Hoffman in the ring. He shouted,

| 20 |

"Hurdles, Tex!" and cracked his whip for effect. The horses came racing past me like a freight train.

My reflexes took over, and I jumped for the pile of hurdles, a fleeting image in my head of stampeding horses from Hollywood westerns jumping over my crouched body. The horses zoomed past me, my excitement racing too. *Good Lord,* I thought, I would have about ten seconds to place those hurdles in position before that stampede made it around the ring.

I grabbed those bulky poles—they seesawed in my arms—and as the last horse barreled past, I dropped a hurdle in place, and then another, and another, remembering they had to be evenly spaced or the horses would be piling on top of each other, and probably on top of me, and I heard those horses snorting and pounding the ground like they were right on me, and I was panting now as much as they were, but I didn't look up. I just ran forward literally throwing the hurdles down in place, hoping they landed right side up.

Suddenly I tripped, but was up in a flash, and somehow the last hurdle was thrown down, and I went running back to fix the spaces and saw a herd of horseflesh coming around the bend, and it was then I felt the whiplash. Snap! A quick flick around my ankles from Hoffman's whip, and I jumped up straight and turned in the ring to stare at him, as the horses galloped past me, stepping neatly over the hurdles.

Hoffman ignored me and went on cracking the whip for effect, and I just stood there in the ring, forgetting I was dressed as a clown, stunned, not believing he had just whipped me in front of the audience.

It didn't hurt, of course, and it was too fast for the audience to see, but my self-esteem was stung. Then I was angry, so I stomped out of the ring and confronted whoever was backstage, saying, "Did you see that? Did you see that?" I pointed to my ankle, but no one took notice.

Big Charlie came over and said, "Never mind…iz nothing. If dat's all you get vile you're here, iz okay. Never mind, c'mon." And that was the end of that.

I peeked through the curtain and observed that the horses were not, in fact, charging like thunderous furies around the ring, but just trotting and prancing, completely indifferent to my recent terror.

The Camel from Tibet

"Showmen were often given names for the city or county in which they were hired. Thus 'Cincinnati Bill' or 'Chicago Jim' would not only serve as well as any other name, but they possess this advantage, that they indicated in a breath where Bill or Jim had been picked up by the circus."

— W.C. Coup, *Sawdust & Spangles*, 1895

We were standing backstage ready for our next entrance, in the second half of that memorable first matinee. It was a simple animal walk-around to show off some of the menagerie as the ring crew cleared the ring.

Big Charlie was to enter the ring, dressed as an Indian fakir with a tall turban wrapped around his head, carrying a large wicker basket and musical pipe. Sitting cross-legged in the center of the ring, he would "play" the pipe, which was attached to a hidden hose in the basket, and a long balloon snake would rise out of the basket, dancing in the air, getting larger as Charlie blew into the pipe.

Meanwhile, as the organ played some strange Eastern rhumba, Little John would enter with a llama, and I would come in leading a donkey. Easy. Just walk the animals around slowly for the kids to see them close up. The signal to exit would come when Charlie saw the set was ready for the next act.

He would then blow so hard the balloon snake would pop, the music would crescendo to a chase, and Little John and Tex would trot around the ring one last time with the donkey and llama and then exit. Okay, I said to myself. I could handle walking around with a donkey.

It was nearly time for our entrance when another of the five infernal Hoffman brothers appeared. "Where's the camel?" He looked around, saw me, and growled to run like hell and get the camel! The camel always goes in this act.

I stood there, dumbstruck, a familiar gnaw gripping my stomach.

"C'mon, cowboy, get that bloody camel over here. *Now!*"

I stumbled out around the back where the camel lay on the ground—sprawled, I should say, legs splayed in every direction, with a rope around his neck, tied to a stake. "Okay" I said to myself, fighting a growing premonition, "I'll get the bloody camel, just this *once...*"

I eyed the creature, talking out loud as I bent down to untie the rope from the stake. "I'm sure you're used to this, done it every day, right? It's all new to me, so...just this once, bloody camel...no offense..."

Our entrance was any second now; my head was a-flutter with butterflies, my stomach crawling with caterpillars. I managed to untie the rope, talking nonsense to the camel all the while, hoping to get him used to my friendly voice. I commenced tugging and pulling to get that blasted camel on its feet, when a ring hand came running to help, shouting that we were on for our entrance.

Achmed the camel (*from Tibet!* shouted the poster of "The Wildest Show on Earth") seemed unconcerned. Unhurriedly, clumsily, he got to his knees, ignoring the tugging, pulling, and cussing of these two idiotic humans, the clown and the ring boy. Finally, he stood up and took one slow step at a time, sporting a dopey smirk on his face.

That old camel must have been arthritic. He couldn't walk straight. It seemed his legs operated in total independence of each other, working in whatever rhythm and direction they happened to decide upon in each step, splaying huge feet in all directions, usually sideways, which had the effect of keeping me hopping and dancing, to keep from being trodden upon by some disjointed leg that kept me guessing where it was going to land.

We made it to the ring entrance. Little John had already entered with the llama. Good buddy Canadia was recruited to walk the donkey. I frantically looked around for someone to take the camel, when a voice said, "Up ya gaw, Tex—ride 'em *cowboy!*" and four hands of assorted Hoffman brothers grabbed my elbows and knees.

With the realization of what they expected me to do, that feeling of calm came over me, a feeling that comes from knowing exactly how to react. I kicked.

Despite my physical protestations, I was picked up bodily and tossed like a saddle onto the camel's back. But there was no saddle, there was no bucket seat, no rope to grasp, nothing but the one hump which I hugged with both arms, lying on my stomach, legs dangling.

Someone yelled up to me not to worry, the fellow who used to be here did this all the time. I didn't have time to ask what fate befell that poor fellow. The camel was given a smack in the rear and off we lurched into the spotlight, my legs flapping in the air at each bounce.

Ah, the laughter of the crowd, music to a clown's ears.

But I didn't hear it; I was preoccupied. I was thirty feet in the air (it seemed) hanging on for dear life, being jostled like a tipsy Tex of Arabia, at each bounce losing my grip and sliding backwards down the hump toward Achmed's tail. I kept scrambling and clawing my way back up as the camel just loped along, unconcerned, haughty, and drooling, following the other animals.

Canadia was looking over his shoulder with his mouth hung open, thinking, no doubt, that he'd been right. I must have gone bonkers to be doing what I was doing.

The act went on for about an hour, it seemed, when Charlie's snake balloon finally burst and the music went double time, the signal for the animals to race around the ring and exit. My fate was sealed, I thought. Trampled by a camel in Wales.

The music raced and so did Little John with the llama and John Canadia with the donkey. I was bouncing frantically on Achmed when I heard Big Charlie's voice above the noise.

Seeing my impending disaster, he yelled for me to grab onto the trapeze bar. "Tex! Next time around, rich up und grab to de sving bar!"

"Wha? Wha—?"

Achmed the Camel was loping around the ring fast, and I had a last chance to look up at the single trapeze bar as I passed underneath. I barely hung on to the bouncing hump and timed it so that next time around, as Achmed bounced me upwards, I let go of his hairs and reached for the bar and suddenly found myself without a camel, hanging wildly over the ring in mid-air.

The crowd roared its approval, so I kicked my legs in response, as if to say, *See, I'm really an aerialist after all.* But now there was nothing for me to do but hang there for the rest of the show, because the ring was empty—even Charlie had made his exit—when I heard the music begin for the next act. The curtain opened and in ran the elephants.

That was a good enough catalyst for me, so I let go of the bar and, hoping not to break my legs, dropped into the ring and rolled into a somersault and kicked my heels to show the audience I was unhurt—just all part of the act, folks—and jumped over the ring curb just in time to miss being the real-life punch line of an elephant joke.

★

I wonder what Achmed the camel thought about all this. He was certainly an odd creature to be of use outside a desert clime. W.C. Coup, circus proprietor, wrote a fascinating memoir of the circus in nineteenth century America, explaining in 1885:

> The first drove of camels was imported in 1847 from Cairo, Egypt. Later, the government made the experiment of carrying the mail from Texas to California by 'Camel Post.' This proving unsuccessful, the animals were turned loose to shift for themselves, until circus showmen created a demand for them. It is said that even now there are a few camels running wild in Western Texas and Mexico.

I imagine the races in the Old West between the Pony Express riders and the Camel Post. I see myself as a rider dashing nonstop from El Paso, Texas, west to Yuma, Arizona, hanging on to the camel for dear life, hugging the mailbags, legs flapping behind in the wind, passing the pony riders whose panting steeds had to stop for water. But not Achmed the Camel (from Tibet!) who, never thirsty, strode across the wild west in all his galumphing wickedness, leaving behind him a trail of legends as The Wildest Camel on Earth!

★

I somehow got through that first matinee show. It was exhilarating, really, like stepping into the pages of a wacky children's book. Soon enough it was time for the evening show. And it came time once again for the animal walk-around. One of the Hoffmans came up, looked me in the eye and drawled, as if to no one in particular: "Ayup, someone's got ta gaw git that goddam camel."

I met his stare and said, all right, I'll go get him, adding there was no way I would ride him again.

He just said: "G'wan, t'other fellow rode 'im every show." I meant to ask, again, whatever became of that fellow, but he turned his back and spat, and there was nothing to do at that point but "git the goddam camel."

I walked over to where Achmed lay sprawled on the ground. Defiantly I started to untie the rope, all the while making my position clear: I told him there would be no bareback riding, no drooling, no snorts of disapproval, no crooked walking, and although we might not become bosom buddies, these terms must be met for us to coexist peacefully in this show.

This speech was delivered with determination and enough conviction, I thought, even for a camel to comprehend. As the knots around the stake came loose, Achmed, who was perhaps hard of hearing, swung his head over to hear better, but being rather dumb, forgot to stop his momentum and smacked his forehead into mine just as I looked up.

I went flying backwards, landing ten feet away on my back, dazed and staring at the swirling stars above.

Time passed in peaceful silence. I said to myself, "I will just lie here until someone finds me, and checks me for bone damage, and wipes the blood from my forehead, which no doubt looks ghastly over my clown makeup. Let them come and see what that goddam bloody camel has done, let them take note and arrest that cussed beast."

I heard a voice directly, yelling for me. It was one of the ring boys, shouting to hurry up, the act was on. I sat up, dizzy, feeling the lump already swelling, and pointed to my head, shrugging, confident there was bloodshed—but no, my make-up was intact, the camel was innocently grazing, so I dragged him into the ring and walked him around, hopping out of the way of his spindly legs, thoroughly disgusted. I knew no one would believe or care how dangerous that one-hump animal really was.

Later that night, having post-performance tea with the clowns in Charlie's caravan, I mentioned the incident. Seeing the bump on my head, Canadia's only comment, smiling sweetly as he passed me the sugar cubes, was, "One lump, or two?

5

Keystone Konstables

*"No one will pretend that circuses are schools of morality.
But to be amused and astonished must be worth something
hygienically. Will we learn nothing from this?"*

—*Vermont Phoenix,*
Brattleboro, Vermont, 1859

When the tent was down—that first night of mine with the show—I witnessed a scene that I came to cherish. The lot was cleared. All that was left was a circle of caravans around the circle of sawdust where the ring had been.

During the final show in any town, the lot is struck with backyard tents coming down as the last acts are performing. Animals are loaded into wagons; concessions are packed away; the big top guy wires are unknotted in preparation for the tent coming down even as the show finale is in progress and patrons are filing out. Roustabouts stack bleacher boards as each section of spectators climb down and hit the grass.

No horseplay at this point with hours of work ahead. It is all business at hand to load out as soon as possible, in order to get two or three hours of sleep before the jump to the next town.

After the hours of load-out commotion—the slamming of sledgehammer to loosen iron stakes, the shouts and curses of tent crew, grunts from the elephants pulling wagons out of mud, jokes from the artistes, who had discarded their spangles and were toiling in dirty coveralls and old work gloves to protect their hands, the children, the bosses, everyone becoming roustabouts after a long day—suddenly it was silence.

By midnight, when all was finally packed up, everyone disappeared into their caravans for a bite to eat, the French over here, the Germans over there, bosses on the far end, roustabouts in the back trailers. Then seemingly on cue, a circus sixth sense, everyone came out carrying piping hot tea, not in dainty teacups, but large steaming bowls which one cupped in two hands.

With calloused palms you didn't get burned; the heat of the bowls diffused through the hands, gratefully absorbed into the full body, spreading out to fatigued muscles. Everyone stood around the circle, and someone would light a fire in the sawdust and the trash of the day was thrown in.

That first night, I was handed a bowl of tea silently by the grandmama of the French jugglers, and we all stared at the fire, sparks rising in the night like lightning bugs. I had an image of leftover spangles from the show floating up to spangle heaven, the last vestiges of circus magic burning out in the night sky—poof!—until the next town the ritual began anew.

I had no idea where to sleep. Canadia John found the back of a pickup truck for his outdoor bedroom. I crawled into the front cab of a big lorry and wrapped my aching body around the gearshift. Bruised, battered, and numb with weariness, I felt like that line from Melville, somewhere in *Moby Dick,* "My whole beaten brain seems as beheaded."

Still, I felt the odd sense that here was a place strangely familiar, where everyone had a part to play, a role to which you simply adjusted your own temperament. It was conventional society gone awry. I liked it.

I knew instinctively this particular Hoffman circus, The Wildest Show on Earth, would be an education in human folly, my own not the least. And yet, despite the sense of anarchism in this company, circus was a clearly ordered world—things simply had to get done, daily and on time. I felt some growing kinship with these folks, who had not planned every little detail of their lives to the point of immobility or tediousness.

As I sank into nothingness, I sensed the truck gently swaying. I was so exhausted it took a while to realize I was in an elephant truck. Since we were headed out of town in barely a couple of hours, the elephant was already loaded inside. This is fine, I thought...it's like the ocean, gentle swaying, rocking waves, sailing along, floating to sleep...

Clunk! Wide awake. The whole truck tilted to one side. I slid down toward the door. Then there was a rasping, sliding noise... Crash! The truck righted itself, rocking on its wheels, and all was quiet. The elephant had leaned against the wall and gently slid down to the floor to rest.

It seemed I had barely closed my eyes, when I was awakened by sounds of truck engines starting, shouts from the bosses, and the circus was moving out to the next town. Freddy Santus, juggler and acrobat, a handsome rogue with a devilish smile, jumped into the cab of the truck, pushed my sleepy body aside, grabbed the steering wheel and shouted in French, and broken English, over the roar of the engine, "Allez, on y va! Wake up, Cowboy!"

Freddy drove the elephant truck in the pre-dawn fog over narrow, winding Welsh roads, overhanging tree branches whipping against the roof and sides of the big lorry. I had the windows rolled down because the heater was broken and stuck on High, roasting us in the cab. I drifted in and out of a drowsy somnolent haze, with occasional jolts of semi-consciousness from being bounced and thrown against the cab door by the fast driving and bumpy, curvy roads.

Actually, I was terrified of Freddy's driving. It was all one speed: fast. After one dangerous curve taken at full speed, Freddy laughing insanely, I sat up straight, wide awake, gripping the door handle. I finally understood his wild gestures, his frantic pointing down to the floor, his fast jerks back and forth, head shaking with crazy laughter: *we had no brakes!*

Horrified, I pushed in the air, while jabbing my finger at the brake and shaking my head frantically, yelling, "Stop? Non?! No Stop?!!"

"Oui!! Non!! Pas de freins!"

I looked out the window. We were barreling along narrow roads with cliffs on either side, an elephant behind, and a crazy Frenchman at the wheel, grinning madly. He seemed to take the predicament for granted. Just another country drive in a typical Hoffman truck with no brakes, a heater stuck on High, and a swaying elephant that threatened to topple us at each curve.

I gripped the door handle, ready to jump out. I stayed in that position for a half hour, until we came out of the hills, down into a flat valley and finally a village, with Santus managing to gradually slow the vehicle with tugs on the hand brake. We slowly pulled up to the circus lot on the far end of the village, when a Hoffman brother ran up and told us to stop with the long truck half into the lot, and the back end sticking out into the street.

Santus stopped the truck and jumped out, grinning at my bloodless face.

"Tex," said Hoffman, "you stay here, and if anyone comes over, just stall." It was spoken as an order. "Huh?" But he was already gone, and I was content to sit in the truck and calm my heartbeat, thankful to have survived.

I managed a nap until being awakened by knocking on the windshield. Two Welsh constables in uniform were pounding on the truck with their sticks and telling me to move the truck out of the road. It was 6:00 a.m., and the town was waking up.

The crew inside the lot was already laying out the tent. I said, "Sorry, officer, the truck is stalled."

"Then push it! Get those men over here!"

"Can't, sir. The elephant's in the back. Too heavy to push."

"MOVE the elephant!"

"I'm not the trainer..."

Frustrated, they asked who was in charge. I pointed out one of the Hoffman boys in the distance, carrying a heavy stack of bleacher boards.

I watched the next scene from my vantage point inside the truck. The windshield made a TV screen, so I viewed what followed as if taking in a silent keystone kop film.

Long shot: the two policemen confront Hoffman. Hoffman escorts policemen into his caravan, politely holding open the door and bowing them in. Four more Hoffman brothers appear around the corner, as if on cue, and enter the caravan. Ah, I thought, they were going to discuss the matter. Fade out.

Short time later: camera fades back in. Medium shot of the caravan, which is curiously bouncing around and rocking side to side, as if dancing. Then the caravan door opens and out flies one constable, horizontal in the air. As he hits the ground face down, the other officer of the law is kicked out—we see only the boot of the kicking foot—and for a moment there is a tangled heap of blue uniforms before the two men leap up and run off. Two tiny figures run off into the distance, getting smaller and smaller.

Well, this scene was like a shot of caffeine, so I left the truck and went to help with the set-up. We did two shows that day and skipped town early the next morning.

I asked Charlie later about this little incident. "Yah, oh sure," he said. "No permits. We vere kicked out-a dis town last year. Hoffman never pay rental for a field. Yah, sure, de po-lice come right and left, no matter. Hoffman's are dere *own* police force!"

Charlie mentioned a similar incident in another village. The crew was struggling to get the tent up in time for the matinee show. Several nervous members of the local constabulary stood in a line, shoulder-to-shoulder, arms folded in a face-off with the Hoffman boys. Peter Hoffman held a can of petrol. Geoffrey Hoffman lit a cigarette. Peter poured a line of gas between them and the police and challenged them to step over the line.

Several cops made a move forward, but Geoffrey threw down the lit cigarette and Whoosh! A wall of flame shot up, constables in hot confusion; they were seen running off in the distance, squawking like a flock of distraught chickens whose dignities had been offended. Hoffman Circus did their two shows that day and skipped town that night.

Just another day at the office.

The Poster

*"There were two lively runaways yesterday morning,
but no great damage was done. One of the elephants
in the procession ran against a street gas lamp
and somewhat demoralized it."*

—*Herald and Globe,*
Rutland, Vermont, July 26, 1883

The posters advertising the show were plastered—without permits, of course—on every available storefront, telephone pole, fire hydrant, and trash can in town. A perusal of the Hoffman Circus poster that year would reveal an eclectic roster of acts. I took one as a souvenir. I look at it whenever I need to shake my head, clear away cobwebs of memory, and put in perspective what I have been doing in the fifty years since.

The memories abide in my mind—and body—in the way that an aroma brings visceral recollections suddenly to the surface.

The opening of the show, after the ubiquitous overture on the organ of "There's No Business, Like Show Business," featured cowboy Hoffman dressed as Wild Bill Hoffman prancing into the ring on horseback: Red's Rodeo *("From the USA!")* exclaims the poster.

He cracked his whip, flashed a grin as wide as his hat, gave a yodeling whoopee, and the show was on! Welcome to Hoffman's Circus—for once truly living up to its hype as The Wildest Show on Earth. Out came the dancing girls—billed as Hoffman's Majorettes—dressed as cowgirls in miniskirts, sequined vests, and white western boots. These gals twirled their batons, spun around in pirouettes, gave little cowgirl whoops and yips now and then, and generally smiled a lot.

You weren't totally convinced they loved their work—but then again, you knew they couldn't be doing it for the money. So you finally come around to thinking, as you watched them, that they were there because no one else was around to do it, and it was sort of fun, and anyway they were obliged to help out, being the wives and girlfriends of the Hoffman boys. Even Charlie's nine-year-old daughter sometimes joined the fun. She of course stole the act with her smile, while dancing, but didn't smile at all when concentrating on catching her baton.

There is a certain smile found in chorus lines. You recognize it as a stage smile when you notice that the eyes work independently of the mouth. They shift, just looking around as if in some other world altogether, perhaps thinking of what's for dinner, while the flashy steps and toothy smile work effortlessly.

These dancing Hoffman majorettes, however, had not reached that vapid level of professionalism. Their smiles varied in charming degree to suit the situation, and in consequence you smiled right along with them.

They smiled when they made a successful pirouette; they smiled with a touch of chagrin when they didn't make it all the way around. They gave a wan smile if they dropped the baton. They smiled bigger when they caught it. They flashed a quick smile at each other whenever they managed to stay in step, or—less often—when they remembered to whoop together on cue after finishing a turn. Meanwhile, the band turned out a spirited, if repetitious and wheezy, medley of tunes from *Oklahoma!*

The first horse act was a Hoffman atop his trusty steed, six-shooter twirling around the index finger in one hand, leading a few horses around the ring. I wondered about those horses. There seemed to be only one bunch of horses in the stable, yet if you read through the poster, you would see listed Norwegian Fjord Horses. Further down the list was Blue Grass, The Amazing Appaloosa Stallion. Perhaps there was a horse in the show named Blue Grass, but a person could look all night, and place bets, but still never be sure by the end of the night which of the horses it was. "Appaloosa" is a fine sounding word, though, and it does look good in bold print.

It would be acceptable to stop there, but no: in bold red letters across the bottom of the placard, one finds the Eight Knapstrupper Troupe, Exciting Equine Number! The brothers were often accused, Charlie told me, of deceiving the public by painting black spots on their gray horses. That may be why they were careful to keep the Knapstruppers out of the rain.

I wondered whether, by the end of the season, that herd of horses were terribly confused as to identity: were they Knapp-struppers, rodeo cow ponies, Appaloosas, Norwegians, or what? I never knew which horse really was Blue Grass. Appaloosan horses are known for their spotted coat, but then there were those spotted Knappstruppers.

The horses were not the only members of the menagerie with identity problems. I was convinced all the animals got together late at night when the circus was asleep. They communicated to each other how to best wreak havoc the next day on the humans: *I'll work the bucking bronco routine tomorrow when Hoffman jumps on me,* says Blue Grass. (The other animals murmur assent.) Achmed the Camel, with a dopey smirk, offers to shake that newcomer Tex around like a rag doll...

There was daily chaos backstage from the animal anarchy. Bo-Bo the Llama *("From Peru!")* spit disdainfully on humans passing by. Buckshot the Mule lashed out with his hind hoof, aiming for anyone's shins.

The Russian bears *("Overstuffed Teddies, From Siberia!")* were not in the show that season. Apparently there used to be an English bloke who dressed as a Cossack and went in the ring to cavort with the bears, but the bottle got to him, and he lost his nerve and ran off with a girl from Brighton. But had he lost his nerve with the bear or with the girl? Sometimes Charlie would go in with the bears by himself—the only one who dared to do so—but the Hoffmans didn't pay him extra, so he no longer bothered.

Then, in smaller print down at the bottom of the poster there is Buffalo—The Only Performing Bison in the World *(From Canada!)*. Buffalo never went in the ring. As far as I could tell, that old Bison didn't do anything, and wouldn't, if anyone were stupid enough to ask him. It fell to my lot to feed him. I didn't like the job.

Out of all the intimidation I endured in the Hoffman circus, from both man and animal, I was most intimidated by that Bison from Canada. He belonged to the wild plains, not chained up alone without his kind, bound to a traveling circus in Wales. We both knew it. It was maddingly wrong.

He tolerated no sympathy. Nothing less than ferocious formality and brusque distance would do. He terrified me. He was old, he was huge, he was shaggy, and unspeakably...gruff. It is the only word that comes to mind, though it is a weak word in this case. He was Anger, Danger, Defiance, Strength, Frustration, Resignation, and Madness personified, tied up at the end of an iron chain.

His manner disdained all frivolous attempts to communicate amicably. His scorn rendered my acts of food-and-water-bearing as gestures of obeisant privilege. His frightful snorts made it perfectly clear that one of his breed was not to be spoken to or approached in any way, so I served his wishes by leaving his sustenance at a modest distance. Never since have I met with such an embodiment of ancient power and righteous indignation, of worn-out anger, and undeniably evocative pent-up wildness, nearing insanity.

★

Despite the circus name, the Santus family was the mainstay of the Hoffman circus. They were a French family billed (for some reason with different spelling) on the posters as The Santos Troupe: Whirlwind Jugglers and Antipodista *(From Portugal!)*. They were a talented group of jugglers, and if you thought you were seeing double in the second half of the show, it was because you saw the Santuses a second time announced as Les Kansas Five, Unicyclists *(From France!)* wearing different costumes, with the same smiles and flashy energy.

Brothers Jean-Paul and Freddy—short, slim, wavy-haired, and athletic, dashingly good-looking in that Mediterranean way—were always hanging around, flirting with the pretty local groupies in every town. Their sisters, Yolande and Aimee, were graceful, charming, independent, strong-willed, and talented. Like typical circus artists, they were multi-skilled: their specialty was foot juggling—antipodista in circus parlance—on their backs tossing and manipulating props with their feet.

Yolande, with pretty, long brown hair in a ponytail, smiled as she asked me if Canadia John was married.

They were a fine traditional circus family: dedicated, talented, resilient, a close-knit clan that practiced, traveled, and worked together. Grandparents, aunts and uncles, and children were fiercely devoted to each other. I was always impressed with that aspect of circus society. The Santus family were good examples. Everyone, no matter the age, had a role in the family business.

The children knew several languages and geography in a natural way. Little toddlers ran in circles around your legs if you stood still for over thirty seconds. One of these little ones could already balance on his head with arms and legs free-floating in the air. It was not uncommon to see the father balancing a toddler upside down in the palm of one hand, a big, inverted grin on the child's face like a carved pumpkin on Halloween, turned bottoms up.

I think if I had grown up like that, I would certainly see things differently, perhaps understanding life from two perspectives, upside down and right-side-up. Which worldview would I see as the truest?

Ill in Rhyl

"A farmer who heard the clown band during the parade remarked: 'Dern me if that beant the wust band I ever heered. We got one in our town that kin beat it all holler.'"

—*Ringling Route Book,*
Lapeer, Michigan, June 13, 1891

The Hoffman show traveled in northwestern Wales at the end of June, in towns with unpronounceable singsong names right out of Tolkien's Middle Earth: Abergwyngregyn, Llanfairfechan, Mynydd Llandygai, Gorddinog. These places were on the eastern shore of the Menai Strait, opposite the Isle of Anglesey. We were not far from the town of Caernarfon.

By the time the circus reached the northern mountains of Snowdonia, both John and I had come down with nasty colds that turned into fevers. We left the circus and managed to find our way to the town of Rhyl, a seaside resort in the Welsh county of Denbighshire, where we rented a room and collapsed. For three days we fell into feverish dreams, day and night. We were desperately ill in Rhyl.

Between interludes of lucidity in my sickbed, reading newspapers, I had a hallucinatory reverie of my next adventure. There was a media uproar in the papers over the upcoming investiture of the Prince of Wales in the Castle of Caernarfon. The coronation was to take place on the first day of July a few days away. The town of Caernarfon was only forty miles from Rhyl.

According to the media, the impending ceremony was being received positively by the majority of the Welsh population. Some nationalists, though, viewed it as part of the subjugation of the Welsh people since the thirteenth century, when King Edward I of England deposed the last native Prince of Wales, Llywelyn ap Gruffudd. I was captivated by these Welsh names and all the hoopla surrounding the coronation.

In my sweat-soaked fever, I envisioned finding my way into the castle a day before the royal ceremonies. Discovered, I am hauled before the royal family where I improvise some comic bits which the Queen frowns upon severely. But before I am cast bodily into the moat by the Queen's Guards, the young Prince of Wales—in an unconventional burst of independent bravado and mercy, possibly inspired by the new status about to be bestowed upon him—the young Prince, I say, has me released and in a fit of rebellious compassion confers upon me the honor of being his personal court jester for the festivities.

Well, I thought to myself in a spasm of feverish logic, crazy things can happen if left up to fate—right time and right place and all that. I saw myself as Danny Kaye in the comic film The Court Jester. I knew John would decline what he called my "absurd folly," but he agreed, in this foolish fantasy, to become a court page. He liked the outfits.

John and I awoke from our fevers after three days. Fortunately, the investiture had taken place without any hindrance from me. The young Prince had intoned his speech in English and Welsh, declaring: "I, Charles, Prince of Wales, do become your liege man of life and limb and of earthly worship, and faith and truth I will bear unto thee, to live and die against all manner of folks."

Amen. That sentiment lent me tolerance to endure further Hoffman escapades.

★

The circus had moved on without us. My plan was to get better and then back to the circus. John thought otherwise. He proposed we head south to London where he had a relative. He had been a good sport and followed me into the circus. It was my turn to acquiesce to his plan. Ah, well. We were back in commonplace reality. Hoffmans and The Wildest Show on Earth now seemed like the fevered fantasy.

Getting back on our feet, we hit the road hitchhiking and our rides took us south. By late afternoon we were dropped off outside a village. We were hungry, low on cash, and needing a place to spend the night.

We started to walk down the road, both wondering what was next, when John stopped and held up his hand. "Hold on," he said, "do you hear something?"

I stopped and listened. "Sounds like music," I said.

John got excited, thinking there was an outdoor concert where we might meet folks our own age and get invited for a meal.

"Right!" he said. "Let's go, I'm starving."

We walked on about a quarter mile, the music getting louder as we approached. Finally, the music took shape, the melody was clear.

John stopped, a look of dismay frozen on his face.

I stopped and listened, grinning.

The tune was—you guessed it—"There's No Business, Like Show Business" on that trusty asthmatic organ. As we approached the circus lot, Big Charlie saw us coming and waved us over. "C'mon in," he said with his German accent. "Tea's on..."

Commonplace reality was gone; we were back. For the next couple of weeks, when I said goodnight, John would grumble: "Another fine mess you've got me into, Mermin."

★

Another other-worldly event occurred on July 20, at 3:58 a.m., British time. We watched the moon landing on a tiny TV in the middle of the night. As Neil Armstrong stepped out onto that ashen astral orb, I too felt that with the cosmological experience of my first circus, I had taken one small step for a clown, and one foolhardy leap towards my dream of someday creating my own traveling tent show.

Tex & Canadia

"At night, slight fight, and this dramatic speech:
'I won't live on the same world with him.
He's got to get off the earth!'"

— *Ringling Route Book,*
Marshfield, Wisconsin, July 5, 1891

Meanwhile, back in the mud on earth, and to get John off the cow's-head detail, I played up the notion to the Hoffmans that we were a clown duo. It seemed like they needed more clowns on the show. "We'll see about that," a Hoffman brother said. I worried that he was already planning a new test for the hapless Tex, American cowboy.

John and I made our auspicious clown duo debut a couple days later, with Charlie's help. We had in mind the Hoffman admonition to "keep up the patter; they likes a bit o' noise." I told John we had to make a quick impression by showing our ability to "yak it up" in the European style. We would parody a cowboy showdown as "Tex and Canadia."

I thought I knew what was required, so I ran in first, yelling out my Hellos! For some reason I automatically slipped into an affected cockney, or sometimes an Irish accent. My greetings always came out strung together: "Ello-ello-ell-LOW!" I once got caught in a discussion with a lady patron, who thought I was from her hometown in County Cork and pressed me for common acquaintances.

I grabbed and shook hands all around the front rows and, having been loudly convivial, commenced to waving my arms and blasting forth with a boastful declaration that I was "Theeee slickest, theeee meanest, theeee fastest gunslinger in the whole Wild West... yup, I wuz."

I strutted around bowlegged, tripping over my spurs, which were forks and spoons tied together, and pushing my hat, which kept slipping down, off the bridge of my nose, twirling my toy water pistol. This was the cue for John's entrance.

There was a loud bellow from behind the curtain, and out came Canadia, decked out as another gunslinger, baggy pants borrowed from Charlie and toy cap pistols from the Santus kids. He ran around in circles, whooping and squawking in a frenzy like a plucked chicken in a barnyard, making a kind of snorting that came from deep in his throat and ended as a high braying noise in his nose.

Amazed, I watched this admirable effort for a while when I up and shouted: "HALT, Varmint! Who IS you?"

He replied, in a shout to the audience, as we had rehearsed: "I'M the meanest, baddest, fastest gunslinger in the Whole Wild West, mister...and you better believe it!" he added, improvising, and pointing hard at me in the chest with his finger. The organist supplied us with an ominous chord, and a cymbal crash came from Frankie the drummer.

I shouted back. "Nope, I was the fastest," and prompted my half of the audience to endorse me, while John answered equally loudly, getting his half of the audience to cheer him on.

We were gratified to get such an easy response from the audience. There was one major flaw in this audience banter: some of the opinions we polled were not very polite in nature, and with the shouting of the crowd and the crying of babies, we suddenly didn't know how to stop the whole debate.

We finally managed to quell the riot and get to the point of the gag—a showdown. We had the usual comic bits: the back-to-back stepping off ten paces, with one following behind the other and ducking when he turned; the pistol that twirls around the finger and flies off; the bobbing up and down in uncoordinated rhythm at the face off; and then the blow-off. That is when John fires his cap pistol, while I surreptitiously pull the string that holds up my baggy pants, which fall to my ankles, exposing my checkered shorts and knobby knees. I would start to run but trip over my pants, and the crowd roars at the silly antics. Piece of cake.

Well, John fired his cap pistol, which didn't go off, so he looked down at it, then up at me and yelled "BANG!" and ran around the ring and disappeared out through the curtain, thinking I was following in hot pursuit.

I wasn't. When he yelled "BANG," I tugged at the drawstring, which immediately made a sailor's knot, leaving the blow-off with me fully clothed and lacking a suitable exit. What could I do but let out a melodramatic anguished, "Ahhhhhhrr!" and clutch my stomach like I was shot, struggling in vain to wrench free that mule of a knot, and pirouetting around the ring, more like a drunken ballerina than a dying desperado.

I gave strange jerks and emitted grunts as I tugged at the string, until finally I just figured the hell with it and ripped open the front of the pants and jumped out of them, yelling, "Ah HA!" I danced a quick jig as the perplexed audience sat there waiting for something more, when suddenly I heard the music change for the horse act.

I grabbed the pants and jumped out of the ring just in time to keep from being stampeded once again by the Norwegian Fjord Horses.

It was my first lesson in a basic law of circus slapstick from Stan Laurel: "When in doubt, drop your pants." Many years later I would hear the addendum to that golden rule succinctly put by Mr. Laurel: "And when your pants are down, always maintain an air of half-assed dignity."

★

The act, thought John and I, had potential. However, we didn't want to go through that charade again with knotty strings, so not knowing any better, we kept the premise and changed the theme. The next time we tried it, I went running in, shouting that "I was Theeee World's Grrrr-eatest Magician!" and John came running in, close on my heels declaring he was the World's Greatest magician, and then... well, the rest can be imagined.

To this day I don't recall what kind of stupid magic trick we attempted, nor what the blow off was supposed to be, though I think it had something to do with throwing water at the audience. It doesn't really matter. Our clown duo did stick it out for the rest of our short time with the Hoffmans. John was happy: no more dead cows' heads, Yolande smiled even more, and we wrangled five more pounds' wages a week for our efforts.

★

Circus tests you. Old maxim, and true. I was paying my dues. I certainly didn't get paid for it much: on payday each week, you had to knock on the Hoffman caravan and hope for a good outcome. The first time John and I tried it, one of the brothers came to the door and just stared at us, annoyed. I mumbled something about payday, but he spat on the ground and slammed the door in my face.

I told Charlie, who told us to try it again. I knocked on the door, and Hoffman looked like he was going to punch me in the face, but then his gaze looked past me and saw Charlie ten yards behind us— bear trainer, strongman, clown, arms folded across his wide chest. That's the only way we got paid each week.

Sometimes Charlie stood out of sight, and when the Hoffman brother opened the door and looked around and behind me—no Charlie—he grinned cunningly. I just stood calmly and waited. When his smirk turned to a frown, I knew Charlie had stepped out from the shadows, arms folded. Hoffman shook his head, grinned again, and with a snort handed us the cash from his pocket. It was all part of the game. Thanks, Charlie.

Ballad of Little John

*"'What's in THOSE wagons?' asked one lady patron.
'Lady, there we keep the ferocious donnikers.'"*
[Circus lingo: the 'donniker' is a toilet wagon.]

—*Ringling Route Book,*
Rutland, Vermont, 1887

Everyone in a touring tent show is a colorful character, whether artists, crew, or owners, and this is true for every circus I've worked with. The cast of characters would make a novelist envious. Everyone has a purpose for being there. There are no idle hands.

And every circus person I know, with the least bit of prompting, with good humor and a wink, will regale a listener with tales of catastrophes, injuries, practical jokes, good times and bad, and the resourceful characters that populate circus society. Here are a few such accounts from the Hoffman Circus.

The Car Wash

A former Hoffman employee relates that somewhere in the mountains of northern Wales, a local garage was opening a new car wash. The Boss—the Hoffman brothers were collectively referred to as The Boss or sometimes The Gang— arranges with its management to put an elephant into the car wash for publicity. Any ill-conceived publicity scheme erupting from the brains of the brothers invariably led to remarkable and often exciting incidents.

On opening day of the car wash, the elephant is led in. The proud owner switches on the car wash machinery. The pachyderm "goes postal" and wrecks the car wash and in an alarmed manner lumbers precipitously down the main road of the town to the panicked looks of startled pedestrians. Enjoying the ruckus—it turned out better than anticipated—The Boss laughs so hard somebody else has to deal with the situation.

Snorty George

Practical jokes were commonplace on a circus lot. One hapless crew member was Snorty George. I misheard the English accent the first time I passed a small caravan on the lot and heard a loud, bear-like grumble. "What was that?" I asked, startled.

"Oh, that's jus' Naughty George," was the reply I heard. I later discovered his story and his Snorty name.

Old George had been on the show for some years handling concessions, menagerie set-up, and other odd jobs. A good-natured fellow, he had thinning hair atop a round, cheeky face and a nice plump potbelly, something unusual around a circus lot where the workload invited a lean-and-mean physique.

George wasn't fat; he was just rounded. He could move fast when the situation was required. But that situation was rare for George. He had a reputation for taking every opportunity for naps in his caravan, an old vehicle barely big enough for his bulk. And when he snoozed, he snored like a bear in deep hibernation, unconcerned with the clamor and commotion of the build-up on the circus lot.

When in snooze mode nothing would awaken George. Snorty George's snores and snorts were as varied in tone, pitch, and rhythm, as the reverberations, crashes, wheezes, and clangs coming from the Hoffman band.

Snorty George was proud of, rather than indignant about the practical jokes he periodically endured. One story had George so fast asleep in his caravan one hot afternoon that the Hoffman boys hitched it up and quietly towed it five miles away and left it in the middle of an empty cow field.

Another story had it that someone had once secured a bag of dead fish to the underbelly of his caravan one hot summer. Day by day the stink grew stronger, and folks made detours around George. His place wreaked of low tide, but it never disturbed his naps one bit. Traveling from town to town, after about a week the rotting fish must have finally dropped off and the satisfying aroma of a circus backyard returned to normal—manure, hay, animal musk, damp canvas, and popcorn.

Old Tired Joe

I never knew the real names of the Hoffman tent crew and they never knew mine. Old Tired Joe was not old, though his weathered face gave that impression. He was a scrawny fellow with long stringy, always-dirty hair and pear-shaped muscles protruding from tough wiry arms. He was a typical circus odd-jobber—whatever needed to get done, he could be called upon to get it done.

Thus, he was an unloader—unloading trucks of bleacher seats and tent canvas. He was a sledge man, who could swing a sixteen-pound sledgehammer with one hand, pounding iron stakes deep into the earth without missing a beat. He was also a billman, hanging poster bills around town in the middle of the night.

Old Tired Joe had his shirt off on hot days, and I noticed a concave, hairless chest with strange wavy-horizontal-tattoo-like markings. One day, as we were hauling bleacher planks from the truck—he could carry a six-high stack of the stringers on one shoulder, while I could barely manage two—I asked him about the tattoos.

WHAM! He dropped the bleachers on the ground inside the tent, wiped his face, grinned and said, in a Liverpoolian twang: "Oi! The what? You mean this?" He pointed proudly to the faded horizontal scars across his chest and snorted what sounded like a short bark. Then he laughed, showing several missing teeth. He went on to tell me a tale as tall as a tent pole. He spoke with a grin, and a spark in his narrowed eyes.

Old Tired Joe told me of the time when The Gang decided to teach him a lesson for some infraction—he didn't rightly recall just what he did to earn such compensation. Any transgression, no matter how minor, was reasonable motive for The Gang to have some fun. They grabbed him by the limbs and held him down on his back as one of them drove the crawler dozer, a kind of small tractor, over his naked chest.

He was quite proud of the tire marks. It finally dawned on me why they called him Old "Tired" Joe. It had nothing to do with him being old or weary—he simply had been "tire-d."

Of course, I didn't believe a word of it. Circus folks do tend to embellish their stories. And yet, having witnessed The Gang in action, well...I wasn't sure. I've found, through personal experience, that what sounded magnified in the telling was often what had transpired.

I wanted to learn everything I could about the circus, including how to plaster a town with posters. So I sometimes joined Joe when he drove around a town in the advance van that carried the posters, glue, brushes, tape, and staples. There was a loudspeaker atop this van attached to a microphone in the cab.

I jumped in the advance truck with Joe one morning. It was great fun. It was also great to be off the circus lot, driving through the small Welsh villages in the northern mountains, advertising the coming of the circus. We posted bills on fences, barn doors, and shop windows, not bothering to ask permission. As we drove at a crawl through the main streets, Joe would grab the microphone and blare announcements through the loudspeaker like the voice of Almighty God, startling bystanders.

> **"Hoffman Brothers Circus! The Wildest Show On Earth! Right Here, Right Now! You there—pretty girl in the pink dress—yes, you... you'll have the time of your life at the circus!"**

The pretty girl in the pink dress on the sidewalk would nearly jump out of her shoes, looking around, flustered and blushing. Joe would proceed to pick out other strangers innocently walking in town and make them jump too. I would follow up with a rolled down window, so I could toss candies at groups of kids, and the occasional free admission tickets to other pretty girls in their summer dresses, as pointed out by Joe.

On the outskirts of a village, back in the rolling countryside, I would grab the microphone as we passed a field and announce to the startled cows that the circus was coming and any of them feeling adventurous were welcome to join up. The cows always lifted their heads and listened with large-eyed curiosity.

The Ballad of Little John

Little John had no need to try and stand out—he was immediately different, due to his midgetary stature, which he sometimes used to his advantage. It was impossible to know just what his private feelings were, what insecurities had led to the forced bravado he projected in public. There was a silent moment when we put on our clown makeup together, staring into pieces of broken mirror as a philosopher/scientist would inspect a foreign creature. Everyone has to deal with the hand they are dealt by nature.

Little John played the game as well as anyone. The circus gave him a job and a role in life. I was reminded of the twin dwarfs, Edward and Romeo Poirier, known as Tooty and Fats, who operated a popular gas station in Taunton, Massachusetts in the 1950s. Whenever a car pulled up to the pump at Midget Twins Service Station, they would dash out and climb up little step ladders to wash your windows and check your oil.

Little John also had his own way of dealing with the world where grownups towered over you and curious children looked at you, and everything manmade was oversized.

Big John and I had no caravan of our own to cook in, so we relied on the occasional meal invitations from the other artists and cheap café breakfasts to fill up on for the day. One morning Little John joined us in a village restaurant. Similar to an American diner, it had a counter up front with round, padded, revolving stools to sit on, and instead of booths, just a few round tables.

The three of us took counter seats. Big John and I swung a leg around our stools like cowboys in a saloon. Little John clambered up on his stool with both hands. The place was filled with early morning working folks. Being circus folks, I couldn't help feeling like we were aliens from a distant planet, who had taken over the bodies of three humans, so we could blend in and observe the natives.

As we waited for coffee, Little John punched my thigh and gestured with his short arm and a sideways nod. I swiveled in my stool to see two pretty girls sitting alone. They must have been eighteen or so, very attractive in their short skirts and blouses, talking quietly with their heads together.

I had a fantasy flash of boldness that lasted about two seconds, in which Big John and I sauntered over with our coffee to say, "May we join you?"

Our confidence came from that unique aura of being in the circus, a confidence which could lead to a flirtatious breakfast, an offer of free passes to the circus if they would like to find us after the show and, since we two had no caravan of our own, perhaps invite us both to their flats that night for...

That daydream quickly vanished as Little John punched me in the thigh again, urging me to go over and initiate conversation. I hesitated too long, using the feeble excuse that I would go over, except there were three of us and I didn't want to leave Little John behind.

Fed up with my timidity, Little John growled, "Bloody 'ell...'eres 'ow yeh do it," and slid off his stool awkwardly, waddled over to the girls, stood between their chairs, his head at the same level as their chests. They sat staring at him, his eyes staring back at them at breast-height.

Big John and I were transfixed, waiting to see what would happen next. Then the bold little guy said, straight off, without any introduction or attempt to keep his voice low, "Ever fuck a midget?"

My jaw dropped and I flushed. The room was silent for a moment, just long enough for me to see the other patrons of the establishment—all grizzled workingmen it seemed—turn their heads to watch, coffee cups frozen mid-air.

That was long enough for another split-second reverie to invade my brain: the men leaping up to defend the honor of the innocent lasses, tables overturned, dishes crashing to the floor, Big John and I throwing powdered sugar into the faces of the angry mob as we grabbed Little John and bodily carried him out the door like an animated sack of potatoes, his arms and legs waving in frustration.

I also had a ridiculously aloof moment of lucid reflection: wasn't Little John a dwarf—large head attached to short stubby legs and arms—so why did he say "midget" which refers to people of short stature with regular physical proportions? Was he using "midget" as a derogatory term, or simply for effect? What the hell?

But there was no chaotic eruption. Life resumed without event. Patrons ate their breakfasts. Amazed, I watched the girls blush prettily, and Little John pulled up a chair between them and started a low conversation we couldn't hear.

John and I ate our breakfast at the counter, feeling abashed and foolish. Once in a while, I glanced back to see if we were needed to rescue the girls, but all three seemed to be enjoying themselves.

We finished our food, Little John waved us over, introduced the giggling girls, then waved us away. "See yeh back at the tent," he said, with impressive audacity. And that was that.

Walking back to the circus lot, I said to John, "Holy Smokes, that was one hell of a pickup line, eh?" There was a pause before he nodded and replied, "And one we will never be able to use."

Later that night after the show, we saw the girls hanging around. I said hello to them, but it was jump night—the tent was coming down and there were a couple more hours of work ahead. A little while longer, I looked around and saw them way off in the distance, disappearing into the night forever.

I asked Little John later what had happened. All I got was a wicked wink.

Hey Rube!

"Coffeyville is famous from the fact that the Dalton gang was shot to death, while endeavoring to rob the two banks ten years ago. One of the men who is said to have killed two of the gang in the running fight that occurred on that fateful day, furnished the show with hay and oats. It was reported that Mrs. Dalton, the mother of the desperadoes, was a visitor at the matinee."

–Ringling Route Book,
Coffeyville, Kansas, September 25, 1901

Hoffman's Circus was no stranger to a "Hey, Rube!" In the old days, this is what American circus folks yelled whenever the local toughs, the rubes, showed up at the show, drunk and looking for a fight. It was Roustabouts versus Rubes, Rowdies against Townies—never a fair match. How could it be? I never could understand why townies would think they could browbeat the Hoffman tent crew of angry, muscle-bound roustabouts, brandishing iron stakes.

"Hey, Rube!" was the call to action to grab a sledgehammer—or anything handy, like extra tent stakes, or a coil of heavy rope, or horse whips—and jump into the fray.

★

W.C. Coup, writing in his 1901 memoir about his mid-nineteenth-century circus adventures in *Sawdust & Spangles: Stories & Secrets of the Circus,* comments:

In these peaceful days it is almost impossible to realize the rough and desperate character of the people...from which the old-time wagon shows drew their principal patronage. In the days of Abraham Lincoln's childhood, 'fighting was in the air,' and the showmen received their full share of it. It was no infrequent occurrence to be set upon by a party of roughs determined to show their prowess and skill as marksmen with fists and clubs. Many years later, when describing this part of my career of battles and circus fights to General Grant, he admitted that my experience in thrilling and startling incidents compared favorably with his own, the difference being that he was backed by a powerful government, while for the showmen there seemed to be little sympathy.

I came to believe the Hoffman brothers relished the occasional skirmish and may have been the instigators more than once. We were often harassed by town councilmen and village constables. It appeared the Hoffmans had nothing but disdain for such bothersome things as fees for local permits, and no doubt they enjoyed a kind of roguish satisfaction in their irregular reputations.

I can easily envision a Hoffman-style Hey Rube. Local constabularies—inflamed and insulted by Hoffman's scorn for their authority—engage the local toughs to incite a brawl late after the show: "Rightio! We'll teach those itinerant circus show-offs a thing er two!"

The Hoffman Gang, with circus sixth sense, hide in the shadows as the townies creep onto the lot at midnight and attempt to cut ropes and slash the tent. I witness it all from the safety of the animal tent. Suddenly the signal rings out—Frankie on drums and the organ blasting out the fighting anthem, "There's No Business, Like Show Business"—as roustabouts with iron stakes surround the ruffians.

Astride the elephants trumpeting, the Hoffmans charge, led by Wild Bill Hoffman riding bareback on a Norwegian Knapstrupper, the Santus brothers running around shouting and looking for someone to throw juggling knives at. Another happy Hoffman brandishes a lasso and snaps a horse whip around the shins of a retreating townie. I ride bareback on a snorting Achmed the Camel, scattering a terrified group of ruffians.

Yolande Santus crouches behind a wagon, stands up and whomps a townie behind the knees with the heavy twirling baton. As the poor fellow limps away, she looks over at me and winks, eyes sparkling with fire. I wink back and shout: "Ah, bien fait!" and ride away under the stars on the haughty camel (*from Tibet!*).

★

These contradictions in circus life, especially apparent in the Hoffman operation, were a throwback to traveling mud shows of a century past, when itinerant show folk were considered disreputable by certain segments of society, either by territorial town officials or the religious-minded citizens appalled by "loose" circus women performing in tights, and of course by drunken townies simply out to break something.

The circus chaos seemed to be standard operating procedure for the Hoffmans—it was simply business as usual. I think they just didn't know how else to do things.

They had no artistic sensibility and no control over their animals and no sense of style or rapport with audiences. They were outrageous. But they kept the show on the road, no minor feat. And they were a family, working and struggling together. You had to like them for who they were, in their own way. They were always grinning! Maybe it was just youthful mischievousness.

I learned a great deal of how not to do things from these guys. I knew, even in the midst of it all: it was a very valuable education. It provided me with a big part of my personal mission: gathering improbable stories to tell when I was old.

A Hoffman Farewell

"Thieves took advantage of the popularity of circus day, ransacking empty houses. Five inebriated individuals were lodged in jail as early as ten in the morning. Several other drunken songsters were added to the assortment, and the concert late that night was enough to take the starch out of any circus poster."

—*Burlington Free Press*,
Burlington, Vermont, 1883

Decades after my encounter with the Hoffmans, I was talking with an Englishman, Chris Barltrop, at a circus festival in London, and I said, offhandedly: "Hey, you know, my very first circus was in Britain, with the Hoffmans."

He got all excited, took my hand with both of his, and shook it heartily. Laughing, he said: "You worked with the legendary Hoffman gang? And survived? Bloody 'ell!"

Turns out that some years after my time, Barltrop had worked for the Hoffmans as bill poster, and later ringmaster as well as artist, performer, director. He gave me some history: Hoffman was not the real family name.

The Gang were offspring of Billy Mack, "a very eccentric show-man," according to articles of the day. He was director of Broncho Bill's Circus in the fifties and sixties. Thinking it would be good pub-licity, Billy had claimed his show to be American and The Wildest

Show on Earth. The first act was a full-grown, angry buffalo, hurtling into the ring with Billy dragged behind, hanging on to a piece of rope for dear life. The show later became known as Circus Hoffman—still living up to its reputation as The Wildest Show on Earth!

A few weeks after meeting Chris, I received a package from him in the mail. It was a VHS copy of a British television newscast about Circus Hoffman from 1970, the year after I had left. It's all there! Achmed the Damn Camel, Charlie with his balloon snake, the Hoffman boys at work, Franky the Face, the Majorettes gamely smiling and dropping their batons.

The broadcaster couldn't quite believe the footage he was showing. The news crew had only intended to film a little piece about a traditional British circus. When they showed up with cameras on the lot, they were astonished and not a little amused by what they witnessed and happily took advantage of the madcap situation. The sixteen-minute black and white broadcast, with tongue-in-cheek British commentary, is hilarious.

It finishes up just after a matinee show with shots of the backlot crew chasing loose animals, a mule kicking a roustabout, the gruff bison on a rope pulling a hapless Hoffman behind a truck, the camels biting each other, the elephant swaying in a dance, seeming to smile, trunk raised in salute to all the wonderful commotion.

Voiceover: "The hardworking Hoffman family can generally be found running hither and yon with apparent determination. [Pause.] And in just one hour, it all begins again."

★

After Hoffman, I lost all contact with my friend John for decades. John focused on business and political science in college, eventually returning to Canada to pursue a career in government diplomacy. The circus in Wales seemed like an ancient mythological beast, dangerous and rarely believed to exist. Having told the Tales of Hoffman for so long, I was curious to find out how much embellishment I had given to the stories. I decided to track him down, and I gave him a call.

"Hello, Canadia? This is Tex, the Fastest Gun in the Whole Wild West." There was a long pause on the line, and then what sounded like a muffled guffaw.

"No siree—I'm the fastest gun in tarnation, dagnabit!"

I laughed, relieved I had found the right Canadian. "Listen, old friend," I said, "I've been telling those Hoffman stories so long—I'm just calling to fact check. What—in tarnation—do you remember?"

"I remember when we started out, you had to settle for the Pink Room..."

"Good Lord, that's right!" I said, amazed.

"...and you saved me from that pile of dead cows' heads...and you ended up bronco-riding that crazy camel...and one of us got locked in the lion cage by Frankie the Face...and..." The words just tumbled out from the other end of the phone, as if a restrained herd of wild horses, corralled for too long, had broken through the fencing and—momentarily stunned with sudden liberation—stampeded in jubilation.

As we corroborated each other's stories, we both felt the relief of validation. It was confirmation that you don't need to fabricate stories of circus life. Veracity is enough.

Thirty years later, I was visiting Gerry Cottle's new circus headquarters in southwest England in the village of Wookey Hole. Gerry was the largest producer of circus shows in Britain, a modern entrepreneur showman with touring tent shows and year-round theatrical productions. He started in the business like me, from the outside, learning the trade after joining up with a show as a teenager.

Gerry took me around back to the tool shop and said, "There's someone here who wants to say hello." Out came Big Charlie—Karl Brenner himself—with tools in his hand, fixing some broken circus equipment. "Hey Tex!" he said in his German accent, "c'mon in, I'll put on de tea."

I sat in Charlie's caravan and out came the marmalade cookies and pickles and crackers with cheese, as if just a single winter season had gone by—not three decades.

I love that about the circus. You can go anywhere in the world and walk up to a circus where you know no one and still be welcomed by ears eager to hear your stories and share theirs. But even more likely, you'll suddenly hear the words, "C'mon in, the tea's on," and someone you worked with decades ago is grinning at your surprised face.

★

I harbored for years the idea that the Hoffman guys were tough characters, real hooligans. As Gerry Cottle told me, "Their shows were what we call in England rough-and-ready. They conformed to their own rules, always changing phone numbers and truck license plates. All the boys were very independent characters," said Cottle, "really from another age; doubtful to see their likes again."

Then I watch that old broadcast video from fifty years ago, and I see they were really very young! I couldn't stop grinning when I first watched it. Boisterous and cunning lads. Mid-twenties to early thirties. Not that much older than I was at the time. I tell these stories and some friends find them implausible. So, I show them the video.

Even now, when I feel down and dispirited, I pop in the tape and my humor returns. Thanks for that, boys...tip o' the hat to yeh.

Even as inexperienced as I was when I encountered the Hoffmans, I knew their show was a throwback to a past era of mud shows. I felt like I was back in the mid-nineteenth century. They were scoundrels, but they deserve a lot of credit: they started young and stayed a long time in the business. I could put up with all the shenanigans and fatigue and hard work; I felt immediately familiar with the circus environment—community, culture, lifestyle, independence, animals, smells, traditions—it all really felt strangely comfortable.

Perhaps by telling these stories, I have redeemed the Hoffman coarseness by providing what they seemed to be striving for, a resemblance to those other five young brothers from a hundred and fifty years ago, the Ringling boys. The difference, of course, is that the Ringling brothers built an institution, one that started as a one-horse mud show and grew to become "The Greatest Show on Earth," with a strict moral code of behavior for its employees.

The Hoffmans more closely resemble those legendary American wild west gangs: The Daltons, the Clanton Gang of Tombstone, Frank and Jesse James... The notorious Hoffman Brothers of Britain! The Wildest Show on Earth, indeed.

Act II

A Clown
in Copenhagen

A Clown in Copenhgen

Facing page: Top, Pete Harrison and Robin, in the Circus Building dressing room, 1973. Bottom left, Antonio & Robin face the mirror prepaing for the the show. Bottom right, equestrienne, Diana Benneweis and ringmaster, Claus Jespersen, 1973, in street clothes.

This page: Top, Robin, Pete, and Antonio, Benneweis "house clowns" 1973-75. Bottom, the Caroli family, with Francesco (left), perform musical finale.

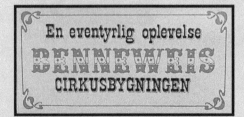

This page: Top, Cirkusbygningen in Copenhagen, 1886. Middle, Les Francescos: Italian clowns Ernesto, Francesco, and Enrico Caroli. Bottom, Benneweis sticker, "An adventurous experience."

Facing page: Top, Renovated Circus Building, Copenhagen, 1977. Bottom, Clown Robin in front of Benneweis poster, 1973.

The Legacy of Marceau

"What I wanted to do is pursue in silence,
with dramatic action, the metaphors of the world,
which carry the weight of the soul. My character,
Bip, is torn on the battlefield of life between
comedy and tragedy."

—Marcel Marceau, interview,
author's collection

I n the fall of 1969, after the summer with Hoffman Circus, I went directly to Paris to study with legendary mime Marcel Marceau, the man who would become my mentor the rest of my life.

The first time I had seen Marceau was in 1965. I was a teenager, home with my family, waiting to watch The Red Skelton Show on TV. The usual variety hour of jokes, skits, song, and dance was replaced with "A Concert in Pantomime," a one-hour episode of silent skits performed by Red Skelton and Marcel Marceau. There had been nothing like it on TV: an hour with no words! I was fascinated.

Four years later, while in college in northern Illinois, I saw a notice that Marcel Marceau would be performing in Madison, Wisconsin. I had to see him perform live! It was mid-winter, and Madison was a couple of hours away. I borrowed a car and drove through a blinding snowstorm. The show was at eight o'clock.

I got to the theater late, but in time: quarter to eight! I ran to the box office, but it was closed. There was a sign on the window: "Sold Out."

When you are nineteen years old with a passion, you don't just give up at the first obstacle. I walked around the block, with the snow falling hard. Down an alleyway, I found an unlocked door. I walked through it into empty hallways, where another door led me to a large walk-in closet full of winter coats. The light clicked on. A man said: "You here to help?"

I almost saluted and clicked my heels as I stammered: "Yes...sir!"

"Well, come on, quick! The show's about to start. We'll put up these folding chairs in the back so the volunteers and ushers can watch the show. Come on!"

I jumped to work. I put up some chairs, opened one and sat right down, a minute before the curtain rose on Marceau. For the next two hours I was mesmerized along with the packed audience. In the back of the program notes, a sentence caught my eye: "Marceau will open his first International School of Mime in October."

I wrote a letter, asking for an application. A short form letter came back, stating simply that classes begin October 3, 1969, 10:00 a.m. at Theatre de la Musique, Paris. That was it. No instructions for audition or resume. I showed the letter to my dad and asked his opinion.

"Well," he said, "you'll never know—if you don't go over and find out." Bless his heart, I had permission for adventure!

I showed up in Paris, on the third day of October, and sure enough, Marceau's brother Alain checked my name off a list of international students. I was in! Classes were in Acrobatics, Classic Dance, Mime Technique, Mime Improvisation, Act Creation, and Fencing.

Marceau loved fencing. Our master teacher, Claude Caux, was French champion in three weapons: foil, epee, sabre. Sometimes Marceau would join the class and challenge us. It was intimidating and awkward to fence with Marceau: he was a master, and left-handed.

★

Marceau's white-face pantomime image was by then known universally, comparable on a global scale to Chaplin's iconic Little Tramp image. Marceau's unique artistry made mime a modern theatrical art form, his name becoming synonymous with the silent art. The depth of Marceau's artistry had a profound influence on my career and shaped my artistic worldview.

I visited with him every year for the next thirty years. He became a lifelong mentor and friend. I was invited as an observer into his world of high society: celebrities, artists, actors, politicians, and movie stars. They flocked to his shows, respectful and in awe of his artistry, while Marceau himself appeared humbled by their attention.

The world of a mime is in theater; the life of a circus artist is in the ring. The theater is a world of fantasy and imagination, life simulated inside a darkened theater. Circus is immediate, physical, elemental, dangerous, a lifestyle between sawdust and canvas. The blend of the two worlds encompasses centuries of overlapping traditions. There is a fascinating history here and stories of the mime masters to tell— but that is for another time.

★

I fell for mime. It fit my reserved personality and I seemed to have an innate talent for it. But I hadn't been able to shake the sawdust out of my clown shoes. Performing mime on stage fed my sense of romantic lyrical poetry, but the boundaries of the stage felt limiting. I missed the magic of the Big Top, the camaraderie of very real characters, the laughter, the animals, the sawdust, and the endless stories. I even missed the mud.

After my year of training with L'Ecole Internationale de Mime, I felt the urge to hit the road and perform again under canvas. It was time to run off and join the circus—for the second time.

Gypsy

"Two farmers during the show at night started to dance on the hippodrome track. One of them easily succumbed to the influence of a lady, who led him by the ear back to the seats."

—*Ringling Route Book,*
Hutchinson, Kansas, 1891

Upon hearing my stories, some people have said I must be either very foolish or very bold. That doesn't account, though, for the private fear I felt each time I set out. Not a fear of danger or disaster, but dread at not being in control in a foreign world. It is self-doubt that haunts the back of your mind, the insecurity of feeling not good enough.

What if I put myself out there and can't handle what happens? What if nothing happens? I needed to find out...

As is my style, I needed a hook, a motivation to take the first step on such a quest. This time the hook was Charlie Chaplin. I heard that the silent film icon, living in Switzerland, would come down from his mountain home with his brood of children to visit Circus Knie, the Swiss National Circus, when it came to his village.

Founded in 1803, Circus Knie is still the largest tenting show in Switzerland and a national institution. It is also one of Europe's most respected circuses, defining the standards against which other circuses are measured. The Knie family is the equivalent of a Swiss royal family.

Chaplin loved the circus and would invite the Knie family and circus artists to his home for a party after the show. I thought how wonderful it would be to perform for the master of mime and silent cinema. This was in 1973, the year after Chaplin, 83 years old, was given an Honorary Academy Award in Hollywood for "the incalculable effect he has had in making motion pictures the art form of this century."

With fifty dollars in my pocket and a cheap plane ticket to Luxembourg, I planned to hitchhike to Switzerland and join up with Circus Knie and take any job available—roustabout, crew, animal caretaker—and eventually clowning. I gave myself a window of three days to find the circus before the money ran out.

My first day out on the road brought me to a marketplace fair in a town on the outskirts of Luxembourg City. In the village square that afternoon, I watched a Romani family perform a small outdoor show. They had hung a colorful curtain between two caravans as a back-drop. A low barrier made of long ribbons, connected by short wooden spikes, delineated their performing ring space.

Two elders in crimson vests and solemn wrinkled faces played earnestly on accordion and tambourine. A swarthy fellow played fiddle. There was a scruffy trick dog, white with black spots, a couple of small horses, some dashingly handsome tumblers with mustaches, several long-haired children collecting money from the spectators, and an appealing teenage daughter with dark eyes, dancing with arms over her head, joyously flinging her hip-length black hair from side to side.

There was a mesmerizing charm in the scene—no fancy sets and lights and technical instruments. It was human scale.

The gypsy dancer was slender and pretty and she danced with a graceful simplicity. The dance was somehow not sexual—it was more a flirtation with the senses, joy of movement as passionate enter-tainment. There was a feeling of delight, watching her, a kind of detached appreciation of sensual beauty.

I felt the serenity that comes with the sense that it is okay to watch a talented artist and feel drawn to the artistic line of a leg, the design of an upturned arm, the nobility of bearing, the tilt of the head, the affinity of gesture with the rhythm of the music. It is like watching a beautiful ballerina, a graceful bareback rider, a figure skater, a confident aerialist. Talent and skill linked with the physical grace of a circus artist is irresistibly magnetic and sexy and authentically beautiful.

There is a superb documentary film about the life of Carmen Amaya: *Queen of the Gypsies,* who was widely considered the greatest flamenco dancer in the twentieth century. A description of Carmen Amaya by Sebastià Gasch—an art critic who saw her while still a teenager in 1929, best describes the young gypsy dancer I had watched:

> *Suddenly a jump! And the gypsy girl danced. Indescribable. Pure Soul. Feeling made flesh. Like all gypsies, she must have been born dancing. Promptly, the viewer feels subjugated, dominated by her fierce hip movements, by the bravery of her pirouettes and the force of her broken turns, whose animal ardor ran parallel with the astonishing accuracy with which she executed them.*

After the performance, with nothing to lose, no place to stay, and nothing in my stomach, I approached one of the gypsy guys. I mentioned I was a mime and clown, and I was looking for a circus. Did he know of one in the area?

He took me over to his family. They looked me over and communicated with each other in a language I didn't understand and waited for the elders to make an assessment. Could I play music?

Yes, I replied, the trumpet. Suddenly a trumpet appeared from one of the mustached brothers. After more questions and negotiations, I was recruited. The terms: no money to pass hands, but they would feed me aplenty and provide blankets and straw for the night on the ground if I would show them some tricks and accompany the accordion in their show.

I suspect the hospitality shown to me was not typical. Possibly the social amiability extended to a stranger like me was for the sake of novelty. Perhaps they may have rightly deemed me harmless, a hapless clown, and had a native sympathy for a lost spirit.

In their evening show I tootled on the trumpet and did mime and a few simple magic tricks as a pre-show. Afterwards, accepted as a fellow itinerant artist, I was invited to partake in a hearty family dinner, which included a spicily seasoned string of chicken char-broiled on an open fire, skewered on what looked like a long knife from their knife-throwing act.

I endured substantial interrogation about life for performers in America, when I really wanted to know about their gypsy life. They were generous with their stories and their laughter. I could see religious icons and flowers and ornaments garnishing their itinerant home as the food kept magically reappearing from the open door of the caravan. Their friendly dogs stayed at our feet, contentedly chomping on scraps.

As twilight gathered around us and the dishes were cleared, there was one ugly incident that spoke of a long history of racial prejudice toward Romani culture. Some youngish punks nearby, swaying from

intoxication, made loud drunken remarks concerning the flowery skirts of the young female dancer. The scowls of her mustached brothers as they stood up was enough to slow the advancement of the rowdies, but still they taunted the family.

The brother who held the knife, lately sheathed with that stringy piece of chicken, rubbed the grease on his pants and suddenly threw it twenty feet to stick in a tree near the ruffians. They halted, swayed in unison in an about-face turn, and lurched down the road like a waddle of inebriated penguins.

Antagonism between "townies" and itinerant performers has a long history for gypsy and circus folk alike. For two hundred years, circus folks were seen as deceitful, disreputable, dangerous dregs of society, menacing the morality of decent town folk.

There was also some history of friction between Romani and circus folks in Europe. In the 1800s there was a lot of competition for audiences among the many traveling shows.

Since the horse-drawn circuses always drew crowds from villages out to the circus field, small itinerant Romani families often followed the shows and set up their wares nearby. Circus owners generally disliked these operations, which they felt distracted the crowds from the circus business. But there were some circus owners who developed friendly alliances with their fellow travelers and welcomed the extra attraction.

Lord George Sanger was Britain's greatest circus showman in the nineteenth century. He retired from circus business in 1905, approaching his eightieth year, to write his memoirs. In *Seventy Years a Showman*, Sanger writes about gypsies performing on the same fairgrounds as his father's show. His description is faithful, if more elaborate, to the family I had encountered:

> *I have seen young gypsy girls—gloriously beautiful—literally draped from shoulders to ankles in silk handkerchiefs of the most costly description, great gold bangles on their wrists, heavy jeweled ornaments in their ears, and flashing rings on their fingers, flaunting their finery at this fair in the forest. With them would walk their chosen gypsy swains, clad in shining velveteen, spangled with buttons of gold, silver, and pearl. Buckles of silver*

adorned their shoes, and peeping from the black, well-oiled locks
that hung to their shoulders under the broad felt hats might be
seen enormously thick gold earrings.

★

Decades later I would visit a popular gypsy circus in Paris beneath a small, raggedy old tent and rickety bleachers, kids sitting on the ground right up to the ring. "Despite the turbulence of the world, our fury for life is not weakened!" declared Alexandre Romanes, founder with his wife Delia, of The Cirque Romanes in 1994. It was the most charming and authentic show, featuring colorful Romanian costumes, dark-skinned Roma acrobats, and musicians playing Balkan music on fiddle, accordion, clarinet, tambourines, and trumpet, all sounding to my ears like furiously eclectic Klezmer music.

The whole affair felt like being welcomed at a gypsy wedding with dancing, swirling dresses, nonstop music and proud performers. I was sitting in the crowded intimate tent between my friends Alla Youdina—former star of the original Moscow Circus on Ice, now Director of Creation for Ringling Bros.—and Tim Holst, Vice President of Ringling Bros. and Barnum & Bailey.

These two representatives of the largest show on earth sat on hard wooden bleachers watching the smallest gypsy show on earth. And they loved it. I saw in their enthusiasm an almost nostalgic regret about the constant pressure for perfection in a big corporate circus, compared to the little family circus before us there in Paris.

Years before that day, in the town square in Luxembourg, I already had an intimation of what I was after: passion over perfection. I determined that someday, when I had my own circus, it would be built on a foundation of style and charm all its own. As Tom Sawyer said to Huck Finn, it's all about style—if you go about doing something—well, do it with style!

★

After the excitement of my day with the gypsy family and the feasting was over, the fire was stoked, and stories commenced about life on the road. The wine flowed. They sang some Romani songs and cajoled a song from me.

In the few seconds it took to stand up, songs flashed through my head, but all I could come up with, inspired by my time as Tex, were some verses of an old cowboy ballad:

"Oh, give me a Home / Where the Buffalo roam / Where the deer and the antelope plaaay / Where seldom is heard a Discouraging Word / And the Skies are not Cloudy all daaay / Home, home on the Raaange..."

I sat down to grins and uplifted wine glasses. They laughed gaily and tossed benedictions of good fortune my way. I needed good fortune to find a circus before my money ran out.

I mentioned this again to the family.

The elder matriarch read my palm, one of the boys translating. I wish I could recall the full fortune she foretold. In any case, would I find a circus?

With flashing eyes and a wave of her hand, she answered in English: "You will."

I was exhausted and ready for deep sleep. I wondered if I should travel with this exotic family a bit. No, I realized as I curled up in wooly horse blankets on the ground. This was a story, for sure, but I had to move on.

Besides, I was getting flirtatious glances from the dark-eyed young dancer and suspicious frowns from her brothers. I surmised she had very few opportunities to speak with any male outside the family.

Content with the adventures of the day, everyone disbursed and found contented sleep. Before the break of dawn, I folded up the blankets, silently shared a muddy cup of coffee with the elder matriarch, the only family member up at that hour, and left a note of gratitude in the bell of the trumpet.

Slipping quietly out of town, I found the road again.

Cirkusbygningen i København

*"The cirkusbygningen [circus building] in the very
center of København, built in 1886, is circular and
topped by a golden dome. The most distinctive
feature of the facade is a frieze located just below
the roof on the periphery of the outer wall depicting
circus motifs from ancient Rome and Greece."*

—*Tourist History of Denmark*

Kids are natural explorers. When I was nine years old, I decided it was time to see something of the larger world beyond my backyard, just for a day. The plan was simple: I'd climb the nearby hill, wait for the right, small cotton puff of cloud to come directly overhead…and follow wherever it took me. Until lunch time. Then I'd retrace my steps and be home in time for dinner.

Adventure would simply happen along the way. Who knows, maybe I'd even bump into a circus. Lighting out for new territory and being led, literally, by the winds of fate was the whole point. Nine is a great age for exploration.

The perfect cloud shape very slowly appeared on the far horizon. When it was directly overhead, I stood up and off I went! After about ten steps I looked up—the cloud had changed shape. Not only that—it was moving quite fast. I had to pick up my stride to keep apace. Then I was running. Suddenly the little cloud was far off to the opposite horizon, changed from a puff to a white galloping horse and...gone.

Only five minutes had passed. I sat down on the earth and studied ants the rest of the day, occasionally glancing up at the passing clouds, occupied with vague big thoughts.

There are beautiful moments in a child's experience, moments extraordinary and deeply personal, when the world shifts. It can be a puzzling, profound awakening. That little boy trying to follow a cloud was left with an uneasy sense that his self-absorbed worldview might be inadequate. Growing up is as often about moments of disillusionment as much as revelation—what we learn depends on which of those moods takes over.

★

As I left that gypsy camp at break of dawn in Luxembourg, I was already losing my sense of adventure, and feeling a looming disillusionment. I looked up and saw a lonely white cloud floating lazily above. Remembering my boyhood, I noted the direction and took the first ride going that way.

I was so tired and disoriented I didn't care where it would lead. With each ride I enquired the whereabouts of a circus. Late in the day, I was dropped off right in front of a large circus big top—in Belgium! I had been heading north, instead of west towards Switzerland and Circus Knie.

With a sinking spirit, I found the Belgian circus director and asked for a job.

"A clown, eh?" he said, looking me over with raised eyebrows. "Okay, watch the show tonight, and we'll audition you in the morning."

I felt no sense of excitement or adventure; something was missing. My instinct was correct. I saw the show that night and was mightily discouraged by the clowns. They were coarse and just...unfunny.

Dispirited, with no place to sleep, I waited until the circus had gone to bed, then crawled under the bleachers, made a pillow of straw, determined to skip town once again at the break of dawn.

Dreams of Charlie Chaplin and the Circus Knie had fast dissipated. It's disheartening how easily high-falutin' plans can vanish when weariness sets in. What the hell was I thinking? Self-doubts creep in and take hold, when you're hungry and alone and sleeping on straw. In a foreign country. With no money. And it starts raining.

★

Day three on the road. Heavy rain. I found a train station and spent the last of my money on a ticket north. I knew someone in Sweden, so I figured I would ride to Stockholm, find my friend, rethink my mission, maybe borrow, or work for, some money for a flight back home.

I dozed on the train all the way to a stopover in Denmark. I had an hour to kill before the connection to Stockholm, so I wandered out of the station to see a bit of Copenhagen.

It was raining in Denmark, too. I felt lost and forlorn, carrying my wet suitcase. Just a few blocks away, I came to the large gate of The Tivoli Gardens, but I couldn't afford the entrance fee. And then, quite unexpectedly, I turned and was astonished to see a beautiful circus building a block away! What!?

It stood on a corner of the city block, a wide, circular building with carved circus figures around the domed roof and a huge forty-foot smiling clown figure over the doors, advertising the World Star-Time International Cirkus Benneweis!

Dripping wet from the rain, I walked up to the box office and inquired about the show. The matinee was about to begin! I had no money, I explained to the ticket lady, but I was a clown with the circus, and...

"Oh! How nice to meet you! Here's a ticket, go right in!" This was my first experience of circus showfolk's easy acceptance of one of their kind.

I was ushered to my seat after passing through a decorative lobby with walls displaying historic circus posters and photos from a century of circus stars who had performed there. Two thousand red velvet cushioned seats faced, amphitheater-style, down to the ring, which was carpeted with a huge yellow star. More sparkling stars, depicting a glittering horse and elephant, decorated the blue velvet ring curtain. A sixteen-piece orchestra sat in a balcony above the ring entrance.

All thoughts of the train departing in thirty minutes for Sweden vanished. That unexpected welcome at the box office, that strange sensation of inevitability—the sense that my world had just immensely expanded—hung over me like a protective umbrella.

I was enthralled.

★

Two hours later, as the audience exited, I just sat there. The show had been unlike anything I had ever seen. It was, in a word, classy. There were elite circus artistes from around the world, great musicians, and a couple of enjoyable clowns. They were listed in the program notes as Pete, an older, bald fellow from England, and his partner, a Spanish dwarf named Antonio.

The circus princess was an exotically elegant and athletic woman with long black hair and stunning smile—Diana Benneweis—who masterfully directed her beautiful white horses while wearing a dazzling Parisian gown. The ringmaster—Claus Jespersen—wore a gray tuxedo and top hat and presented the acts with smooth composure, in a relaxed voice, as if entertaining friends in his living room. It was all very gracious, quite different from American-style circus bravado and ballyhoo.

Someday, I thought, I will return to Copenhagen and perform in this building. It will probably take me twenty years, gaining experience in smaller shows, training with master clowns, getting jobs in ever-bigger shows, and ultimately: the circus building in Copenhagen! I now had a reasonable long-term goal in life. Twenty years, I figured—yes, I'll be back in twenty years.

I was thinking these thoughts as I watched the ring boys sweeping the ring and cleaning around the seats. One of them awoke me from my daydream: "Can I help you?"

"No, uh, thanks. I was just thinking about the show."

"Did you enjoy it?"

"Oh, yes, fabulous! Actually, I work in circus, I'm a clown, and I—"

"Clown?! Really? Want to meet the director?

"What?! No! I just—"

He grabbed my arm saying, "Come on, why not? His dressing room is just over here."

"No, no. It's alright—I'll be back in twenty years! "

He knocked on the dressing room door and shoved me in. I found myself facing the ringmaster, Claus, nonchalantly sitting on a couch, holding a glass of brandy, and wearing nothing but underwear.

As we stared at each other, Diana Benneweis walked out of the bathroom—also holding a small glass of brandy—dressed in nothing but a white cotton towel, her long black hair wet from the shower. Without missing a beat, she came over to me, flashed her brilliant smile, and handed me her glass: "Hello, I'm Diana."

I don't drink—but I downed the contents of that glass in a gulp and gaped at them both.

Claus and Diana were in their late twenties, a strikingly handsome couple. Claus came from a Danish military family and trained with horses at an early age. He had an erect bearing, wavy fair hair, and young Richard Burton good looks. Diana had waist-length, jet-black hair and classic Mediterranean beauty. She was the adopted daughter of Eli Benneweis, who was born in 1911, and became one of Europe's most successful circus entrepreneurs.

★

The origin of Cirkus Benneweis dates to 1887, making it one of the circus world's oldest family dynasties, still operating after one hundred and thirty years. In 1973, when I showed up, Eli Benneweis was still touring with the Cirkus Benneweis tent show, Denmark's premiere traveling circus, while Diana and Claus ran the highly regarded Benneweis show in Copenhagen's famous century-old cirkusbygningen.

I learned later that Claus was the creative innovator, hiring the acts and directing the programs with a confident, youthful vigor. Diana was the business brains behind the operations. She was the no-nonsense, strong-willed producer with disarming charm behind a willful temperament. He was the fun-loving playboy with an inventive artistic sensibility.

They were two extremely indomitable lovers, living in a highly publicized and contentious partnership.

The two stared at me, glanced quickly at each other, then back at me, expectant. I stood there nonplussed. I introduced myself as Robin—the name my Scandinavian friends knew me by—and mumbled something about the great show I had just seen.

They asked about my experience. I stammered something about having worked in the circus ring, not mentioning the Hoffman gang, and having trained with Marcel Marceau. That caught their attention.

Claus called out for a ring boy to fetch Peter Harrison, the old British clown in the show. When he came into the dressing room he was still in costume, but without the bald clown wig. He was no old-timer after all: his brown bushy hair and long narrow face matched mine! We stared at each other, looking like twin brothers, the same age.

Claus and Diana looked at the two of us with bemusement. Claus was the first to speak: "Pete, what do you think—shall we try him out?"

Later I'd learn that Antonio, Pete's clown partner of short stature, was unwell. Antonio had been a fixture in the circus building for twenty years, first with Cirkus Schumann when they operated the building, then with Benneweis. Already in late middle-age, Antonio was having health troubles related to kidneys, beer, and dwarfism; he often came to work rather unsteady.

Pete agreed to work with me the next day to teach me their routines on a trial basis. We shook on it and decided to meet at ten the next morning.

Dazed by this turnaround of affairs, I was still acutely aware of my situation: I said to Claus that I had been on my way to Sweden and had no money or place to stay the night. He looked at Diana, who simply nodded. He reached into his pocket and handed me 400 Danish Kroner. We shook hands, and that was that. I would be in the show the next night!

My self-predicted twenty years had passed—SNAP! —like that.

★

Ten o'clock the next morning I showed up with nervous antici- pation, only to find the whole circus company out on the sidewalk in front of the building, elephants, artistes in full costume all lined up, horses prancing in place with nervous excitement. Pete saw me and frantically pulled me aside: "Robin! Quick, get on your costume!"

"I have no costume," I replied, puzzled at all the commotion so early in the day.

"Sorry I forgot! The parade is about to start! Come with me, quick!"

I followed him up to the dressing room where he threw one of his clown outfits at me—we were the same size, which didn't matter anyway with baggy pants, suspenders, and huge flappy clown shoes. I plopped on a red nose and down we ran to join the company outside. Claus saw us and shouted "You two! In front!"

It was the annual Royal Parade through the streets of Copenhagen. Pete and I were at the head of the procession, waving to the cheering crowds lining the sidewalks, throwing confetti and candies to kids. Behind us was Denmark's royal family in an ornate Cinderella-style carriage pulled by six white circus horses, the leading two ridden by Claus and Diana. They were followed by Spanish jugglers, Bulgarian acrobats, dancers from the Royal Ballet, and the Benneweis elephants, trailed by the ring boys in their elegant outfits with shovels and trash buckets. It was exciting, baffling, momentous, fun, and hallucinatory all at once.

I glanced back at the royal carriage. The Kingdom of Denmark was a constitutional monarchy—Queen Margrethe II had ascended to the throne just the year before, in 1972. On her ascension, the Queen became the first female monarch of Denmark since 1375. The crowds celebrated joyously as she passed by in her carriage.

I felt dizzy with bewilderment. I had been thrust right out of time into some Hans Christian Andersen fairy tale.

First Night

*"The marvels of acrobatism and horsemanship and
the drolleries of clowns are presented in a manner
to which no captious critic can take exception.
The attendants are polite and there is an utter lack
of that offhanded brutality and suspicion of
toughness often inseparable from traveling
entertainments under canvas."*

—*Ringling Route Book,*
North Dakota, 1895

I felt numb. My first night of performance at Benneweis had the quality of a lucid dream: I was aware of being in it, but I was not in control. It felt like I was living in a Twilight Zone version of a make-believe Hollywood movie set. I got my clown makeup on early and went downstairs to sit in the shadows in a corner of the large backstage area.

One by one, the other performers came down to warm up. I watched quietly, unobserved. Disoriented, like waking from a long coma, I had a feeling that something was wrong, that somehow, those twenty years of missed experience should have happened. It was all a mistake in another dimension, an alternate reality where I did live those two decades...but somehow there was a technical glitch in the system, mistakenly erasing that timeline, and suddenly here I was, popped into this reality. I was Rip Van Winkle with a clown nose.

The dressing rooms were up a spiral staircase and down a long circular corridor on the second floor of the building. The clown dressing room was the first room on the left, because we needed to get down to the ring fast. We were "ring clowns," making seven or eight entrances between the regular acts as equipment was being changed in the ring.

We became known as Pete, Robin & Antonio, the "house clowns" for the circus building. Our job was to keep the transitions between acts flowing, fast and fun, often by making clown parodies of the previous star act. With so many two- or three-minute entrances, our characters could develop throughout the show and become familiar to an audience.

Pete was the boss, always giving absurd directions to me, Robin, the quiet one who, like a confused Stan Laurel, would look for backup from Antonio, who was his own obstinate character, usually outwitting us both at the gag blow-off.

In the ring, Pete talked and gestured excitedly during a gag. I was the silent clown. Antonio seemed to be always grumbling to himself.

Early in my tryout week, something happened that only served to emphasize the surreal quality of my experience. With all the running in and out of the ring—dashing upstairs to get props for the next gag and rushing down again to be ready behind the curtain, two shows per day—there was little time for a proper meal. The artist canteen was not far from backstage.

I sometimes grabbed a hot dog for a quick snack when we were not on for several acts. And then, one time...

"Clowns!"

I froze, hot dog halfway to my mouth.

"CLOWNS!" The shouts echoed from backstage to the artist canteen where I sat, stunned. The other performers sitting at their tables looked over, and someone yelled: "GO!"

I jumped up, grabbed my hat, dropped the hot dog, spilling mustard and ketchup onto my oversize polka dot tie, and ran out, expecting to meet Pete backstage. I slid to a stop behind the ring curtain and glanced around searching for my two clown partners, still upstairs in the dressing room.

In a flash I saw Pete flying down the stairs, only to slip at the bottom and fling his arms out to break his fall, hurling clown props all over the floor. Antonio stood at the top of the circular staircase, paused in confusion. Claus, the ringmaster, stood by the ring entrance, waving me on, shouting "Go!" as the curtain opened.

I ran past one of the Bulgarian acrobats being carried out with a twisted knee. The circus orchestra had changed its normal music from the Bulgarian teeterboard act to lively clown music. Without thinking, I ran into the ring...

I suddenly found myself standing alone in the middle of the ring, facing two thousand expectant spectators in Copenhagen's prestigious Circus-Building-by-the-Tivoli—one of the most renowned circuses in the world—with no partners, no props, no idea of what I was doing, and wondering why the hell I kept getting myself into these outlandish situations...

Then I had an out-of-body experience.

My awareness zoomed up to the top of the dome ceiling and looked down at this hapless clown, standing there. I recall thinking, from up there, how spontaneously such things happen, out-of-body/out-of-time, nothing gradual about this kind of thing. I watched myself from above as clown Robin started to perform a mime routine. At that thought, almost with a "Pop!" I was suddenly back into myself, in the ring, and improvising...

I pantomimed setting up an invisible tightrope about shoulder high across the ring, an easy enough illusion. It was an old Marceau routine. I stepped a few feet in front of it to take a "Ta-Daa!" bow to the audience, mimicking the Bulgarian acrobat style with head bowed, heels clicked, and one arm extended with an index finger pointing to the tightrope. I turned and sprinted back, "forgetting" the tightrope was there and pretended to run smack into it, getting thrown onto my back. That got some laughter.

I proceeded to mime-walk the rope with wobbly knees, scared of the height, faking tricks. Finally darting to the end, I jumped off to applause, turned to rush out of the ring—only to again forget the invisible tightrope was still there. I bounced off it with another pratfall and more laughter.

As I ran out of the ring—this time ducking under the mimed rope—I saw Claus nod his head. Other performers had gathered to watch the scene. "Well done, mate," said Pete, clapping me on the back as we headed to the canteen for another hot dog, my heart pounding.

I knew something important had just happened, but my exultation was short-lived, and I needed to figure out why. Later that night I tried to sort it all out, replaying the scene in my mind. Sure, on one level the adrenaline rush carried me along on a current of energy. Sure, my theatrical instinct and mime training proved I could improvise in the ring. But that wasn't it, exactly—there was something deeper to understand.

The mime technique was something I could add to Pete's acrobatics and Antonio's clowning experience. But when I ran into the ring alone, I had sensed the mime technique was too stiff, too technical for the circus. I knew instinctively a silent clown needed to relax. My walk, my movements needed to become more casual. To emotionally connect with everyone in the audience, the clown's—and my own—personality and way of moving needed to be less stylized, more natural, the feeling more genuine, the character more authentic.

Theatrical clowning on stage is different from circus clowning. The mood, running into a circus ring, is special; I felt immediately comfortable there. I understood why I never much connected with most clowns—they try too hard to be funny. Kids know when a clown—or any grownup—is being artificial.

On a normal stage in a theatrical spotlight, each movement of a mime is choreographed like a dancer. Every motion is suspended and projected. Each gesture pushes through space as if the air were a tangible substance. Each breath follows the rhythm of the gesture. The dynamics of movement are subtle, the sense of time is malleable.

While miming had added economy of movement and clarity to my clown gestures, I would learn to forego a formality of technique for the more personal expression of character. I would not be a mime actor playing the role of clown. The clown would be, more simply, me.

Duck Hunters

*"Pete Jenkins' opinion: 'I liked the limber, slippery
cuss that did the bending and twisting, and stood
on his head and feet at once and run all around his
neck. There must be part snake in him. He must have
packed his bones in his trunk before he came out
to show his bendabilities.'"*

—*Ringling Route Book*,
Chariton, Iowa, 1893

I t was all very thrilling, but certainly not effortless. In truth, it
was pathetically unamusing to run into the ring with Pete and
Antonio, try a new comic gag, and watch Claus grimly, silently, shake
his head as we ran back out. We were likable as a trio. There was
nothing coarse or vulgar about us.

Our gags were just not funny.

Pete grew up in show business. He had recently been performing
internationally with Johnny Hutch and The Herculeans, a British
comedy acrobatic troupe. Johnny Hutch was one of Britain's most
beloved comic personalities in circus, stage, and TV. The Herculeans
wore old-fashioned, white one-piece pajamas with red trunks
and large, exaggerated 1890s fake mustaches. Their routine made
remarkably antic, acrobatic pyramids with a very British, straight-
faced, "bosh, nothing to it" attitude.

Circus historian Dominique Jando described them this way: "The Herculeans, a group of turn-of-the-century mustachioed acrobats in white leotards and red bloomers, was perhaps Johnny Hutch's most successful act, and certainly the most imitated"—noting another later Johnny Hutch troupe of eccentric character acrobats, The Halfwits.

Pete had left The Herculeans after a recent Benneweis engagement, to marry a Danish girl who worked at the circus building. He had great acrobatic comic timing—but was new to ring clowning. Antonio had been in circuses his whole life. He was getting on in years, forgetful and unwell.

Pete the acrobat, Robin the mime, and Antonio the short clown— we looked good. It was just challenging for us to create a repertoire of a dozen or so fast, visual two-minute gags. As the ring boys moved equipment in and out for each act, Claus would stand on the ring curb by the curtain and keep an eye on us as we three tried to be funny.

Claus was strict at keeping the show moving. When the ring was just about clear and ready, he would give a short tweet on his whistle to warn us to wrap up whatever we were doing and get out of there. As we ran out of the ring, he would invariably do his head shake, as if to say "Nope, not funny."

Back in the dressing room, as Antonio took a nap, Pete and I would discard that gag and desperately wrack our brains for a new idea— which we would try in the show the next day, after which it would invariably be discarded. This went on for weeks and was not fun.

We got pretty good at keeping an eye out for the cleared ring, aiming to finish the blow-off of our gags before Claus got out his whistle. But we were still laughably unfunny.

We played our gags seriously: clowns in the ring don't know they are funny. They simply act according to the absurd laws of their clown universe. Our inexperience was evident: we should not have thrown out a gag after doing it only once or twice, just because Claus shook his head. The gags were fine—we just needed to work them out in front of audiences. It's how we did a gag that needed refining.

Like a writer with a first draft, not quite right, needs to edit and rewrite and make it better—you don't just immediately throw out the whole draft.

An example is The Duck Hunters gag. I didn't think it was funny. But the audience laughed. The usefulness of the bit was in its simplicity of plot and staging: we were able to adjust the timing of the blow-off. We could cut it short or extend our comic "business" as needed by the ring boys, busy clearing the ring.

We Duck Hunters came tiptoeing out in a spotlight, like Elmer Fudd hunting Daffy Duck. Pete, the boss, wearing his oversized striped suit, big shoes, red nose, and bald wig, carries a big. obviously fake, wooden rifle. He looks around and beckons me to follow quietly. The bumbler, I wear a too-large hunting hat with—for no obvious reasons—a dozen fishing hooks dangling from it. With several fishing nets and three pairs of binoculars strapped all around me, I struggle to carry all the hunting equipment.

I beckon Antonio to follow quietly. He comes out, making a racket with a duck call, quacking with every other step.

There followed the usual slapstick bumping into and shushing each other. Kids giggled, and we shushed them, which caused more quacking noises from Antonio. After each silent pause in the spot-light, Antonio was great at timing his next "quack" step and freezing, as we all looked around to see where the duck was—which of course was impossible: there was a small plastic quacker in Antonio's shoe.

I would keep one eye on the ring boys, and one eye looking around the audience with binoculars. When it was time to finish, I tapped Pete on the shoulder, pointed up, and he raised his rifle straight up to the roof. On a BANG! from the drummer, a hundred rubber fish fall from the ceiling and briefly flap around the ring.

The band played fast music, kids clapped with glee, the ring boys dashed in to clean up the fish, and we ran out triumphant, Antonio happily quacking.

Rubber fish, and an occasional rubber chicken, from the sky? Not necessarily funny. But rubber fish is on the clown culinary list of things, like banana peels and pickles and cream pies, with inher-ent comedic potential. It was ludicrous, of course, and I don't know why audiences laughed with delight—maybe it was the absurdity of clowns earnestly hunting ducks, only to land flying rubber fish.

The Duck Hunters was the one gag we didn't throw out right away because of the expense of a hundred rubber fish. We worked it for a few audiences until the timing was right. They laughed, and we learned. It was not some well-thought-out, logical plot that made it work—it was about timing and how we played our characters.

The Clown from Benneweis

*"Johnnie Carroll was presented tonight with a loving
cup by his friends in the dressing room. The loving
cup is one of the kind that grows on trees and is
often seen around the pump on a farm. Tybell and
Harry Zella made presentation speeches in such
touching words that two of the camels died."*

—*Ringling Route Book,*
Leadville, Colorado, 1891

The citizens of Copenhagen loved their circus. All around
the city there were hot dog carts, one on the corner outside
the circus building. Often when I encountered a vendor anywhere in the city, a typical conversation would ensue: "Ah...where
are you from?"

"America."

"Are you enjoying the city?"

"Yes, I work here."

"Oh, really? What do you do?"

I would pause, waiting for the pleasant moment of revelation:
"I'm the clown from Benneweis." Invariably an expression of surprise
and delight would appear. Free hot dogs were forthcoming, anytime
I mentioned who I was: "The Clown from Benneweis." It was like a
secret identity I could hide at will.

The circus building sat on the corner of Jernbanegade and Axeltov, smack downtown, a mere block away from the world-famous Tivoli Gardens. On the side of the building there was a tall iron gate, an entrance to the circus backlot. Its iron was ornamental and heavy, slow to swing open, and wide enough for elephants and caravans to go through. It was the portal to another realm, the circus kingdom, a world of which the public, strolling by on the busy streets of Copenhagen, had no idea.

I was living for the season in a room at a boarding house for artists, recommended to me by a circus agent. It was a large apartment owned by Madame Schumann, who still lived there. She had married into the extended Schumann circus dynasty, which had operated the circus building since 1887, until Eli Benneweis took over in 1969. She rented out her rooms to performers engaged at the concert halls and stages of Tivoli and other venues.

I missed the community of caravans around a big top tent out in the open sky, but this was the next best thing. One large room had a grand piano. I enjoyed hearing a classical pianist practice before her concert with the Danish symphony. It was very comfortable knowing the other tenants were also performing artists. It felt like a 1920s boarding house for itinerant vaudeville performers.

From April through October, Cirkus Benneweis performed seven days a week, ten shows weekly: evenings at "klokken 20:00—Wed, Sat. & Sun. at 14:00 and 20:00." I liked to show up early, sometimes to build props and play trumpet duets with Pete, or to practice new circus skills with other artists. I was always the first to sit down at our long makeup table in the clown dressing room to get ready for the day's shows.

Our clown trio, putting on makeup in our narrow dressing room, slipped easily into a routine. I would sit quietly and stare at my face in the mirror, not a thought in my head. It was a time of transformation from regular Rob to Clown Robin. Then Pete would bound in, immediately breaking my fuzzy existential meditation. He'd slap me on the back of the head with a cheery, "G'day, mate...!" and toss off some new ridiculous gag idea or practical joke.

Antonio was predictably the last to show up, saluting us with a wave and a grunt. He was a small man with a very deep voice. Pete and I would stop what we were doing and observe him climbing onto his chair. According to the degree of Antonio's inebriation, we would silently adapt our gags that day.

Pete and I were like twins—similar skills, sense of humor, both age twenty-three. Antonio was more than twice our age. A Benneweis house clown for twenty years, he was an iconic fixture to the Danish public.

I respected Antonio. He treated me kindly and had the manners of a gentleman. He could swear in multiple languages and was fond of telling ribald jokes. But anytime a visitor came to our dressing room—often friends of mine from outside the circus—he quickly hopped down without a word and offered his chair to the guest, accepting no objections.

Circus was his whole life. As a young Spaniard, he had learned to walk the low wire— necessarily low, given his diminutive stature—and he spoke Danish, English, Spanish, French, and German. When he was sober, he was a library of classic clown gags. I picked his brain as much as possible. Whenever he showed up late and was wobbly, Pete and I gently said, "We've got it, mate," and let him sleep it off.

Sometimes Antonio would show up in the ring in time for the finale of the show, when all the performers marched around the ring, carrying flags of many nations on long poles. We stood around the circle as Claus bid farewell to the audience. I made sure to stand close to Antonio, who invariably started swaying, his flagpole wavering. I held both my pole and his, so he could brace himself for the march out again.

I liked the moments we three sat at our makeup table, staring at our mirrors, lost in our own thoughts. Performers have their own personal pre-show rituals. Actors, already a nervous species, might

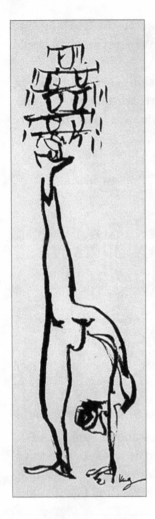

wear a lucky talisman underneath their costumes, and wish bad luck to fellow actors with "break a leg," an ironic wish to pre-empt and avert bad luck.

Athletes have their quirky habits: a baseball pitcher wearing the same lucky socks in championship games; a basketball player bouncing the ball a specific number of bounces at the free throw line.

Circus performers—elite athletes of another kind—are interesting to observe backstage. It's a charged moment: lives and careers may be at stake, twice daily. Their rituals are personal, often religious gestures, not for public display, moments before the curtain opens.

In the clown dressing room, we fell into our own unspoken ceremonies. Facing our personal makeup mirrors, which were cracked and bordered with a dusting of talcum powder, Pete sat on the far right, I was in the middle, and Antonio sat far left, nearest the door. The daily ritual of applying clown face was done quietly, and could take twenty minutes, or five in a hurry.

Pete's makeup kit was in tidy order. Mine was in predictable disarray. Antonio applied minimal makeup, a dab of red, a bit of white around the eyes, and then he sat and quietly stared into his mirror. Occasionally Pete would crack a joke, but generally, we each fell into a personal space.

When you stare into a mirror, whether you are a woman applying makeup for an evening out, or a man shaving every morning, you see yourself keenly, almost as if looking at a different person, observing yourself the way others might see you. It is face-to-face—or mind-to-soul—communication, deeper than a mere glance to check appearance.

★

The makeup table was long and narrow. Upon it, each in its own exclusive place, sat the following implements of the clown trade:

- a large tub of Clown White cream

- a tub of Clown Red cream

- black outlining pencils

- baby powder

- a white sock to fill with baby powder, to "powder off" the face after makeup was finished, dusting ourselves and the mirrors in the process

- soft brushes to brush off the excess powder

- sponge applicators for makeup base

- cold cream makeup remover

- baby wipes and tissues

- clown noses to apply with spirit gum with a sharp gluey smell that bonded to your senses for a lifetime

- spirit gum remover, a secondary eternal scent

An organic assortment of debris hung from the walls and might include at any time: scissors, cotton swabs, rubber chickens, rubber fish, various wigs, clown shoe polish, towels tinted red with makeup, and sundry musical instruments, including two trumpets, an English concertina, harmonicas and saxophones of all sizes, a guitar and ukuleles, variously-toned honking horns, and a dented tuba whose bell looked as if it had been hit by a hundred mini-asteroids.

You might find a supplementary accumulation of other functional clown detritus. The backroom was filled to the ceiling with juggling stuff, magic props, racks of costumes, and a veritable hardware store of tools for building props that may or may not survive the whole season.

Pete and I spent many hours at toy shops and hardware-and-plumbing-supply stores. A hardware store is a veritable paradise for creative ideas. I still never know what to say when the hardware clerk asks the purpose of the object I am seeking, which is never, of course, the normal function of the object.

And they never know how to respond, when I say, "Oh, nothing really...it is just for this exploding, collapsing umbrella, that shoots water from the handle," or some other wonderfully absurd gag prop. It's fun to watch their blank expression when a grownup like me says such things in a serious voice and pays in cash.

To this day, whenever I enter a hardware store just for something normal—a lightbulb, screwdriver, duct tape—the clown adrenaline kicks in. I can't help wandering around, eyeing things voraciously, with images of great new props to build. It's an obsessive habit. If I'm with a friend, and they see a glint of avarice in my eyes, I count on them to quickly hustle me out of the store before I overspend on useless items.

Is there a CA group—Clowns Anonymous—to get some healing from this affliction? "Hello, my name is Robin...and (gulp) I'm a clown."

Even though I haven't been in the ring or touched clown makeup for years, once you've done it, it's not easily shaken. It's in your system for life. You're stuck with it. The sawdust remains in your veins.

Parody

*"When leaving, a circus star exclaimed to a local
maiden, handsome as the heart of a dream, 'The story
of my burning love has never, never passed these
lips before.' 'Then you must have talked through
your nose,' said she, 'when you told it to me last
winter.' O dusty, dirty Reedsburg. We'd linger
longer, but we can't no longer linger."*

—*Ringling Route Book,*
Reedsburg, Wisconsin, 1892

Typically, the acts from the trio billed as Pete, Robin & Antonio featured Pete, the boss, and Robin, the sidekick, attempting something absurd or devious, only to be foiled by the surprise appearance of Antonio, the real boss. We rarely resorted to slapstick just for the sake of slapstick. We stayed true to our characters and how we individually responded to a situation.

Sometimes our best attempts at a gag would go awry in real time, requiring quick improvisation due to Antonio's state of insobriety. For example, we did a classic Bank Robber routine. The ring boys carried a large safe into the middle of the ring.

Lights were off in the building as Pete and I, in a single spotlight in the dark, came tiptoeing down from the top of an aisle with bags over our shoulders and masks over our eyes, shushing people quiet. We look for something under their seats and hats and handbags, until

Pete grabs me and points to the safe, sitting in the middle of the ring in another spotlight.

We climb over the ring curb and dump our equipment. We make a racket, along with sound effects from the band, trying everything to open the safe: rubber crowbars that bend u-shaped; huge stethoscopes as we noisily spin the combination locks; wooden sledgehammers and foam rubber chisels.

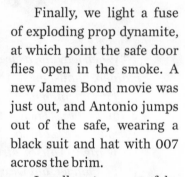

Finally, we light a fuse of exploding prop dynamite, at which point the safe door flies open in the smoke. A new James Bond movie was just out, and Antonio jumps out of the safe, wearing a black suit and hat with 007 across the brim.

I pull out a very fake rubber gun and pretend to shoot at Antonio, and the bullet—a plastic bullet pulled in slow motion on an invisible fishing wire—is supposed to bounce off Antonio's chest. He would then chase me and Pete out of the ring to fast James Bond theme music.

Once when I "shot" the slow-motion bullet, poor tipsy Antonio forgot what he was supposed to do, so he grabbed his chest, let out a yell, "Yer got me!" and fell over dead.

It just didn't look good, shooting a dwarf clown. He lay there on his back, as the ring boys did their job removing the safe prop. The band played fast music, and Pete and I had to carry out Antonio, stretched out flat and snoring. Claus, watching by the curtain, soberly shook his head.

Another time we were in the middle of the bank robber gag, when the whole circus building erupted into chaos. I had just pulled out my clearly fake rubber gun when a whole section of the audience rose to its feet and ran crashing right into the ring.

Startled, I looked up to see a half dozen men in black suits, with necks thick as bulls, coming straight at me. What in the world!?

Before I could think, one of them karate-chopped my gun hand, two others wrestled me to the ground and pinned my arms behind my back. Little Antonio, bless his heart, only as tall as the man's waist, kicked him in the shins.

Bulgarian acrobats ran in and joined the fray on our side. A brawl in the ring! The audience was confused: was this part of the act? For once, Claus was frozen speechless. It all happened so fast. The show stopped for fifteen minutes. Backstage I was frisked, shaken, and interrogated.

It turned out the exiled Greek royal family was in the audience. There had been a coup against King Constantine, who was forced to flee the country with his family. In 1974, as we performed the Bank Robber routine, a second referendum—for which the King was not allowed to return to Greece to campaign—confirmed the establishment of the new Greek republic and the abolition of the monarchy.

King Constantine's royal family sat calmly in their seats, watching the hullabaloo in the circus ring. Kids in the audience loved it. The bodyguards, however, had only reacted instinctively when they saw a gun. The ex-king later graciously apologized to us.

Just another day at the office.

★

Some of the most fun gags our trio came up with were classic parodies. In every new Circus Benneweis show there were new star acts from around the world. Each season ended with a three-week Circus Festival when there would be an all-new roster of performers. In pre-season, we would sit with Claus and get the list of performers.

Some of the acts were easy targets for parody. Our job as clowns was to bring down to earth the stars who had just amazed us with their god-like skills and physiques, to remind us all to laugh at ourselves when hubris looms too proudly.

The Dobritch Troupe from Bulgaria was with us one year, performing two acts in the show, a teeterboard act, and a perch-pole balancing act. We made parodies of both. The first act had two long teeterboards, seesaws with pads on each end to stand on, and a tall platform for the "jumpers."

Their large troupe of acrobats—in blue spangled jumpsuits with white billowy sleeves and matching spangled vests—came running into the ring, clicked their heels in circus style, while briefly nodding heads with one arm pointing forwards in acknowledgement of the audience. Then they all clicked heels again, turned and nodded to each other solemnly, and ran skipping into place.

Two of them climbed up on the platform, locked arms around their partner's waist and waited to jump down together onto the raised end of the teeterboard. Another performer stood on the other end of the teeterboard, ready to be thrown into space, somersaulting, and twisting in mid-air to land on the shoulders of a three-high pyramid behind her.

After each trick the performers would turn to the audience and do the quick bow/point/nod in acknowledgement of the applause, while shouting in unison "HUP!" before running to their places for the next astounding trick.

When their act was finished and the equipment was being removed, clowns Pete, Rob & Antonio came running into the ring in oversized acrobatic spangled jumpsuits. We set up our own mini-teeterboard, with lots of "HUPs!" and "HEYs!" to each other with clicks of heels, solemn bows, one arm pointing: Pete to Robin, Robin to Antonio, Antonio to Pete, repeating this until everyone got confused.

We placed the mini-teeterboard in the center of the ring and a short step ladder in front of one end, with many more heel clicks, bows, and hup-heys. When it was time for the blow-off, Antonio stood on one padded end of the short board, Pete stood several steps behind him in a half crouch with arms over his head ready to catch him on his shoulders. Meanwhile, I climbed up the step ladder and got ready to jump on the raised end of the board, aiming to fling Antonio in the air with one somersault, to hopefully be caught by Pete.

We suddenly stopped horsing around and got serious. This was not an easy trick for a stout clown with very short legs. This was clearly not a trick to attempt, if Antonio were to show up to work a little tipsy from Danish beer. We had another gag ready in that instance.

But here we were, ready to demonstrate some skill: Antonio had to time his jump off the board perfectly in sync with my jump down, and Pete had to concentrate on the catch, according to variations of Antonio's somersaulting flight in the air.

The audience had already seen some acrobatic skills from me and Pete, and now they were quiet: What the heck? Would we actually pull this off? No, they couldn't...could they?

The music stopped, a low drum roll commenced, the lights dimmed to a spotlight centered on the three of us, and the audience hushed, not sure if these clowns were really nuts enough to attempt such a trick. Then, when the mood was right, taking our time because we knew Claus would not tweet his whistle on a spellbound audience, and all concentrating hard, Antonio raised his arms and slapped his thighs, signaling readiness.

Pete froze in anticipation, arms up...I jumped down onto the teeterboard, and...SNAP! The board broke in half over the fulcrum with a very loud crack, leaving Antonio standing on one end, me on the other, looking at each other, bewildered.

The music suddenly blared again with the rousing Dobritch Troupe theme, as Pete, Robin & Antonio hopped forward together to click heels and bow solemnly to the audience, to each other, and run out, as if we had just performed the most difficult acrobatic feat in the world.

We played it seriously to the end. Clowns, after all, do not know they are being funny. We always caught the audience off guard and got the laugh each time the teeterboard snapped. Already broken, the board was held together by tape and a thin wood piece underneath, breaking with a loud sound.

There are different types of audience laughter. This was a moment of surprise-and-release, a short kind of laugh. Key to getting the laugh was for us to act as if we had just done a miraculous stunt, solemn, as we exited. That's not so easy when you are wearing slap shoes, and a red nose, and people are guffawing.

★

In the second half of the show, the leader of the troupe, Dobritch, came out again, this time with a perch pole act. For the finale trick, he balanced a twenty-foot-high shiny aluminum pole on his forehead, his strong neck bent backward.

His partner climbed up onto his shoulders and shimmied up to the top of the pole. Dobritch then proceeded to climb like a monkey up to the top of another twenty-foot-high steel pole—which was braced to the floor with a supporting steel apparatus—while balancing the pole with his balancing partner, who commenced doing headstands at the top of her pole way up there. It was a very impressive display of balance and strength.

Well then, here comes Pete & Robin in earnest, ready to recreate that awesome trick. I climb onto Pete's shoulders. Pete ascends a short

step ladder. He hands up to me a long dowel and a stiff clown doll. My intention is to balance the clown figure in an upside-down headstand on the end of the rod, which is balanced on my forehead, while still standing on Pete's shoulders. We had practiced this trick and had it down pretty well...

One evening the trick misfired in quite an unexpected and implausible manner. I climbed onto Pete's shoulders—only slightly problematic with big clown shoes and baggy pants—and bent down to grab the wooden rod and the clown doll. It is not so hard to balance something on your forehead while standing on someone's shoulders—it is the job of Pete, the understander, to adjust and stabilize any off-balance of Rob, the upstander.

This time, though, I had stepped onto Pete's shoulders a bit off center and I felt myself leaning too far to one side. I didn't bother to modify my stance—knowing Pete would adjust for the imbalance. I proceeded to raise the rod to my forehead while a part of my consciousness thought: Huh, I'm really off balance here, but Pete will correct it, I'll just continue what I'm doing...

Suddenly, I realize I'm falling in space, holding the rod in one hand and the clown doll in the other, falling straight as a board, face down, looking at the floor rising up to meet me. I recall flinging my arms to the sides like a flying squirrel, so as not to land on top of the sharp rod.

The next thing I know, I find myself climbing back up to Pete's shoulders, a surprised, open-mouthed expression on his face. After that awkward blunder, I felt the need to finish the act with panache.

When we exited back through the curtain, I was faced with stunned looks from the acrobats who had witnessed the farce. I felt slightly embarrassed— falling from a simple two-man high? Sheesh—until one of the Bulgarians said in astonishment: "How the hell did you do that?"

"Do what?" I asked.

He said, "C'mon, I'll give you a hundred bucks if you teach me that trick."

"What trick?" I looked around at Pete, who was grinning and shaking his head.

Apparently, I had stayed stiff when I flung my arms out. And I seem to have hit the ground flat out and bounced, like a cartoon stick figure, right back up onto my feet—and then calmly finished the act.

I had no recollection of that whatsoever. I can only surmise that somehow the body's own intelligence knows what to do under extraordinary circumstances of danger—if we just get out of our own way and let it take over.

I have no explanation for how it worked physically. My chest did ache a bit for a couple of weeks. Probably from a couple of broken ribs. The acrobats were annoyed that I wouldn't share my secret skill. They joked with me for days, calling me The Bouncer. I should have taken their hundred bucks.

Artistes

"Orrin Hollis was to-day kicked by his horse and rushed into the dressing-room holding his hands over the right side of his chest, exclaiming in a lovelorn voice that the kick had landed just over his heart, which 'had been broken many times before'—but was assured that the heart was on the other side."

—*Ringling Route Book,*
Marshfield, Wisconsin, 1891

I n three years with Benneweis, I watched and studied the dozens of world-class acts that came to the building. I witnessed the artistry, style, and personalities of traditional circus professionals at the top of their game. Aside from their highly disciplined work ethic, competence, and generosity, a sense of play and humor was always in evidence.

The Yong Brothers were famous for their hand-to-hand balancing act. One of their opening tricks, on a rotating circular platform, had Johnny Yong balance on his head while his brother took hold of his ankles and then slowly lifted himself upside down. He put his head on Johnny's feet and simultaneously they let go of their hands, arms spread wide as the platform rotated, both balanced by their heads.

It was a strenuous seven-minute act performed in slow motion, with perfectly synchronous movements. Also impressive to me was how Johnny went to his dressing room after finishing the act and reappeared a bit later in a black tuxedo. He stood to the side of the curtain opposite the ringmaster, Claus, in an "at ease" pose of watchful readiness, hands clasped behind his back. Johnny Yong was pure circus: after his star acrobatic turn, he now acted as show master, keeping a hawk's eye out for anything happening out of place in the ring or with the rigging for each act.

We clowns made a quick parody of the Yong Brothers hand balance act: "The Old Brothers." A parody needs to be acted seriously, so, once again, we played it deadpan. Our movements were slow and awkwardly elegant. Graceful movements are inevitably embellished by floppy shoes and baggy outfits.

Pete was excellent at handstands from his acrobatic days with The Herculeans. So, after some ungraceful hand-to-hand attempts with me—including the requisite head nods to each other and bows to the audience after each failure—the big blow-off was called for by pointing up to band leader John Voler in the balcony, who quieted the band and called for a crescendo from the drummer.

The audience of course expected nonsense, but we had an unexpected twist ready. Antonio had steel braces hidden up his jacket sleeves. With great ceremony, he lay down on his back and raised his arms, his palms hiding the handles of the steel braces. Pete took a deep breath, pushed back his sleeves, which promptly fell back down, an action repeated several times until he finally whipped off his bulky jacket and threw it onto me.

He prepared to grab onto Antonio's hands—actually the handles of the braces, supported on the ground and still hidden inside Antonio's jacket. When Pete went up into a perfect handstand, it truly looked like little Antonio was supporting him—a great sight gag!

The typical ending to such a gag—the reveal—is for the straight man clown, in this case Antonio, to get up while Pete and I take our bows, roll up his sleeves to reveal the braces, and then chase us out while the audience laughs at our fraud.

The question for us was this: should we expose the secret at the blow-off and play it for laughs, or play it deadpan all the way, the three of us standing in a row, taking our bows—apparently having done the feat—and stride off proudly like the Yong Brothers?

Which ending would be funnier? The easy laugh or the improbable trick? Both ways would work. You decide.

★

European audiences would be familiar with the names of their favorite award-winning circus stars, and I enjoyed watching their different styles, though everyone displayed a smooth, old-style grace. Bob Bramson with his astounding hoop juggling, suave and smiling, worked in his jacket and tie like another day in the office.

Jean LeMoine's plate spinning comedy was a frantically paced version of a classic vaudeville/circus act. The exuberant Sandros jugglers—father and son wearing shiny black leather pants and wide grins—gave the impression of seals having great fun, with infectious smiles the audience couldn't resist mirroring.

Guzman and Monique: Guzman rode his Harley Davidson motorcycle across a high wire stretched taut under the dome of the building, with Monique dangling below the wire doing tricks from a trapeze connected to the bike frame. Three years earlier she had broken her back in a fall, she told me, but here she was, fearless, under the speeding motorbike on the wire.

Manfred Doval danced without a balance pole on a forty-foot high wire, walking on stilts and balancing on his head on the wire. He used a round "donut" headpiece for that trick, placing his head on the ring and slowly going upside down, legs and arms waving in the air to keep balance, without a net or safety wire attached.

One night he just couldn't find his balance for that dangerous trick. He finally tossed the donut down to an assistant below and proceeded with the act. As he came out of the ring, I asked him if the donut had been faulty. "No! It's not the donut," he said angrily to me. "It's never the donut!"

Calming down, he explained that the equipment is never at fault, even if it was—never blame the equipment. It's the performer's responsibility to check his equipment before every show, and to be ready for any adjustment to the act. He was angry with himself.

Lily Yokoi, The Girl on the Golden Bike, is another prime example of how a solo act in traditional one-ring circus style, announced graciously into the ring by a ringmaster, can captivate and astound an audience. She was renowned as one of the top bicycle-riding balance acts worldwide. She entered elegantly in a gold costume, riding a gold-framed bicycle and performed stunts truly difficult to describe in words.

But aside from the daring tricks she made look effortless, it was her style that won the hearts of the public. Born in 1929, Japanese American, her unpretentious grace, charm, skill, and bright smile conveyed her lovely, modest, almost shy personality offstage. A class act by a classy lady.

Ray Dondy had the audiences howling with his eccentric comedy acrobatics, jumping off a diving board onto a trampoline made up as a swimming pool.

The Great Fattini entered as a sophisticated drunk party goer in top hat and tails, swaying on his feet as he looked for a light for his cigar, finding it atop a forty-foot-high sway pole, which he climbed hand-over-hand to do handstands—still tipsy drunk—as the pole swayed alarmingly over the screaming audience.

I would see him coming down the spiral staircase from his dressing room before his act—walking on his hands! He was in his mid-sixties.

Rogana was a striking beauty who deftly climbed a swaying ladder, while gripping in her mouth, by its handle, a sharp dagger whose tip balanced a long sword, point-to-point. Balanced on the top of the vertical dagger-sword was a tray holding several full wine glasses.

While she ascended the ladder, her head was tilted back to balance the swords. This position shifted the sword/dagger alignment until the point of the sword faced down directly over her throat. One's mind gazed at the danger of what she was doing, while simultaneously marveling at the long bare legs and statuesque form. Where does one look: at the swords or the legs?

Another example of evocative femininity were The Dors Sisters, a classic rolling globe act. Three bare-legged women, each standing atop a large thirty-inch diameter ball, with a wiggling side-to-side motion, "walk" the globes up three steeply inclined platforms. It is a graceful and dangerous act, especially once they reach the top platform. Then they would walk backwards down the incline, avoiding running into each other.

Pete and I considered doing parodies of these women's acts—but after consideration, we passed. We couldn't make fun of their beauty. And really, we were in awe of their strength of body and character. There were a few circus folks we didn't mess with. Besides, I was enamored of the younger Dors sister, but too shy to do anything about it.

Claus Jesperson was a fan of magic, so he booked several great magicians over the years. Finn Jon performed a stylish routine I never tired of watching. Tall, slim, handsome in his Scandinavian way, he was both friendly and private, as magicians tend to be. They carry secrets as part of their personality. Finn Jon was known in magic circles as an innovative close-up performer, a pioneer in the art of levitating and animating objects.

It took Claus several years to woo him into the circus building. Finn Jon performed his Floating Ball routine in a spotlight in the center of the ring, to the haunting melody of the Adagio from the Concierto de Aranjuez by Rodrigo. His movements were slow, graceful, and silent.

Wearing a stylish gray dress suit, he walked into the ring and approached a small round table on a slim stand and placed a large silver sphere on the tabletop. Then he walked about twenty feet away. He slowly pointed a magician's cane at the sphere, which began to tremble, and then slowly rise above the stand and start to float towards Finn. It was as if he were projecting silent mental commands. No wavy magic gesturing, just silent concentration.

The silver sphere floated, hovered, balanced on the end of the wand, seeming to have a life of its own, dancing in silence, aloft in the air around Finn's body. By the end of the mesmerizing act, Finn Jon, still at a distance, gestured toward the stand. The sphere very slowly floated back to its place and settled onto the tabletop, perfectly timed to the end of the music.

From Finn Jon, I learned to levitate small objects, having them rise and float and dance. Many years later I would create a signature piece: "Papillon, World's Only Performing Butterfly." I came out with a small stand, upon which there sat a little vase with a flower. A small silk butterfly rested on the flower.

As the music began, the butterfly fluttered its wings as if awakening. Then it fluttered up to land on my arm. It quivered up to my shoulder, back down again, and danced across a string "tightrope" held between my hands. It fluttered onto a spectator's open hand and danced around the flower.

Twenty-five years in the future, Molly Saudek, a young apprentice in my own circus, would become a world-class tightwire dancer, winning top honors in circus festivals in Paris, Budapest, Stockholm, and Moscow. In the off-season from performing in European circus, she was booked as a featured act in European cabaret venues, like the renowned Tiger Palace in Germany. She told me about some of the other star performers with whom she worked, old-timers such as Finn Jon, "a brilliant magician, and really, really nice guy."

I smiled hearing that. The circus world was indeed a relatively small community, where "old-timers" continued to work as colleagues alongside younger generations.

Lee Pee Ville & Co. was another magician Claus booked one year, a Las Vegas-style act with large equipment and sexy assistants.

For the finale, a large empty cage was wheeled into the center of the ring. A huge cloth was thrown over it—"One...Two...THREE!"—and whipped off to reveal the cage now completely full, with a dozen of the show's performers including me and Pete and Rudy Omankowsky, Jr., the star of Les Diables Blancs, The White Devils, a top high-wire family from Czechoslovakia.

Rudy would one day mentor a few prominent modern highwire artists—including Jade Kindar-Martin, another former teenage apprentice in my company, Circus Smirkus, in the 1990s. He was playful and friendly, and you couldn't help but like his confident style. A highwire performer comes naturally by that confidence, a necessary trait for being able to do what they do. He was best known for his performance taking a 1.25 kilometer-long skywalk between two mountain tops in France.

Without revealing Lee Pee Ville's whole method for his cage finale, with a dozen of us magically appearing, we had all initially been squeezed intimately, like standing sardines, hidden in the very tight dark space behind a fake wall in the magic cage. When getting ready for the act backstage, we all jockeyed for positions, hoping to get sandwiched between our favorite performers of the opposite sex.

Rudy was a handsome, charismatic devil with a flirtatious smile and laughing eyes. He always positioned himself behind Diana, and in the dark I would hear Diana's heaving breathing and some wiggling, and I could imagine roving hands and a flirtatious Czechoslovakian grin.

Diana and Claus had separated earlier that year. Given the dynamic libidos inhabiting the vigorous physicality of circus folks, it was not unreasonable to expect a bit of indulgent hanky-panky now and then when opportunity arose...in the dark...inside a cage...being bumpily rolled out in front of two thousand spectators.

There was always some fun to be had in the circus...

The Joke Show

*"Dude Goetschius sings: 'I've been out East, I've been
out West, I've been as far as Fargo/But a devil such
a town I never saw as the city of Chi-car-go.'
Lemonade vendor yells, 'Don't let your ladies
go home dry.' O'Brien sings: 'With all her troubles
and aches and pains, I love her still.'"*

—*Ringling Route Book,*
Fargo, North Dakota, 1893

For one night every season, Claus Jespersen, before opening
the show, would announce to the audience in a mock disap
proving manner: "Ladies and Gentlemen, I ask your indulgence for
tonight's performance. The rumor has it the artists intend to disrupt
the usual proceedings and, yes, sabotage tonight's performance
with unauthorized playfulness. I will endeavor to keep things under
control, but in all honesty, things are out of my hands. So let us
begin—and good luck."

It was the annual Joke Show.

This was purely for the artists and staff, a way to let loose and
break the daily routine with unpredictable fun. Anyone could play
minor pranks on each other or alter their usual act in some unexpected way. The only rule was to avoid disrupting the show so much that
the audience would not be entertained and get their money's worth.

Of course, as the house clowns, Pete and I believed it was our responsibility—our duty—to make sure the audience did get their money's worth of surprises. The other artists eyed us warily all that day. We were known to pull the occasional practical joke during the season anyway, but usually backstage, not in the ring. This night was different. The audiences enjoyed being in on the joke once they realized what was going on.

The stolid Yong Brothers, for example, might enter the ring and solemnly proceed with their hand balance act—while sporting blonde wigs and Groucho glasses. Pete and I went up into the bandstand over the ring entrance with a bucket of carrots. We had informed the band leader John Voler of our intent during Franz Althoff, Jr.'s equine routine.

He was old-time circus. Dominique Jando writes in Ciropedia.org:

The German Althoff dynasty dates back from the sixteenth century and is Germany's (and perhaps the world's) oldest. During World War II, Carola Williams, née Althoff, and her brother Franz sheltered in their circus many Jews, whether circus artists or not, whom they protected from Nazi inspections by hiding them behind a double wall in the back of the circus's laundry wagon.

After the war, Franz Althoff went on to run Germany's largest circus, where he presented a remarkable "liberty act" (a horse act in which non-mounted horses are presented as an ensemble, with the trainer standing in the center of the ring); it consisted of 48 horses of different breeds—an exploit that has remained unique to this day...

Franz Althoff's nephew, Franz Althoff, Jr., known as Franzi, was considered his heir in matters of horsemanship and as a circus director, he created his own Circus Williams-Althoff in 1976. He had risen to fame when he worked with Ringling Bros. and Barnum & Bailey in the seventies with a tiger riding a horse!

★

This was the distinguished Franz Althoff, Jr. who was about to enter the Benneweis ring with his horses in the Joke Show. We were out to test Franzi's sense of humor.

Up on the bandstand, Pete and I waited for Franz to get halfway through the act. The horses were marvelous, pure strength, beauty, grace, prancing in style around the ring. Franz gave signals mostly through gestures, raising his arms, pointing with the long thin whip, like a fly fisherman's rod swirling through the air. With ten horses galloping around the ring, the flow of a whip circling in air was a visual signal to indicate a specific movement, turn, or pace for the horses to follow.

At one point, Franz would signal a few horses to break ranks from the circle, one at a time, and stand in a row in front of the curtain. One horse was singled out to display solo tricks with Franz.

This was our cue. Pete and I crawled to the front of the bandstand with our buckets full of carrots. Leaning over the balcony, we carefully started dropping one carrot at a time in front of the horses standing by the curtain. One by one, the horses found the carrots and began snuffling and munching happily, like workers on a break standing around the coffee machine, totally missing the visual cues Franz was sending for them to rejoin the act.

He looked up to the balcony, and I'm sure he saw me and Pete duck down, too late. We hadn't realized how successful our prank would be; we were a little apprehensive at disrupting his act. But all was well. As we snuck down from the bandstand, we heard laughter from the audience.

Franz, grinning, stopped to join the horses for a munch of a carrot, then fed them the rest, with some friendly snuffling and neck hugs, patting them down calmly like it was just a break from a rehearsal. Then, with a signal up to the bandleader, Franz straightened up in performance posture and recommenced the act, to outstanding applause. It gave the audience an appreciative glimpse of the loving relationship between Franz and the horses, his kind nature, and the improvisational style of circus.

Claus Jesperson had his own brand of childlike fun. For all his handsome Lawrence Olivier/Richard Burton movie star presence, he had a core personality of youthful irreverence. I think he appreciated the times that Pete and I pulled off some backstage tricks, wishing he could step out of his ringmaster responsibilities and let his guard down.

He surprised us all with a well-played gag during the evening show. He could barely contain his playful anticipation as he gave me and Pete a heads-up. He usually introduced the Dobritch Troupe teeter-board act by formally listing their great accomplishments: "Ladies and gentlemen, this next act hails from Bulgaria. They have won special awards from top European festivals, etc..."

My Danish was pretty sloppy, but I understood enough to hear Claus add this at the end of his introduction:

"And besides their numerous awards, this amazing company of artists is special in another way: all the performers in the troupe are... deaf. They communicate with each other in the act through nods and gestures. And they have asked me to request from you, dear audience, since they cannot hear your applause, if you like their tricks, please wave instead of clapping. Thank you. And now, here they are, The Dobritch Troupe!"

Claus knew the Bulgarians didn't understand Danish. They came running out to their places, all eight of them, with arms out and a snappy bow of heads and fast-paced Bulgarian music. Silence from the audience.

The troupe nodded to each other in readiness, and did their first amazing trick, a female acrobat somersaulting high in the air off the teeterboard... As they took quick bows, not a sound came from the audience, just a sea of two thousand hands waving in the air.

The Bulgarians looked at each other. Then they ran into place and made their next amazing trick. Two thousand silent waving hands. The build-up of anticipation during each trick was absolutely hilarious for those of us watching at the top of the aisles or peeking from behind the curtain. Claus stood stiffly at the side of the curtain, struggling not to smile.

The poor confused acrobats seemed to communicate non-verbally with glances, shrugs, and gestures, but they readily took their bows and clicked their heels after each trick and gamely carried on with every degree of professionalism. By the end of the act, they caught on. You could see some brief consultation as they ran into places. They finished their last trick—to a drumroll from the band and the waving hands.

Claus explained that he would like us to incorporate into the act all the best gags from classic soap routines. And he wanted to be in on the fun. We framed the act around the classic Bill Posters routine. This act had been in the repertoire of circus clowns for generations. With Antonio's long experience in circus, and with Claus directing, we commenced rehearsals.

To make our soap mixture, we experimented with brands and found the best soap to be brick-like green European bars. They were expensive but made the perfect thickness. Everyday Pete and I were up in the dressing room with a large trash barrel, the two of us sitting, facing each other on either side, grating innumerable bars of soap into flakes, using the largest kitchen food graters we could find.

Scraping those flakes felt like Pete and I were in the army on kitchen patrol KP duty, peeling tubs of potatoes as punishment for clowning around. When finished, Pete would take out an electric drill rigged to a large eggbeater, add water, and with great fanfare and lots of noise, concoct daily tubs of soapy glue for posting the Bill Posters on a tall kiosk.

There is one great problem every comic confronts when rehearsing new routines. There is no audience! Without that spontaneous feedback, there is no way to know what's funny. I felt an ominous sense of impending disaster. Our rehearsals were a literal mess: we lugged out a thirty-foot diameter round vinyl mat to spread around the ring, and by the end of a rehearsal, everything, including us, was a sopping wet mess of soap suds.

Then we had to roll up the heavy mat, haul it out to the concrete yard behind the building and hose it—and ourselves—down, Pete with the hose, and me with a large broom pushing the heavy soap solution off the mat.

Was the act funny? I had no idea. Before opening night, I was a nervous wreck. Claus had given us a big spot in the show. For a clown, there is nothing more embarrassing than running around frantically as the audience sits there in silence. You feel more a fool than a clown.

Knockabout humor was not my style, though I loved watching the slapstick of the great silent film stars—Charlie Chaplin, Buster Keaton, Laurel & Hardy, Charley Chase, Harold Lloyd, Mabel

Normand, Harry Langdon. Ah, well, I thought—another learning experience in humiliation was about to occur.

The soap act went like this: Claus, the ringmaster, stands on the ring curb near the curtain entrance and graciously announces to the audience that there is a special guest just for that evening—a prima ballerina from the Royal Danish Ballet.

Katja, a charming, very pretty, young ballerina recruited from the Royal Danish ballet school, glissades to the center of the ring in white form-fitting costume and white tutu. Behind her, as she danced, there stands a cylindrical twelve-foot-high wooden kiosk with a large placard advertising the Royal Ballet.

About a minute into Katja's classy routine, Pete, Robin & Antonio come barging through the curtain completely interrupting poor Katja. We wear the white rubber jackets and white pants and white caps of house painters ready for work, waving our arms and shouting commands at each other.

Katja freezes, the band stops playing, and Claus strides angrily over to order us out. Meanwhile the ring boys set up a long table and a twenty-foot A-frame ladder near the kiosk, along with buckets of foam.

Pete pulls out streams of paper, showing Claus our contract to post a fresh placard announcing the newest Royal Ballet program, and to do so "toot sweet!"

I do my best, unsuccessfully, to carry several bulky tubes of rolled-up posters under my arms, multiple huge paint brushes tumbling out of my pockets, oversized painter's cap dropping down over my eyes, as I push a wheelbarrow full of white foam, splashing out.

It is pure Laurel & Hardy: Pete plays Ollie, the boss, while I am the bumbling Stan Laurel. Antonio carries two buckets by the handles, one in each hand, more white foam for the posters overflowing at each wobbly step.

Pete argues with Claus with shouts and wild gesticulations. Claus takes a step back and bumps against the wheelbarrow placed by me—inadvertently, of course—behind him. He falls backwards right into it, splattering white "paint" all over his beautiful tuxedo. The band launches into our fast clown theme music.

A ring boy runs in and pushes the wheelbarrow out of the ring, with Claus still sputtering in it. Meanwhile, Katja stomps out, first slipping face down on the already wet vinyl carpet. Then we go to work.

Pete shouts orders at me, and I confuse all his commands. Antonio looks baffled and gets in the way. Pete shouts for me to roll out a large

poster on the table. He stands at one end, ready to slap a brush full of wet glue onto the poster—which I dutifully roll out— but with a SNAP! it rolls back up when I let go, and Pete's brush slaps me with glue, and I slide on the slippery vinyl, wet from Antonio's overturned buckets, while Antonio slides under the table.

Pete lunges to grab the poster as it rolls up, instead sliding face down the length of the table and somersaults off it. After five more minutes of slapstick bedlam, Pete climbs the high A-frame ladder and sits on top, holding a wet poster, ready to glue it onto the kiosk. He yells down for me to send up a paintbrush.

I put a short board on a small sawhorse fulcrum, place a brush on one end and step on the other—"Hup-Hey!"—and the brush tosses up in the air, end-over-end, to land right into Pete's open hand.

He calls down for a bucket of glue.

I obediently place a full bucket on the little teeterboard, which I then dutifully step on, sending the bucket full of soap foam spinning into the air, and upending over Pete's head. Bucket on head, Pete pitches forward, ladder and all, to land on the ground with a tumbling somersault.

More wet pandemonium ensues until Claus returns with Katja to finish her act—but they only get more soaked as Claus finally chases us out.

★

The act was a success. What's the best thing I can say about it? I am happy to have done it. It was great fun to let loose like that, pure silliness without an artistic thought in your brain to slow you down. I now know what it is to do a soap gag and have never done one since.

The act went on for ten minutes, which sounds short but is plenty long enough in real time when you're getting soaked nonstop with slushy white stuff.

Here's the thing I learned about slapstick style: we had a dozen hectic tricks within the frantically paced routine—but we did it all too fast! The audience started laughing right from the get-go and never stopped the whole time. I had never before heard the roar of real belly laughter from something I was doing. I was more used to the giggles and smiles and short laughs from my more subtle style of comedy. This was something entirely different!

Each messy slap in the face with a brush, each slip onto your butt, each fall and slide got new explosive guffaws. It was a shock—and exhilarating. And nonstop.

We soon noticed that the audience seemed to be missing some of our gags. Some falls lacked the laugh explosion. We had too many gags, one after another. They saw a funny bit, for example, and were still laughing at it, while we, meantime, completed two more tricks. There was no relief from the constant laughter.

Pete and I had many discussions about this during the first weeks. We had to learn to adjust the frantic pace of the slapstick, so that the gags did not overlap so much—and of course the rhythm of laughter changed with every audience. There is a special timing to slapstick. We started to listen to the first laughs of the crowd and adjust our timing, orchestrating their reactions.

We learned not to rush into the next gag until the laughter from the last one had almost, but not quite, died down. Before this, I had no idea that such broad knockabout humor required an artful awareness aside from a timed choreography.

Circus clowning is not an easy art! As an old Shakespearean actor once said, when asked if it was hard to die: "Dying is easy. Comedy is hard."

The Chef's Hat

*"During the afternoon performance, two rustics
engage in a fist contest. They are arrested, tried, and
convicted. The trial is held in the menagerie."*

Ringling Route Book,
Paris, Tennessee, October 16, 1895

The soap act of 1974 was memorable in many ways, though none so dramatic as how it affected our health. Opening night was April first. The previous month had been spent in rehearsals for a bunch of new, short reprise acts as well as the soap entrée.

The weather can be quite cold in March in Copenhagen, with an onslaught of blustery winds that chill your bones right through your winter clothes. After our rehearsals, Pete and I had to hose down the heavy vinyl ring mat; there were no ring boys to help. We had to clear the ring immediately for Diana's rehearsal with her horses.

We dragged the mat outside and despite our winter jackets and rubber boots, it was shivering cold. We went from hot and sweaty to wet and chilled. Only after all that could we hurry upstairs to take hot showers. And then change clothes for rehearsing our other short acts.

We both got bad colds that lingered through March. When the show opened in April, we had no respite from sore throats and sneezes. We made seven entrances between the acts, running up and down the spiral stairs to get new props. After the Bill Posters act, we had just enough time—two other acts—to run upstairs, shower off the soap, grab a towel to furiously rub dry, dash back to the dressing room, throw on fresh costumes, grab props, and scoot downstairs in time for our next entrance.

During intermission we washed the mat, which the ring boys had dragged outside for us. It was still shiveringly cold in April.

We got sicker and sicker. Poor Antonio lasted only a few weeks. He spent the rest of the summer in and out of the hospital due to complications with his liver. He would often show up to the dressing room just before showtime, clearly intoxicated, swaying on his feet, looking sheepish. I'd lean over to Antonio and quietly say, "It's alright, mate—we'll take this one."

"Bollocks!" he would exclaim, then go into the other room to nap it off.

The soap gag was too fast and chaotic and dangerous for us to let a less than alert Antonio get in the way. After a while, we kept a grateful Antonio out of it and did the soap routine as a duo.

Meanwhile, Pete and I had no chance to recover from our colds. On the four days with no matinee, we could sleep in until late afternoon, then straggle to the building to make more buckets of soap for the eight o'clock show. Working seven days a week, month after month, you fall into a daily pattern.

We found our plateau of hoarse throats/coughs/sneezes leveling into a habit, as if it were normal to run around wet and sweaty and chilled. Medicines kept us going. The obvious question after the fact is: Why keep it up? I remember thinking at the time— the kind of thinking of a young twenty-four-year-old—that we'd be more ill if we stopped. We'd collapse and be laid up for weeks like Antonio.

Every performer knows the conundrum of feeling not sick at all when on stage or in the ring. Only before and after your act, do you feel badly. Maybe it's the chemical rush of adrenaline and other mysterious body mechanisms. Maybe it's some invisible energy life force that overcomes physical distress and compensates with a supernatural surge of vigor. It felt like our bodies needed that magnetic resonance with the audience to transcend our illness.

We started to check in on each other first thing on arrival at the circus building. Whoever arrived first just sat at the make-up table, staring in the cracked mirror. We would sit silently for a while, then a concerned Pete would blow his nose, look over and say, "Okay, Robin?"

I would sniffle, blow my nose, and answer, "Okay, Pete. You?" We figured for sure the colds would run their course. It couldn't last like this for seven months.

But it did.

By the end of the season, we were both depleted. The cumulative effects of fatigue took a toll. We were athletes and despite everything were physically fit—we just weren't aware how fragile our nervous systems had become. Then Claus asked us to perform in the three-week Circus Festival he produced at the end of every season, with all new artists from around Europe. He wanted the soap act and a few new reprises for the show.

We had three days to prepare after the main season closed. Of course, we said, yes!

For one of the new reprises, we decided to do a comedy chef routine, juggling eggs and fruit, and tossing around plates and pots and pans. Exhausted as we were, we thought we could have some fun doing it, and looked around for costumes. We found a high-end haberdashery in the city and agreed to meet there the next morning to buy a couple of real chef's hats.

What happened there is a painful and scary memory.

We met outside the shop and stared at each other. We looked like a pair of disheveled street characters, pale faces, noses swollen, and eyes red from the longevity of our colds. Pete told me to tuck in my shirt. This was a fancy store, selling tuxedos, uniforms for butlers, diplomats...and chefs. We straightened our backs, nodded to each other solemnly, and opened the door.

A little bell tinkled and a well-dressed man in tails came swiftly to greet us. He seemed rather prim, like a character from a BBC period costume drama, gray hair immaculately brushed back on his head. He looked us over with pursed lips and raised eyebrow, sizing us up warily, as though we might be shoplifters.

We couldn't help mimicking his prudish manner. We automatically fell into the tone of the place. I was too far gone to speak. I felt my body beginning to tremble inside from fatigue.

Pete, always the boss, thankfully took charge. "We just need a couple of chef's hats...please...if you don't mind," he said in his best British accent, though he spoke fluent Danish. "Sir," he added as an afterthought.

I nodded once, almost with a curtsey, ever the straight-faced sidekick.

We were not trying to be funny; we were way too tired to play games. We just wanted to respectfully acknowledge the formality, get our hats, and get out of there. Our attendant inclined his head slightly in a smug deference to our wishes. He estimated our head sizes and whisked himself away.

Pete and I looked at each other, letting out a deep sigh, as if to say, Thank goodness, so far so good. We nodded at the few other patrons who waited patiently.

Our man returned with several boxes of hats in different fancy styles. He carefully opened each box and gingerly picked up a hat. Pete pointed to the simplest style, looked at me and asked, very politely, "Yes?"

I politely nodded my assent, adding a gesture of acquiescence with an upturned palm. Our man disappeared again.

We didn't move, trying our best not to cough or sneeze or even smile. There was something about the place that seemed to demand propriety. We were blissfully unaware that the more we tried to act respectably, hiding our jagged nerves, the closer we came to falling off the edge of the Cliffs of Decorum.

Our man reappeared. In the controlled movement of Oliver Hardy, Pete daintily placed a tall white chef's hat on his head. Perfect fit. Tall, pleated, with a poof-mushroom top. In proper French tradition, the height of the toque blanche, the white hat, indicated the rank of the chef.

Now it was my turn. That hat fit perfectly, too. I shook my head. "Too small for me," I said, adding in Danish, "For lille til mig."

The clerk looked at me, deadpan.

"Storre, tak," I said. Larger, please. He hesitated only briefly then departed.

Pete nodded silently. I nodded back.

The next hat fit me loosely, the wide mushroom top flopping a bit. "Storre, tak," I said again, politely.

The clerk frowned and started to say something, looking at Pete for support. Pete moved not a muscle. The clerk left. Other customers in the store glanced over at us as we stood there, both of us staring straight ahead, stifling a few coughs.

Our clerk brought back several boxes this time. I opened each new box and held up the hats, comparing sizes. Then I chose the very largest and walked over to a mirror. When I placed it on my head, it slipped right down to my shoulders, completely covering my head. I stood there for a long moment, then turned blindly back to the counter.

I pushed the hat back up to my forehead to look at the clerk and started to raise my hand to speak...and the hat fell back down over my face. "Perfect," I said in a muffled voice. I raised the hat again and said, "I'll take it."

Pete stood deadpan. The clerk was unamused.

I looked at Pete, who said, "Yes, quite perfect." The hat fell back down.

The absurdity of the situation was evident—but only to me and Pete. He started laughing. Then I started to laugh. Several times I held the hat above my head, and let it fall back down over my head, repeating it, delighted.

Everyone else in the store was frowning, maybe even a little frightened at these two hooligans making a scene. The clerk tried to grab the huge hat away from me, and we struggled over it, while Pete guffawed, doubled over, holding his stomach. With one hand I held onto the hat, and with the other, took some money out of my pocket and tried to pay. The clerk would have none of it.

Pete, through his laughter, which had turned into a coughing fit, tried to explain we were the clowns from Benneweis, but by then the distraught clerk had gone for help from his manager. The other customers left brusquely, while I happily went back to the mirror, the hat up and down on my head. My glee had turned into a sneezing fit with the hat over my head. I couldn't see and bumped into Pete, who fell, sitting on the floor, just as the manager appeared.

We both tried, but we just could not control our laughter. Laughing and miming, Pete showed the manager how his own hat fit just fine, then turned to me to show how we wanted mine to be too big. So, I put it on again. We both broke up in laughter, holding our hurting bellies. I tried to put my hat on Pete.

The struggle to restrain ourselves led to our gasping for air, and violent hiccups, which only led to more laughing, which really started to hurt. We tried holding our breath, mouths closed, but that turned into nasal snorting and squeaking mousey sounds. We were looking at each other with grimacing, contorted faces, unable to stifle the snorts. Determined not to make a scene, our every attempt to suppress jagged nerves, to keep a straight face, only fueled the fire.

We were literally falling on the floor, holding our stomachs, tears streaming from helpless laughter. It was hugely embarrassing and started to feel scary. Pete finally managed to throw some money on the counter before we grabbed the hats and stumbled out the door.

Back on the street, standing outside the shop, we stood bent over, hands on knees. Our breathing slowly abated. Our nerves stopped trembling. We said nothing. We both understood how serious that scene had become. I imagined the headlines: Clowns from Benneweis Have Nervous Breakdown in Danish Haberdashery.

Finally, we looked at each other, nodded soberly, and left in different directions for home and a long nap.

Back in the circus building later, we put the chefs' hats away. It had been a clown entrée that could have been hilarious in the ring, but it wasn't, now that we'd experienced it in the real world. We were afraid of losing it again, the body memory, too strong. We scrapped the chef routine before even starting.

The sight of those chefs' hats scared the hell out of both of us.

Fly Through the Air

*"The mouldering wrecks of numberless steamboats
destroyed during Grant's siege of Vicksburg lie in
the bed of the Yalobusha. Town Marshal says there's
a million dollars at the bottom of the river, and
everyone has a sudden desire to go in swimming."*

Ringling Route Book,
Greenwood, Mississippi,
November 11, 1895

In the seven-month, seven days-a-week season at Benneweis, there was only one day off in the middle of the summer. I forget now what the special Danish holiday was, but it felt very strange to have a whole day and night off. What to do?

I stopped in to the cirkusbygningen out of habit, expecting the building to be empty. I figured the other performers would be scattered, like kids after the last day of school, off to the beach or on some day trip, drinking beer and wine on some faraway picnic.

I heard noise coming from the ring. The Flying Palacios had set up their net—and the whole family was there working on their flying trapeze act. The backstage area was busy with the jugglers practicing. Diana Benneweis was roaming around impatiently, waiting for her time in the ring to give the horses their daily workout.

I should have known. These were circus pros at the top of their game, always taking advantage of free time to practice. No drinking and carousing—their bodies were their careers. And there were animals to care for. Circus—especially traveling tent shows—is not unlike the old nineteenth century whaling ships. It's not an hourly job, it's a full immersion lifestyle.

I watched the Palacios for a while. The act originated in Mexico in 1940 and achieved renown around the world. I was friendly with little twelve-year-old Rafael Palacio. He was being groomed for starring in the flying trapeze act, the youngest of the extended family which included the parents, older brothers and their wives/girlfriends, teenage sister, and various relatives.

They were a class act. It was a double flying trapeze act, two flyers swinging off the platform on parallel trapezes and two catchers swinging from the other end. What impressed me right away about their act—besides their smooth flying elegance and gentle land-ing back on the high platform, besides their refined, modest poise acknowledging applause with a graceful raising of one arm, a short turn of the hand palm up, from the women a slight bend of the knees, a little flirtatious curtsy of respect to the audience, from the men a friendly smile and curt nod of the head, as if to say, "Oh, thanks, really it was nothing...but it was gracefully done, wasn't it?"—yes, besides all that, it was their take-no-little-thing-for-granted professionalism that struck me. Every detail was classy, real style.

For example, their costumes. They entered in colorful large Mexican sombreros and glittering capes, which they swirled off to reveal the scant costumes typical of flying acts. There could be no frills getting in the way of their difficult aerial routines. The men were bare-chested with tight white leggings. The women's bare-legged outfits could have passed for revealing swimsuits on the beaches of Mexico.

I noticed with appreciation the care they took to coordinate the colors of their wrist bands to the color of their waistbands, which matched the color of the tape wrapped around the swing bars, changed for each show. It was not for the audience; it was for them-selves, their professionalism, their style. Very classy.

In between shows I would sometimes hang out with skinny little Rafi in our dressing room and teach him magic tricks. He was short for his age and sported a big Cheshire-cat grin that stretched from ear to ear like a bright horizontal crescent moon. He kidded me about my unease with heights, until finally I agreed to try the flying trapeze during one of their rehearsals.

It was not easy to lean forward in space, holding onto the metal bar, just before the cue to jump off the platform. But the swinging was exhilarating, like slow motion flying over a vast distance, the white ocean of the safety net far below. It was silent, all senses consumed in the flight.

What really had been worse, though, was the climb up the skinny rope ladder just to get up to the platform. It swayed with each step! I grabbed onto the platform, which seemed far too narrow for four people.

The Palacios brothers, assisting on that platform, encouraged me: "You can do this, non problemo...Just don't look down." They said this with a grin, because, of course, then you couldn't help but look down.

I experienced a numb fear. A single thought repeated in my head: "What in the world were you thinking, you idiot!"

I was reminded of that feeling years later, when I saw a documentary film on George Plimpton, the famous "participatory journalist," who wrote wonderfully amusing books about going a sweaty round with boxing champ Archie Moore; pitching an inning in Yankee stadium against Mickey Mantle, Willie Mays and others; being a hockey goalie for the Boston Bruins; quarterbacking for the Detroit Lions; and...attempting the flying trapeze in a Clyde Beatty/Cole Bros. Circus performance.

In the 1971 documentary film, *Plimpton! The Man on the Flying Trapeze,* Plimpton relates his excruciating experience with The Flying Apollos. He looked like a giraffe in pale pink leotards, his six-foot-four-inch frame way too big for a trapeze flyer! The Apollo catcher quipped how his arms had been stretched a foot after grabbing Plimpton's legs.

Poor George had only a couple of weeks of disastrous practice before making his flying debut in front of an audience. I say "disastrous" because falling straight into the net, in the wrong position, can bring you a broken neck, or bounce you right out onto the hard floor.

In the film, the ringmaster announces George Plimpton to the audience as a guest flyer: "He will attempt to hurtle into space...," and we see George climbing the rope ladder with a look of despair and desperation on his face, like a prisoner climbing the scaffolding to be hanged in front of a cheering crowd of thousands.

"At breakneck speed...," adds the ringmaster, as George, now on the platform, holds the swing bar with one hand, the other grasping the platform's frame in a panicky grip.

"He will release himself in midair, be caught by his ankles...," while the catcher begins his swing, hanging upside down by his knees, arms out for the catch, "and then pirouette back to his own trapeze bar, and return gracefully to the high platform."

"Well," George adds in a voiceover in the film, "here goes nothing!" It is humorously painful to watch.

Many years later, I found myself in Plimpton's Upper East Side apartment in New York at one of his crowded parties. I'd gotten an invitation by courtesy of the *New Yorker* cartoonist Ed Koren, a friend and neighbor from Vermont. I bumped into George near the kitchen. He was curious about my life in circus. I asked about his trapeze fiasco.

With a smiling grimace, a glass of wine, a waving gesture, and in a patrician voice reminiscent of his friends in the Kennedy clan, he said, "Absolutely terrifying. I have immense respect for the braveries of the singular circus population."

In 2017, I was invited by the Smithsonian Folklife Festival to participate in their weeklong festival celebrating American cultural heritage on the National Mall in Washington, D.C. The theme that year was Circus! Brightly colored Big Tops gave the Mall a welcoming festivity.

Ironically, this was the same year that Ringling Bros. and Barnum & Bailey Circus—after a hundred and forty-six years, the closest thing to a truly American cultural institution—closed its curtains for the last time. It was the end of the Greatest Show on Earth. "It had become an unsustainable business," said Kenneth Feld, owner/producer of the company.

I was in the audience at the Smithsonian festival, watching one of the Big Top shows, dazzled by the beauty of a duo aerial "straps" act, performed to a live orchestra. I knew the female aerialist, Dolly Jacobs. Daughter of the legendary clown Lou Jacobs, Dolly had started her professional career with Ringling Bros. and Barnum & Bailey Circus in 1976. Inducted into the Ringling Museum's Circus Hall of Fame in 1999, she had become a living legend in the aerial world.

Dolly's partner for this beautiful festival act was someone I didn't know. He was not a tall man, but his huge muscles nearly threatened to burst through his skin. Imagine a short, sturdy, yet graceful Arnold Schwarzenegger in a leotard up in the air. His handsome face had deep furrows like crevices in dry riverbeds.

He looked formidable as he stood in the ring, until he smiled, and all those crevices turned upward. Except for his astounding muscles, he seemed too old for the act. But he easily flew in slow, high circles over the ring, hanging onto a strap with one hand and carrying Dolly around the waist with the other, as she performed graceful maneuvers—all without a net.

The act was pure style, strength, and grace. It was moving to witness such an act performed by artists no longer young.

And then the ringmaster announced their names: Dolly Jacobs and—Rafael Palacios.

What?! Rafael?...little Rafi...Palacios? No, it couldn't be the same skinny kid from 1973! Forty-five years ago? That would make him about fifty-seven years old. I felt a warm shiver up my spine.

Rafael was from a fourth-generation Mexican trapeze family. He and his family had also been inducted into the Circus Ring of Fame and had performed for the likes of Prince Rainier and

Princess Grace of Monaco and Pope John Paul II. Rafael Palacios had been awarded the coveted Lifetime Achievement Award from the Cirque de Monte-Carlo. He had also performed as an illusionist for twenty years. But all this I was to learn later.

For several mornings prior to this performance, I had seen him sitting alone over breakfast at the dining hall reserved for festival participants. Now, having learned who he was, I wanted to go over and say hello, but I was shy about approaching him. No way would he remember who I was. Back in 1973, I had only just wandered into the job at Benneweis, a young, inexperienced twenty-three-year-old clown, awestruck by the other performers—including the world-renowned Flying Palacios.

Finally, on the last day of the festival, I grabbed some coffee and approached his table, still intimidated by his bulging muscles and rugged face. He watched me advance and paused over his full plate of bacon, eggs, potatoes, and coffee. I started to say, "Copenhagen, 1973, Cirkus Benneweis, you were..."

He interrupted me: "I knew you looked familiar! Hi, Robin! For the past couple days, I noticed you having breakfast over there..." His crevices broke into smiles and his eyes sparkled. "Sit, please...sit." His voice was gentle, his whole demeanor, mild and friendly. Forty-five years vanished on the spot.

"You showed me some rope tricks in your dressing room," he said.

"Yes, that's right!" I said, astonished he remembered.

"You got me started..." he said. That's when I learned he had been performing magic in Las Vegas and other nightclubs, besides performing the aerial acts. Our breakfast conversation was warm and affable. Others in the room disappeared as we were caught up in that preternatural matrix where time was malleable. We were two old pals flooded with intersecting memories, impossible to fully reconcile as we tried to carry on a normal breakfast conversation.

We were both touched by the truism of that circus farewell we both knew so well: a handshake, a wave, and "See you down the road."

Why the Hell Not?

*"Travelling circus...is something in the blood,
an attitude to life. A circus is a magic wonder
of light and sound, the magnetism of which
draws all beholders to it for a couple of hours
of undiluted pleasure."*

A.H. Kober,
Circus Nights and Circus Days, 1931

Forty years after my time with Benneweis, I was visiting Circus Sarasota, a beautiful one-ring traditional show in a European tent, created by Dolly Jacobs and her partner Pedro Reis. Watching a dog act begin, I had that familiar warm flash of memory. It was David Rosaire!

When he came running into the ring with his signature energetic style, followed by a dozen yapping Pekinese dogs, "David Rosaire & His Perky Pekes," I felt myself flash back to Copenhagen. It was the exact same act, same routine—the only difference was David's now white hair.

These were new dogs, no doubt; but otherwise, nothing had changed. A dozen fluffy pekes lined up in an orderly row, with one unkempt mutt hiding out in a doghouse. Here came a disobedient baboon dressed in cowboy gear, driving a stagecoach pulled by a huge Great Dane. When some performers create a very successful act early in their careers, they stick with it. Why change a good thing?

The Rosaire family carried a respectable circus pedigree. David is fifth generation of a renowned British circus family of animal trainers, mainly horses and dogs. I remembered David as clever, professional, a sharp, ready wit, a very British kind of humor, always friendly and extremely caring of his four-legged troupe. It is not a simple task to travel the world with large props and a troupe of animals in several caravans.

David's act was fast-paced and fun. He put the Pekes through their paces, riding a scooter, pushing each other on mini-swing sets, sliding down slides, and running back to their platforms all properly lined up and strictly obedient. But every time David turned his back, the shaggy mutt would tear out of the doghouse and do the same tricks in double speed, outperforming the pekes—until David saw what he was doing and, with pratfalls deflating his dignity, chased him back to the doghouse.

This disobedience repeated itself for the whole act, children in the audience howling with delight at the antics of the rebellious canine.

After the show, I wandered to the backyard where the performer's caravans were lined up behind the big top. I hesitated, wondering which one was David's and if he would remember me from Benneweis. Suddenly, down the line, a caravan door opened, and David stepped out. He saw me standing there, and called over: "Oi, Robin! C'mon in—the tea's on," and went back inside, disregarding superficial boundaries of conventional propriety.

I smiled. Once again, I enjoyed the intrinsic hospitality and forthright demeanor of circus folks, "down the road." It's a nice feeling to know that I can travel the world, find a circus somewhere, and be welcomed for tea and biscuits.

★

Another comical reunion occurred in 2016, when I was invited to Seattle's world-famous Moisture Festival, which is billed as the world's largest Comedy/Varieté/Cabaret festival, running for four weeks each spring. It features "the weird and the wonderful, keeping the tradition of Vaudeville and Burlesque alive."

The performers are mostly a new, younger generation of talents from the worlds of circus, vaudeville, and cabaret. As I hung out in the Green Room backstage, chatting with performers my own age, an older couple sauntered by.

When I asked, I was told, "That's Freddy Kenton." Freddy was an old-time juggler, born in the Netherlands in 1938, seventy-eight-years-old when we met at the 2016 Moisture Fest. His wife, an elegant, attractive lady younger than Freddy, with a very pleasant smile, performed as his assistant on stage.

I had never worked with Freddy and had not seen his act before. His appearance on the bill with all the other much younger artists was a highlight of the program: "The Fabulous Freddy Kenton, Gentleman Juggler with his lovely assistant Evelyne." As soon as he entered on stage, you knew this was something different. His was the old style, the uniquely personal mannerisms of a performer from a bygone era.

He strode onstage elegantly dressed in cloak and top hat. Evelyne wore a sparkling evening gown, tossing the props to Freddy with the graceful gestures and smile of a seasoned professional. Her smile and style, poise and charm, seemed vaguely familiar. When I heard her name, I felt pretty sure she had worked in the Benneweis circus building...maybe in 1974? Forty-five years ago?

Evelyne was born into the legendary Bouglione circus dynasty. As a young performer at Benneweis, she had worked with her sisters in The Dors Sisters Rolling Globes. I recalled their act for its sensuality. Three lovely young women flashing bare legs and arms, standing atop three large rolling globes, dangerously wiggling their way, higher and higher, to the top of several inclined platforms.

Freddy's career had been astonishing, and like any old-time circus man, he could regale you for hours with stories of the itinerant life, dropping celebrity names casually. For instance, his eyes sparkled when he mentioned touring with Edith Piaf, and working in The Moulin Rouge in Paris in the seventies, where he was invited to drink champagne with Catherine Deneuve and dance with Brigitte Bardot.

Backstage at the Moisture Festival I saw elegant and lovely Evelyne sitting alone, so I mustered up some courage and went over.

She was a few years younger, probably in her early sixties. I said: "Hello. By any chance are you one of the Dors sisters?"

"Oui. Yes, I am." She offered her hand briefly, intrigued by my question.

I introduced myself, then said, "Copenhagen, Circus Benneweis. Pete, Robin & Antonio?"

"Robin?!" Her eyes lit up, and we sat a while, talking about the good old days. We hadn't really known each other back then. We were young. We may have spoken only in passing.

Freddy saw us chatting and laughing gaily and came over with some glasses of wine. I stood up and introduced myself, worried that he might think I was flirting with his wife.

"So, you two knew each other in Copenhagen, eh?" He raised his eyebrows and put on a mock face of intimidation.

I didn't know he was putting me on. I swallowed and said something like, "Well, we didn't REALLY know each other..." but he interrupted me and sat by Evelyne.

"She is still very lovely, no?" he said, holding her hand.

"Even more beautiful than when I knew her, when she was a teenager," I said.

He handed us both some wine glasses and grinned. "So you knew her when she was a girl, in the fair blossom of youth?"

Evelyn smiled and said: "Hardly a girl; I was a young woman. I remember watching Robin and thinking, *He's a very sweet American clown.*"

I said: "Really? I was watching you in that scanty costume, all beautiful legs and arms, and I thought, she is the prettiest of the sisters. But I was too timid to say anything."

"No!" she said, "I was too shy!"

"What?!" said Freddy. "You mean you were attracted to each other, at that ripe age, and you didn't do anything about it? You never had sex?!"

We both shook our heads.

"Well," he said, mildly scandalized, "why the hell NOT?!"

Clowns

*"Here Today and Gone Tomorrow, [the circus]
is a state of restless American achievement,
a pioneer peddler with magic in its pack and a
timetable in its pocket—a spangled, sparkling
girl with a date in a town a hundred miles away
tomorrow morning."*

—*National Geographic,*
"The Wonder City That Moves by Night,"
March 1948

There were many famous clowns coming through Copenhagen during those years. Les Francescos, Toto Chabri & Co, Joe Jackson, Jr, Galetti... It was a privilege to watch their classic routines and study how audiences responded to their different styles of comedy. What made them great? Why were they so universally beloved by audiences young and old?

Many of their routines I found not especially funny. Then again, I'm not one who easily laughs out loud. The gags were predictable and old-fashioned, like hearing a joke that has been around for a hundred years. And yet, night after night, I witnessed audiences laughing at the same sight gags, the same jokes, at the same times and places in a routine. The old-time clowns were unfailingly engaging and popular. What was it?

Modern sensibilities may not appreciate the comedy style of those traditional European circus clowns. Perhaps it's not important. Like the ridiculous debate of who is better, Chaplin or Keaton? That misses the point. They are both masters, with different styles. And all of us have our different preferences. Those silent films from a century ago still make us laugh!

Laughter is an involuntary reflex. It's a matter of taste—you react, or you don't. The impulse comes first. The thinking about it comes later. As critic Walter Kerr writes in The Silent Clowns, his insightful book about the silent film comedians: "Keaton was the most silent of the silent clowns...the best athlete of the comedians. Chaplin the best mime."

The American screen critic, James Agee, wrote an influential essay for *Life* magazine in September of 1949, "Comedy's Greatest Era," comparing styles this way:

> *The finest pantomime, the deepest emotion, the richest and most poignant poetry were in Chaplin's work. He was the first man to give the silent language a soul. Keaton was the only major comedian who kept sentiment almost entirely out of his work. Deep below his lack of emotion, giving a disturbing grandeur to the foolishness, for those who sensed it, there was in his comedy a freezing whisper, not of pathos, but of melancholia.*

For traditional one-ring circus clowns, the key to our fondness of them is not just what they do, but who they are, as they do it. To put it another way, as Chaplin once said: "If what you are doing is funny, you don't have to be funny doing it."

We can watch Chaplin in *The Kid,* or *City Lights,* or *Modern Times* many times over, and know by heart what will happen. And yet we still laugh with delight, anticipating the familiar gag. The great circus clowns are like a family reunion's favorite uncles, whose jokes and funny stories you have heard so many times, but you still ask for them because, well, you simply love the uncle telling them.

James Agee writes with extraordinary perception about the personalities and styles of the silent film clowns. He knew those performers had all learned their trade first in circus, vaudeville, and music halls, before they ever arrived in Hollywood. Agee's description of film slapstick perfectly captures the physically demanding techniques of what a circus clown might do, in the ring, night after night:

> *When a modern comedian gets hit on the head, the most he is apt to do is look sleepy. When a silent comedian got hit on the head... it was his license to be as funny as possible physically, without the help or hindrance of words. So he gave us a vision, a kind of poem for lost consciousness... He might make a cadenza of it—look vague, smile like an angel, roll up his eyes, lace his fingers, thrust his hands palm downward, hunch his shoulders, rise on tiptoe, prance ecstatically in narrowing circles until, with tallow knees, he sank down the vortex of his dizziness to the floor, and there, signified nirvana by kicking his heels twice, like a swimming frog.*
>
> *These are the fine cliches from the language of silent comedy in its infancy. The man who could handle them properly combined several of the more difficult accomplishments of the acrobat, the dancer, the clown, and the mime.*

Agee goes on to describe a classic circus clown gag, and how clowns aim to "one up" a gag to milk the most surprise laughs from an audience. In the circus we call it, "topping a gag." He writes:

> *In an old, simple example of topping, an incredible number of tall men (or clowns) get, one by one, out of a small auto. After as many have clambered out as the joke will bear, one more steps out: a midget. That tops the gag. Then the auto collapses. That tops the topper.*

★

Pete and I always had great fun brainstorming the most outrageous toppers you can imagine and trying them out with a live audience, springing the cleverest number of "tops" before it becomes too much. The audience gave us the best and most immediate feedback. But we always kept an eye on ringmaster Claus, who was our best critic.

I am fortunate to have learned from an older generation of clown artists. Two very different clowns made a deep impression on me: Charlie Rivel and Francesco Caroli. These two famous clowns exemplify the all-around circus skills inborn in artists growing up in the circus world. Charlie Rivel, who began his career as an acrobat, is a good example of the difference between intimate European clowning and the stylized, broad slapstick of Ringling-style American circus clowns. Francesco, and his Caroli brothers, started out as equestrians.

Charlie Rivel was born in 1896 and died in 1983. Watching Charlie perform felt like witnessing circus history. He was still performing well into his elder years because, in true circus fashion, age didn't matter. Circus was his life. In his younger days he was a strong acrobat. In later years he was known for his exquisitely slow movements and childlike clown character. I learned from him the power of taking your time.

He took forever, attempting to climb atop a wooden chair and play his guitar. Placing the chair in just the right spot, he puts the guitar on the ground so he can use both hands to pull himself up to stand on the chair and sit on the back of it with feet planted on the seat. Then he notices he has left his guitar on the ground.

Slowly turning around, he manages to finally slide down the legs of the chair to get the guitar. Then the problem of how to sit on the top of the chair with the guitar begins all over again. This already has taken several minutes. Finally, in frustration, he bawls loudly like a two-year old child, ending with his trademark howl: "Oh-WOOOoooooo!" which always elicits applause from the audiences who eagerly await that familiar plaintive cry.

Charlie is a good example of the respect and love for clowning from the European circus-going public. Clowns in America just don't gain that recognition or status. Raffaele De Ritis, an Italian director known for his modern circus productions, writes:

> Charlie Rivel is one of the few clowns ever to have achieved true international stardom. Like Grock and the Fratellinis before him, Rivel was beloved all over Europe, feted by royalty and popular audiences alike; he received every honor and accolade open to a performer. Spanning eighty-two years, Rivel's career deftly blended superb artistic skills, a talent for pantomime, and a flair for public relations. He developed a totally original clown character that stands as one of the twentieth century's greatest circus icons.

Charlie's slow, childlike persona evokes in me the image of that two-year-old baby clown I was, atop the picnic table, trying earnestly to roll a rubber ball down a ladder...

★

Francesco Caroli, 1922-2004, and his brothers, Enrico and Ernesto—the clown trio known as Les Francecos—played the Copenhagen circus building for two seasons when I was there. I was awed by the out-of-time sense of connection to circus history whenever I got the chance to speak with Francesco between shows.

He sometimes came into our dressing room to hang out with me and Pete and Antonio and tell stories of circus life. I cherish a cassette tape of him I recorded one day, singing Spanish and Italian songs in his tenor voice, accompanying himself on guitar. Antonio's deep, gruff vocals joined in the chorus in the background.

The Carolis came from a large family of Italian artists, who were known for their acrobatics and pyramids on horseback, performing in all the major shows in Europe well into the 1970s. According to Francesco, the big turning point came for him in 1939, at the age of seventeen, when he was asked to replace the white clown in the Circus Blumenfeld in Germany.

The Blumenfeld history—a family of Jewish/German descent—is both fascinating and tragic. As early as the seventeenth century, the family performed as traveling actors, acrobats, and tightrope dancers. Their family dynasty grew to ownership of traveling circuses in Germany and a circus building in Magdeburg.

There is a long history of great Jewish families in the circus—Blumenfeld, Strassburger, Bronnett, Sosman, Lorch, among others. The Blumenfeld family died in the concentration camps during the Holocaust.

In European clown trio tradition, the White Clown, played by Francesco, is the respected authority, while the Auguste clowns, Enrico and Ernesto, play the bumbling, competitive fools. The brothers soon incorporated clowning into their repertoire, along with the family equestrian act.

Francesco was in the 1956 film, *Trapeze,* starring Burt Lancaster and Tony Curtis, and was also friends with Charlie Chaplin. "I put all his daughters on horseback," he told me. He played the saxophone, in addition to the clarinet, trumpet, guitar, and piano. He was fluent in Italian, German, French, English and Russian.

In 2004, European papers reported that Francesco Caroli, hailed by his admirers as the "most famous white-face clown in the world" had died. As one paper detailed:

> In 2003 Francesco Caroli entered the ring for the last time, exactly on his 80th birthday, after 75 years of circus life. At this farewell performance in Munich, spectators, artists, and Francesco himself cried. "It's a job with a heart," Caroli said. "It wouldn't fit if someone was a bad person." He showed that to his audience every evening. During his time at Roncalli, his greeting "Come in, leave your grief outside. Be a child again" became his trademark.

★

Of the many star clowns who came into the Benneweis ring, Les Francescos had the most influence on my thinking of traditional clown entrees. Here, finally, was the venerable clown trio to study, mentors of life in the circus and clowning in the ring. I never tired of watching him and his brothers through two different seasons in Copenhagen. They took their time, their movements were natural, nothing frantic about them.

Francesco always entered in a spotlight, playing a beautiful tune on his saxophone with the band, dressed to the nines in his elegant costume with flashy spangles under a blue velvet cape. After the song, he would engage the audience directly as if they were old friends and in on the joke, amused by his bungling brothers, who always interrupted him, the way children might annoy a parent who is patiently trying to entertain guests at a party. He would tolerate their nonsense only to a point, before putting them to a test with some practical joke.

One of the highlights of my memories with Les Francescos was their musical clown routine. After fifteen minutes of business with all manner of wacky instruments from the bumbling brothers—exploding tubas, collapsing chairs, rocketing music stands—Francesco still tries to play serious music.

The routine ends with the three brothers on trumpets and other members of the Caroli family—adult sons in tuxedos playing three-foot long Aida trumpets, wives joining in with cymbals, even a grandchild dwarfed by the big bass drum he keeps banging—all march around the ring in line, playing the popular song, "Those Were the Days." The band filled the circus building with a loud brassy sound that sent a chill up the spine, especially after all the silliness of the clowning. The audience would automatically clap in time to the beat, adding more resonance. Often you could hear the audience join in, singing the chorus.

Pete and I asked Francesco if we could sometimes join them with our trumpets. It truly was exciting to run in and join the marching parade around the ring, with so many trumpets blasting out the music, the drums and cymbals, and the band up in the balcony, blaring away, the audience keeping the beat and singing, the building awash in powerful music.

Playing along with the Caroli family, my senses overflowed with awareness of the many generations of circus history in the ring and of my own blessed, Zelig-like place in that moment. I can feel the thrill now, fifty years later. The memory of boisterous trumpets and syncopated clapping and singing in the enclosed, ancient world of the cirkusbygningen, seems now ever more poignant:

> *Those were the days, my friend.*
>
> *We thought they'd never end.*
>
> *We'd sing and dance forever and a day...*
>
> *We'd live the life we choose,*
>
> *We'd fight and never lose!*
>
> *Those were the days, oh yes, those were the days!*

Handicap Day

*"It is Caesarian, Napoleonic, Bismarckian in effort
and in accomplishment, more than can be said of
Alexander the Great. The latter conquered the world,
but the Ringling Bros. pleased it."*

—*The Winona* [Minnesota] *News,*
June 12th, 1894

An extraordinary event occurred every year in Copenhagen's circus building on one day in the middle of the summer. On that special day—Handicap Day— the entire building, inside and out, was full of remarkable activity. For two full days before the event, children with disabilities, chronic disease, and life-threatening illness arrived in Copenhagen by boat, bus, and train from across Denmark to come to the circus.

On the morning of show day, buses and vans encircled the streets around the building, methodically unloading kids in wheelchairs and with crutches assisted by flocks of nurses and attendants—an assemblage of four thousand souls for our two shows that day.

The first time I experienced the event I had no idea what to expect. I asked Pete, "Should we adjust our acts? Maybe we shouldn't do the window washing gag." This was a pantomime where Antonio came right up to the front and pointed out invisible "dirty" spots on a nonexistent wall around the ring curb. Pete had a spray dispenser of water, which he sprayed at the spots, while I mimed cleaning the wall with a washcloth as we moved along the ring curb. Pete mostly used the spray nozzle, but once in a while he would turn the nozzle to send a long stream of water over the first few rows of the audience—the invisible wall, an illusion, providing a good laugh whenever the audience got wet.

I had watched the unloading of the buses earlier in the morning. These were mostly young people with pretty severe disabilities, lots of wheelchairs, children with lost limbs, some barely able to stand or move without help, many paralyzed, or shaking with involuntary tremors. It took quite a while to fill the seats, but both matinee and evening shows were filled to the rafters.

I had two concerns. I was worried that our clowning antics with the audience might not go over well. I also felt anxious about the disparity between the athletic bodies of the circus artists and the bodies of the audience. Wasn't it highly insensitive to show off perfect physical prowess and physiques and high energy in this situation? The tension of watching the crowd arrive, unload, and struggle to get seated for hours was distressing.

I needn't have worried. We decided to improvise a pre-show meet-and-greet. We had a bagful of red foam clown noses for just such an occasion. By the time the seats were almost half-filled, Pete, Robin & Antonio sauntered out into the ring. We stood there for a moment awed by the scene. Then we jumped into action.

The three of us clapped our hands once in unison as we shouted, "Hup!" and opened our arms for "Hey!" We taught the crowd to imitate our clap-hup-heys. Then we spread out into the audience getting high-fives from all the kids we could reach.

We picked out kids who were in wheelchairs—some with twisted hands, some with hand or arm amputated—and saw the huge smiles on their faces when we high-fived their stumps and shook their crooked hands. Antonio had the bag of clown noses in hand and gave each participant a clown nose.

We borrowed a pair of crutches from a kid in the front row and we helped him to sit on the ring curb. I climbed onto Pete's shoulders, and he handed me a crutch, which I balanced on my forehead.

Then, after a brief consultation, Pete ran quickly around the ring on the crutches, ending in front of me. He raised a knee to step into my cupped hands, and I flipped him backwards as he let go of the crutches—which I caught—and he landed on his feet.

We got "hup-heys" from the crowd, and the kid got his crutches back and more applause when he took a bow with us.

We pulled into the ring a few hesitant nurses and showed them how to do some silly tricks to make them heroes with their patients. We generally had a lot of informal fun until the building was full. By the time the actual show began, and we clowns made our first official entrance, we were greeted by two thousand "hup-heys" and were cheered as old friends.

What a responsive crowd! What delight and enthusiasm on their faces and nonstop bursts of screaming laughter throughout the show! What energy they gave back to us!

The steady movement of the audience, its swaying, tremor-like motion never ceasing, looked like an ocean of choppy waves in high winds from the ring. It is one thing to be fully in the presence of an individual with disability, but it is another experience altogether to be engulfed in the charismatic ambiance of four thousand exceptional children released from the quiet frailty of their daily routine.

My first reaction was a jolt of altered awareness. The wide range of the human physical condition, the extreme octaves of humanity's existence were acknowledged and saluted that day.

The audience's applause and cheers and stomping were thunderous after every acrobatic and aerial trick from smiling circus artists. It was a long, exhausting day of high emotions—and a highlight of every season.

★

Decades later, when my own Circus Smirkus company of teens had been created and were performing around New England, we would visit actor Paul Newman's "Hole in the Wall Gang" Camp. This was a summer camp dedicated to giving seriously ill kids "a different kind of healing"—a place that celebrates fun, friendship, and a spirit of childhood where, according to Newman, "every kid can raise a little hell."

In our show there, the audience was a mix of children, some in wheelchairs, some hooked up to life-support machines, or bald from chemo or some life-threatening disease. One of our young Smirkus performers, Kerren McKeeman, now a star aerialist in Cirque du Soleil, shared her own initial awkwardness, similar to my own at Benneweis. She wrote: "How can I possibly inspire these children whose lives and experiences are limited by their physical conditions? How can I perform handstands and acrobatics for children in wheelchairs?"

Kerren had arrived expecting to inspire other kids, but she herself was transformed. "To my absolute delight," she wrote, "the children cheer more enthusiastically than any audience I have ever seen. Those who can, rise out of their chairs, clapping and yelling, their faces radiating complete joy."

Dan Brown, another young Smirkus performer—now a Hollywood stuntman—wrote: "We knew some of them didn't have much longer to live. So, when they gave us a standing ovation, that was hands down the most memorable moment of my life. It wasn't just knowing that we were able to bring them a slice of happiness. This experience trivialized everything else in our lives, every silly bickering moment."

★

Twenty years later, I was traveling to elementary schools around New England creating "Circus Residencies." In one- or two-week sessions, I would immerse the whole school in the world of circus, and on the final night, we put on a show for the community. The most memorable circus residency was at a small physical therapy institution outside of Boston for kids with severe physical disabilities. I was invited to create a circus there with its thirty young residents.

Whenever I work with any group of kids in schools, my approach is similar to the best circus animal trainers. I don't immediately show off, or even try to win them over. I watch them, and they observe me. They choose to get involved at their own pace. It was my job, not to work with their disabilities, but with their abilities and potentials— and to create something with their total input.

At this Boston residential school, there were young kids in wheelchairs, some all skin and bones; older kids missing limbs; some with juvenile spinal disc degeneration; and teenagers with all kinds of attitudes—some eager to play, others wary and waiting to assess me. I talked casually with the group. We agreed that we were all dreamers. What daydreams did they have?

From their responses, together, we framed their circus show with a story. It would begin with them all getting ready for bed, falling asleep—and sharing the same fantastical dream. They were performers in the dream world of circus, where anything can happen, a place where seeming disabilities become abilities that no one else had in the same way.

By the end of the week, we had a performance ready for staff, parents and families, the board of directors, and invited guests. And what a show it was! I acted as ringmaster, playing it as cool and calm as Claus Jesperson.

As in dreams, anything goes, and anyone could try anything. That is what circus is about: sharing what each human body and imagination and spirit can achieve. One kid with twitching limbs from a nervous system disorder found out he enjoyed playing percussion. He banged out a pretty good drum roll on a bongo. Shake, Rattle, and Roll, as he put it.

We levitated another boy, who had crutches. It's an old vaudeville gag. The kid lies down on his back on a bench, covered up to his neck in a black cloth, with only his head and feet sticking out. The magician makes his magical passes and sure enough: the head and feet and the horizontal body under the cloth slowly rise and float!

It's quite a good illusion, done correctly. Then came the comic blow-off. The magician took his bows, the assistants, who had originally brought out the cloth, "inadvertently" walked away with it as they exited—revealing the boy holding his crutches horizontally in mid-air, with shoes attached at the ends, before he sat up to audience laughter and cheers.

A blind boy in our circus was blindfolded—with wonderful illogic—as The Knuckleheaded Knife Thrower. A parent from the audience was "volunteered" to stand against a door, also blindfolded, with arms spread to her sides, holding a couple of balloons. The blind kid grasped a large kitchen knife and was spun around—and when he stopped, he was facing the audience.

As he raised the knife to throw it, all kinds of gags ensued—including taking off the blindfold so he could "see," and then replace it—until finally he mimed throwing the knife at the volunteer, while another kid popped the balloons. The grinning, knife-throwing boy took his heroic bows and went offstage, purposely bumping into everyone, leaving the stage littered with kids, and a relieved parent volunteer.

The show had folks—and me too—laughing and clapping and teary and marveling at the spirit and energy the group put into their performance. There was a daringly choreographed acrobatic wheelchair routine and wild animal trainers who attempted to train one of the house cats.

One boy in a wheelchair was the star of the juggling act. His condition caused constant movement of his body, a dyskinesia with swaying in the chair, head at an angle, hand tremors, arm spasms in the air—which he figured made him a natural juggler. So, we gave him colorful silk juggling scarves, which floated down nicely as his uncontrolled arm spasms tossed them up in all directions.

Two other small kids were his assistants: as the scarves floated down around the boy, they ran around his wheelchair, frantically keeping them from touching the ground, while putting them back in the boy's twitching hands. Tossed in a kind of lyrical, flaying rotation of arms, a kaleidoscopic riot of colorful scarves flew and floated around the wheelchair.

The boy laughed joyously as he juggled with abandon, rolling his wheelchair around the stage, with his assistants scrambling to follow, scarves falling everywhere. We all joined in his infectious merriment. Afterwards, one physical therapist said there had never been real laughter in the building like that, ever.

Earlier in the week, the boy without limbs had provided inspiration, saying he sometimes dreamed of flying: "After all, my body is like a bird's, no clumsy arms or legs getting in the way of flight. I just need wings." So, for our finale, I soberly announced that the closing act was "Laughingly Ludicrous, Sensationally Serious, and Absurdly Dangerous," adding a stern warning: "Do Not Try This at Home.

Try It at a Friend's House! We had to fight the local authorities to allow it to occur at all: The Human Cannonball!"

The homemade cannon, a large painted trash barrel in a wheelbarrow, was enthusiastically wheeled in by cavorting clowns to the theme music of *Indiana Jones*. Then the boy without limbs, while standing upright in a red wagon—wearing protective goggles, a football helmet, a white aviator's scarf around his neck and a pair of wings strapped to his trunk—bowed his head to applause while being elaborately rolled around the room.

The cannon was raised at a 45-degree angle. The other performers knelt and saluted in earnest anticipation as the boy was placed inside. A clown lit a wooden match to light the fuse, we got the audience to cover their ears—but just then, the director of the facility ran up, waving his arms, and shouted "HEY! STOP! No Matches Allowed in School!"

He blew a loud whistle, and the Clown Fire Department came running in with an old garden hose, getting the director tangled up in it, while some clowns had buckets of water which, of course, they threw at the audience. General whoops and howls of laughter, then finally the countdown began as the director himself lit the fuse.

The drummer boy played a drumroll on his bongos, and we all shouted in unison: Three!... Two!...ONE!

There was a flash of light, from flickering light switches, then a big puff of "gun powder" (really talcum) and a boom from somewhere offstage—and two therapists pulled the Human Cannonball out of the barrel and carried him high overhead across the whole room...and into a very big fishing net held up by the custodian.

Thunderous applause filled the room as the Human Cannonball, grinning ear to ear, was carried by the rest of the cast on their shoulders. The audience spontaneously rose in a standing ovation, laughing and weeping. Confetti was thrown, balloons were popped, and Sousa music blared the grand finale of The Wildest Show on Earth!

After it was all over, and goodbyes were being said, I had that feeling of exhausted mental, physical, and emotional relief after a challenging project was successfully completed. One elderly grandmother, with shining eyes and a laugh in her voice, startled me with a memorable line: "Thank you, dear," she said, putting her hand on my arm. "You froze a smile on my face!"

We all have our share of personal disabilities to deal with. No one gets away in life without physical, psychological, or emotional struggles hitting us hard at times. I know first-hand the difficulties of surviving cancer, depressions, a broken neck, living with Parkinson's, and other common and profound ailments of living. We usually handle these difficulties privately, not in public. But some disabilities cannot be hidden.

I drove home in the rain with visceral flashback visions of the Handicap Days in the circus building in Copenhagen. I choked up with a few tears, wiping my eyes as the windshield wipers wiped away rain. I thought about why I had taken on this career of clowning. I was not an extrovert. I was not a satirist or sarcastic comedian. I preferred the silence of mime to the cacophony of words. I preferred the ridiculous, the silliness of a child's sense of humor.

It was my job to encourage idealism and nourish a sense of fun to mitigate the difficulties of living. It was easy with kids. They laugh easily when they play. But grownups forget how to play for the sake of it, abandoning old scorekeeping, rules, and needless competition. Adults get too serious about games and tend to develop CPD syndrome: chronic play disorder.

That night of silliness with the kids performing in front of people was nothing new to me. But I was taken aback, as often happened, by the strong emotional reaction of that audience of adults: their open-mouth surprise, uninhibited whoops of delight, and their feelings of unabashed love, tears streaming down their faces.

I don't really know why I was so moved, driving home. I wasn't crying for the boy with no limbs, and not for all the other kids who, with grand courage, embraced humor and tenderness that night. I think I was just overcome by the splendid tenacity of the human condition.

Antonio

"Big crowd, thick as blackberries. Hot weather,
and our faces leak. Tent well filled with 'lots of peep,'
as friend Arcari says for 'lots of people.' When Arcari
took gas at the dentists' to-day, he heard bagpipes and
bumble bees buzzing, and exclaimed, as he faded away,
'Cover me over with beautiful flowers.' When he awoke
four teeth were lost, strayed, or stolen."

—*Ringling Route Book,* Stevens Point,
Wisconsin, 1891

O ne of the enduring images I have of Antonio was the opening
night of season 1975, my third year in Copenhagen's circus
building. There were always special guests in the audience, Danish
politicians, celebrities, and members of the royal family. The party
after the opening show was held in the ring and it was a lavish, dress-
up affair, ladies in sparkling gowns, men in suits or tuxedos.

I always felt awkward at these shindigs, never comfortable at small
talk with people outside the circus business. They asked too many
questions with champagne glasses in their hands. I could see other
artists feeling the same, though everyone looked great. Dressing up
was like wearing another costume. I carried a red clown nose in the
pocket of my tuxedo, in case the situation called for it. You never know
when it could be handy, and it would look great with black tie and tux.

I didn't stay long at the party. I was tired. I could see Antonio
looked pale and was having a hard time. Antonio had undergone a bad

winter. We didn't know if he could handle the new season. I told him I'd had enough of the party, and would he care to join me and slip out?

He nodded. He looked very smart in his child-size tuxedo and top hat. All the performers had been given flower bouquets. Antonio carried his as we made our way outside. He had been drinking at the party. He looked at me with a long gaze and nodded. I pushed open the large iron gate, and we stepped out. It was well after midnight. The sidewalks were empty, and a foggy mist hung over the streets.

We had one of our silent pauses, just looking at each other. It always felt meaningful, but I never really understood why. It could have been a look that said, yes, we both know what is going on...that he wouldn't recover his health. I can only compare it to the steady gaze, years later, from my canine partner Rufus in his declining old age, when he was clearly trying to tell me something and our thoughts met in a silent gaze.

Antonio nodded again and turned to go his way home. I stood there a while, watching, before heading off in the opposite direction. He was near the end of the block when he stopped for a second and stepped from the damp darkness into a spotlight.

The image it created in my mind made me catch my breath and is vivid to this day—a film noir image, the little man in top hat and tails in the mist, eerie and beautiful. Then the moment passed, and Antonio stepped back into the darkness. I turned and went my way.

★

Antonio entered the hospital early in the season, with a shot liver and other age-related complications. He died the morning of opening night of the Fall Circus Festival. The newspaper ran a photo the next day, front page, of me and Pete in our Gunslinger Showdown routine from that opening night. The photo captures the moment at the end, when we meet each other in the ring, pointing to each other, as we jump up joyously, feet up off the ground. But it was not a joyous time. The Copenhagen headline read: "Clowns from Benneweis Go on without Our Little Man."

Antonio's funeral was surreal in an unexpected way, like waking in a lucid dream when you know you are dreaming, yet are conscious in the dreamscape, aware of bizarre illusions all around you.

Every year in the show, we had at least one routine where Antonio was hidden inside a large prop, which was carried into the ring by four of the ring boys in special outfits, looking snappy, with gold embroidered lapels across red velvet jackets. For example, there was the Bank Robber gag. As Pete and I fooled around, coming down the aisles, making noise with all our safe-cracking tools, the audience would be distracted from the boys carrying in the safe—wherein lay Antonio, waiting for his cue, and hopefully not taking a nap.

Now, outside the church in a drizzling rain, I stood with Pete and the rest of the circus company as a hearse drew up to the curb. Four ring boys in their special outfits slid out a child-sized casket. It felt freakish, watching the ring boys carry the box into the church, as if it were a clown gag, Antonio hidden inside—just waiting to jump out at the right dramatic moment.

My jaw dropped; I glanced over to Pete who returned my look with wide and wet eyes. We both half-expected him to pop out of the casket with his arms raised, gruffly shouting, "Bollocks!"

Back in the dressing room before the evening show, I took out Antonio's personal trunk. It was all that was left of him in this world. An old box of clown makeup; a wig glued inside a hat; a toy pistol that pops out a little tattered flag with BOOM printed on it; some other gag props, and a small scrapbook of photos. Pete and I looked over the objects, silent.

I took the toy pistol that went BOOM and several old black and white photos of a very young Antonio. One showed him outside, behind a circus tent, standing in the middle of a slackwire, low to the ground, practicing his balance. I didn't know he could walk a wire. My favorite photo showed him in a tuxedo, conducting the circus orchestra, standing alone on the ring curb in a long, white spotlight.

For the rest of that circus festival season, Pete and I left Antonio's things as they were at his spot, his makeup box and little hat in front of his cracked, talcum-dusty mirror, a couple of those photos stuck loosely at the corners of the mirror. I still glanced over, silently, when I put on my own clown face.

It was a reflexive habit, that sad glance, which now felt something akin to a prayer.

The Showdown

*"The state penitentiary is located here, and our
zebras set up a jealous howl at the sight of the many
striped trustees who walked about the streets."*

—*Ringling Route Book,*
Joliet, Illinois, 1899

Once in a while, some young American lad would show up in our
dressing room, saying he was a clown. This happened a few
times. I say "young lad" even though we would be about the same age,
early twenties. They thought I must be an old-timer, the same way I
first thought about Peter.

These guys would invariably introduce themselves as former
clowns from Ringling Bros. and Barnum & Bailey. Having read
the playbill notes that said I was an American, they would remark:
"We thought it was impossible for American clowns to work in
European shows."

I would just look blank for a moment and say, "Right," continuing
to take off my makeup.

These fellows had gone through Ringling's Clown College, an
eight-week intensive course in makeup, prop building, act creation,
clown history, juggling, stilt walking, acrobatics, slapstick, and other
Ringling-style group knockabout routines. After auditioning, a handful of the students would receive contracts to go on the road with The
Greatest Show on Earth.

It was a great experience for them to be in that show, even though the broad clowning, generic costumes, garish wigs and frenzied slapstick routines—eighteen clowns frantically racing around three rings in huge arenas for eighteen thousand people—suppressed individuality and character. That's why they were impressed to discover a young American clown working in a more subtle style in a Danish circus.

They would ask if they could audition. I would smile and take them to meet Claus. I didn't know much about Clown College and, frankly, I was impressed. I had great respect for anyone who had worked the Big Show, something out of my range of experience.

Later that season the legendary John Ringling North would visit our show. JRN had not only booked acts for The Greatest Show on Earth; he owned the company. He lost interest when the show gave up the Big Top and moved into arenas. He sold it to the Feld family in 1957. It was Irvin Feld who created Clown College in 1968. Ironically, twenty-five years later, his son Kenneth Feld invited me to co-direct that same Clown College! "Our clowns need to learn how to be funny," he said.

It must have been nerve-wracking for those young American clowns trying out for Benneweis. Claus would arrange for an audition in the ring the next morning and invite anyone from the show to come watch. I had never auditioned for a show and couldn't imagine doing so. I had just shown up and let things take their course. I felt sorry for the Ringling guys, but I respected their efforts. I took them out for beer and a hot dog afterwards.

I later thought about how my story must have appeared from their perspective. It made me ponder the odd occurrences and fantastical string of events that had led to my being where I was, doing what I was doing. Maybe they had just followed a different cloud.

★

One of the most fun acts that Pete and I performed that season we called The Showdown. It was a parody of the western trick roper, Bob Rosetti. Bob did a classic "gentleman cowboy" act, complete with whip cracking, gun-slinging, and rope-twirling, along with a fancy vest, boots, and a lovely long-legged cowgirl assistant. What made our Showdown clown act different than the usual clowning was its extreme slowness...

The ring goes dark. Two spotlights appear at the top of the aisles on opposite sides of the building, highlighting two cowboys, standing still, in a threatening bow-legged pose. Pete stands in one spotlight wearing cowboy chaps, bright red Mexican style vest, a shoulder belt displaying rows of fake bullets across his chest, large holster, and a big cowboy hat, pulled low over his brow so that only a big red clown nose is visible.

Robin stands across the wide expanse in the opposite spotlight. I'm dressed in a gunslinger outfit also, but everything is too big: baggy pants held up with red suspenders and clothespins, a shoulder harness, and holsters around my waist holding water pistols. Forks and spoons made clunky spurs on my clown shoes, clanking at each step. An oversized, floppy cowboy hat hung low, hiding all but a red nose.

The band plays the ominous theme from The Good, the Bad and the Ugly by composer Ennio Morricone. Pete and I stand frozen for a bit, eyeing each other across the wide-open space. Then, each at our pace, we take a step and stop. The audience, below us, turn in their seats, straining to watch as we make our way down the aisles, very slowly, stopping at each step. With heads tilted down, our faces can't be seen.

Occasionally, a giggle sounds from someone in the row I'm passing. I stop and slowly turn in that direction, lift the brim of my hat to look...more giggles from that side. I slowly turn back but halt my step as some chuckles sound from my left. I do another Clint Eastwood glare in that direction. My solemn gunslinger attitude is completely incongruous with the silly image of my costume and the clank of my fork-spurs.

Pete performs the same way across the aisles. We really take our time. I remember watching some Harry Langdon movies, another great silent film clown. What made Langdon different from Chaplin and Keaton was his glacier-like pacing. The slower he went, the more delayed his reaction time, the funnier he was. Where another comedian might do a double-take, baby-faced Langdon would do a double-take, pause, do a triple-take, look at the camera in confusion, do a slow look back, and start the double-take all over again.

As gunslingers, Pete and I discovered the slower we went, the more comical the buildup. The audience reacted with smiling anticipation and the occasional guffaw, giggle, chuckle, or snort—which of course made us react.

It was tempting to move quicker. Occasionally, halfway down the aisle, I might stare down an impulsive giggler, draw my water pistol slowly, point at the kid, then squirt the parent, which set off more laughter. I loved the kids' giggles.

Finally reaching the ring curb on opposite sides, Pete and I stand in spotlights. We face each other in showdown pose, hats still pulled down, faces covered with bandanas pulled up like outlaws. The theme music stops, as we step into the ring. With each halting step toward each other, the bass drum thuds. The circus building never was so quiet for so long with a full house.

We stop, just five feet apart, bow legged knees slightly bent, hands ready near our holsters. The drumbeat stops. Then Pete raises his head and lifts the brim of his cowboy hat. I do the same. Suddenly, he stands up straight and says loudly in surprise, pointing at me, "ROBIN?!"

I look at him in happy recognition. "PETE?!!"

The band kicks in with lively theme music from *The Magnificent Seven,* as we hug each other and go skipping out through the curtain together to happy applause from the audience. Claus enjoyed the act and allowed what might have been a quick two-minute reprise to turn into a six- or seven-minute routine.

★

Several years later I was on tour with my friend Paul Gaulin and his Canadian mime troupe. Paul had also been a student in 1969 at Marceau's school in Paris, and we were now successfully touring theaters throughout Ontario and Quebec.

One evening, the troupe was hosted by the Ontario Arts Council at a celebratory awards dinner in Toronto. We all got dressed up for the soiree and were on our best behavior. During the cocktails, I wandered around the room trying to look sophisticated with a glass of wine in hand. I found myself standing near a trio of elegant Arts Council ladies and couldn't help but overhear their conversation.

One lady asked another about her recent vacation in Scandinavia. She said, "I really enjoyed Copenhagen. The people were so friendly! And everyone rode bikes in the center of town; it was really quite wonderful."

The first lady replied, "I agree! And did you get to the Tivoli Gardens? Just beautiful, eh? I was in Copenhagen a few years ago. It was in 1974...yes, the summer of '74. Did you see that fabulous circus in the building near the Tivoli?"

That caught my intention. I nudged a bit closer to the group, not wanting to miss a word.

The second lady had missed the circus. The first lady continued, "Oh, it was wonderful! It was quite a classy affair. Even the clowns were funny."

What!? Was she talking about me and Pete?

I started to get nervous and looked casually in the opposite direction. My ears got hot. I heard the first lady say, "There were these two clowns coming down the aisles dressed as cowboys in a funny show-down...and they really did nothing, but somehow it was very funny! I'll never forget, they moved so slowly. They were like actors, not the raucous slapstick clowns we see here. More like mimes..."

I felt myself blushing, and in a sweat of dilemma. My first impulse was to interrupt and exclaim, "That was me!" and to bask in a glory of compliments, and modestly autograph the napkins they would thrust at me. But for some reason I held back. I was bashful! I'm not sure why.

And yet, how sweet to surprise the ladies—it would be a story they would tell later. But no—then the mystery of my secret would be diffused. I liked the anonymity. But hold on...maybe I was destined to know one of those ladies better...start a relationship...fall in love... revisit Copenhagen together...start a family of kids, who would grow up to be clowns...

The moment passed. It was too late to interrupt their conversation. They had moved on to other things and were walking away, dispersed in the crowd. I felt silly and embarrassed by my social timidity. Hesitancy causes missed opportunities in life, sometimes regrets. Nonetheless, I let it go and felt serenely happy the rest of the evening.

It was a very warm feeling: the Unknown Clown from Benneweis had made his mark.

Act III

Mule Wrangler
in Lapland

Mule Wrangling

This page: Above left, American clown Joe Jackson, Jr. Above right, Rob attempts to ride Kansas the Mule, Cirkus Scott Swedish tour, 1976.

Both pages: Karl Kossmayer and his iconic Unrideable Mule Act in the ring, circa 1970s. Rob and Karl partnered in the act on the 1976 Cirkus Scott tour.

At Liberty

"This little Everyman character, Kossmayer, brought to the ring a perfect history of the universal, retired middle-class type, life dominated by his wife's discipline, wasting in a few minutes all his life's boring dignity, to run off and join the impossible world of the clowns."

—Kossmayer obituary, Dutch News Source
December 24, 2000

The Three Princes of Serendip is an ancient Persian morality tale. Some travelers set out in good faith, lose their bearings, and serendipitously stumble upon good fortune. The story reckons that you don't reach the shores of Serendip by plotting a well-thought-out course. You set out with good intentions, a yen for adventure, and trust in fate to see where your troubles will land you.

I was about to set out and land on the back of an uncouth mule, who would teach me exasperating lessons in humiliation, and how—when an irksome jinx is upon you—all your efforts to avoid embarrassment are futile, because the cause of ensuing calamities is no one but yourself.

★

It was a blustery morning in October, the day after the 1975 Benneweis Circus season had closed. Always orderly and busy, the day after closing has nothing leisurely about it. Some of the acts with a few props had already gone off into the night. By morning the animal acts were already moving out. Everyone was packed and ready to disperse to the four winds, back to home base, wherever that was, or on to another show.

The clown trio of Pete, Robin, and Antonio had ended. Antonio was gone. Pete would soon be traveling with a new wife and a comedy act with seals and dogs. Three years had passed, and I had worked with first-class artistes from around the world. But I'd been performing indoors long enough. I missed the open road, the close camaraderie of a traveling community, the smell of international foods coming from the neighborhood of caravans, the bawdy roughness of the tent crew.

Once again, as vaudeville acts used to say when out of work, I was "at liberty." I wanted more experience with traditional circuses traveling under canvas. But I didn't know where, or what, to do next. My apprenticeship with famous European clowns was over. I'd worked with icons like Charlie Rivel, The Francescos, Bubi Ernesto, Toto Chabris, Galetti, Karl Kossmayer...KOSSMAYER!

I jumped on my bike and rode furiously through the streets of Copenhagen to get to the circus building before it was too late.

One of the funniest acts to come through Copenhagen's circus building had been Kossmayer's Unrideable Mules. Karl Kossmayer came at the end of the regular season of 1975 to be part of the annual three-week Circus Festival. The mule act was nonstop motion, and very strenuous for Karl.

He was sixty years old and had a bad back—and there he was chasing mules in the ring. I was a bit intimidated by Kossmayer. I never spoke to him during the festival, but I learned a lot about comedy timing and animal training from watching him.

★

I stopped Kossmayer, just before his truck and caravan was about to pull out. "Do you need any help with the mules next season?" I asked, out of breath.

He looked me over. Then on a scrap of paper he wrote an address in the Netherlands. "Can you be there, first of March?"

I nodded.

"Okay," he said, sticking out his hand. "See you down the road."

Circus folks are known for avoiding drawn-out farewells at the end of a season. A handshake, a nod, and—circus-style—our business was done.

Good for me, I thought, as I watched his caravan disappear, pleased with myself for acting on impulse. Too often I'd had an impulse and not acted, but instead considered and pondered and worried until any action was impossible.

That thought was followed by a vague foreboding. Once again, I may have gotten myself into another fine mess.

★

Karl was heading to his homebase in the Netherlands with his wife Sjoukje Dijkstra, Holland's famous Olympic gold medalist figure skater. Karl was born in 1917 and came from a long line of German animal trainers. He had done some clowning in his early years, but Karl became renowned for one of the best-known comedy acts in the circus: The Unrideable Mules.

I arrived in Hilversum, Holland, in March of 1976. Karl had already built sleeping quarters for me inside the medium-sized box truck, where I would sleep with the mules for the next six months. There were four narrow stalls behind the cab. The four mules slept standing, side by side, facing front. Behind them was my bunk.

There were no windows and barely room for a narrow mattress. A half-wall separated me from my bunk mates. My head abutted the butts of the mules in their stalls. There was just enough space next to my bed to walk the mules, backward, down the heavy wooden ramp, out the back door of the truck.

It's amazing how quickly one gets used to the scent of earth— the redolent mixture of manure and mud, mule urine and straw. I fell asleep with the soothing sounds of four snuffling animals, softly stomping their hooves in happy, mulish dreams of chasing me around the ring.

We had a contract for the season in a beautiful fifteen-hundred-seat Big Top with Cirkus Scott, the largest tenting operation in Sweden at the time, formed in 1937 by the Bronett circus family. Over the years, Cirkus Scott became one of the most respected in the

European circus world. It traveled from the southern tip of Sweden up to Lapland, home of the Sami people, above the Arctic Circle.

We did two shows a day and jumped to a new town every night. It was a nonstop operation that required a highly efficient, hardworking workforce. On our way north from Holland, Karl drove the mule truck, with me riding shotgun. Sjoujke drove the pickup, pulling their large caravan. We headed for Sweden's city of Malmo to open the touring season.

I had spent the winter studying Swedish, only to find out that Cirkus Scott had contracted the Magyar Nemzeti Cirkusz—the Hungarian National Circus—to work the whole season under the Scott big top. I switched gears and attempted to learn Hungarian—basic profanity, no doubt—from the Magyar Cossack riders. Guest artists that year included the great American tramp clown, Joe Jackson, Jr., with a classic breakaway bicycle act—and Kossmayer's Unrideable Mules.

In Malmo, the Magyars gave us space for the mules in their horse tent, my new daytime home. Their sixteen horses were groomed by Ahmad, a young Arab fellow. At first, he eyed me and the mules with distrust, pointing me to a corner of the tent. I got the mules situated and went to look for straw and hay, glancing back at Ahmad, who was clearly unhappy about mules invading horse territory.

I was uneasy, too. I knew nothing about the care and training of horses or mules. There had been just a few weeks in Karl's winter home in Holland, and no space for teaching me the act. I knew the routine from watching Karl every night in Copenhagen—but I had no experience performing with the mules. Karl had seen me clowning and must have figured I could handle it.

My earlier vague foreboding returned and hung over me like a shadow of my Hoffman experience with Achmed the Camel (*from Tibet!*). But heck, chasing a mule around the ring would be a lot of fun. What could possibly go wrong...?

Mule Wrangling
in Lapland

*"It was no uncommon thing, if the weather
turned cold, to have a snowstorm, and then we had to
build bonfires in the tent to melt the snow on top and
prevent its being crushed in. The performers shivered
around little charcoal stoves in their dressing rooms.
The animals curled up in the corners of their cages,
and everybody cussed the weather."*

— George Conklin,
The Ways of the Circus, 1921

The legendary journalist for the *New Yorker,* A. J. Leibling,
wrote several remarkable sports books. In *The Sweet Science,*
he tracks his personal connection to the history of boxing:

*It is through Jack O'Brien that I trace my rapport with the historic
past through the laying on of hands. He hit me, for pedagogical
example, and he had been hit by the great Bob Fitzsimmons, from
whom he won the light-heavyweight title in 1906. Fitzsimmons
had been hit by Corbett, Corbett by John L. Sullivan, he by
Paddy Ryan, with the bare knuckles, and Ryan by Joe Goss, his
predecessor, who as a young man had felt the fist of the great Jem
Mace. It is a great thrill to feel that all that separates you from the
early Victorians is a series of punches on the nose.*

I could easily adopt a similar link to posterity by perusing the chronicles of *The Unrideable Mule* acts in circus history. In 2005, I acquired two miniature donkeys named Figaro & Jiminy for the Circus Smirkus Pinocchio tour. That was, for me, a personal connection to my season with Kansas the Mule, thirty years earlier, which, in turn, is connective tissue to Kossmayer's decades of comedy mule riding.

That connection goes back to Chaplin's ornery mule in the hilarious silent feature *The Circus* in 1928, and further back to famous clown Dan Rice, entertaining President Lincoln, and Mark Twain's descriptive version of the act in *Huckleberry Finn*. It is "a great thrill" to feel all that separates me from the Victorian past is a series of bites on the butt by an ornery mule.

In the traditional version of this act, the performer pretends to be an audience volunteer, attempting to ride the mule or horse, but soon is revealed to be what he is, an accomplished circus equestrian. The audience is in on the joke almost from the start.

Karl, on the other hand, was bald and portly, a middle-aged, nondescript "Everyman." Wearing a rumpled suit and tie, he seemed a befuddled college professor, very believable as an audience member, and out of his depth in the ring. He didn't look or try to act "funny," and that was the key to his success and fame.

Even by the end of Kossmayer's Unrideable Mules act, the public had no clue that Karl and I were both plants in the audience. The mules always won! No one could ride them. The mules were clearly having fun, putting us hapless humans to rout.

Karl sat in the audience, third row center section of the bleachers, surreptitiously signaling the mules. I posed as one of several volunteers, invited by the ringmaster to try and ride an innocent-looking mule just once around the ring. In contrast to Karl, still in the audience, we volunteers were all young, athletic, and confident.

Fast-paced music begins, and the mule trots confidently around the ring, while the ringmaster sends in one volunteer at a time. Each can barely catch the mule, let alone jump on. When it was my turn, I was to chase after the darn mule, take falls, jump out of the way of kicking hind legs, hop on, get thrown off, and run for safety. The mule chases me, trying to bite my butt, as I jump over the ring and fall into the laps of people in the front row.

My job is to make the act fast and funny, especially if the other volunteers are boring or intimidated. When I jump on the rear end of the galloping mule, holding onto his mane with one hand and his tail with the other, I manage to ride him halfway around the ring. The audience cheers, the band plays rousing music, while the mule, galloping past the center bleachers with me desperately holding on, sees Kossmayer in the audience take off his hat and wipe his brow.

That's the signal for the mule to stop suddenly, swing around, and run in the other direction. The result? I get thrown, somersaulting in the air, landing on my back in the sawdust. As I dust myself off, the mule runs behind me and snaps malevolently at my rear end.

At that point Karl volunteers to give it a go and attempts to climb into the ring, but his fussing wife—played by Karl's middle-aged sister in a dowdy dress—pulls him back to his seat. Later on, he gets up again and jumps into the ring with me.

The wife jumps after Karl, and they both slip, face down in the sawdust, just as the mule jumps over them. Helpful Karl grabs the mule around the neck and signals me to climb over him to get on the mule. The mule flips me off, and Karl jumps on backwards, facing the tail, which he desperately holds onto as the mule starts to run.

Chaos ensues! I jump out of the way, the ringmaster gets knocked over, the mule stops short, and Karl slides off, face down. The mule manages to pull Karl's pants down around his ankles, and the audience is hooting happily as Karl's shocked and embarrassed "wife" hustles him out of the ring and out of the tent.

★

The first of April, Malmo, Sweden, and it is opening day of Cirkus Scott, two shows scheduled for two o'clock and eight. I had spent a cold night in the truck, the mules offering some pungent warmth. Nonetheless, this was Scandinavia. I pushed open the back door—an inch of snow overnight!—and slipped on the wooden ramp, spraining my ankle. Limping, I got the mules fed, groomed, brushed to a shine, and ready for the two o'clock matinee.

I sat in the audience, halfway up the right section of bleachers. The ringmaster brought out Kansas the Mule, so named because Karl had bought him in the Midwest when he had brought his act to the US with Holiday on Ice. Yes, mules on ice!

Kansas was big and muscled, black as midnight, and obstinate. His stubbornness, I was to learn, was the sign of high intelligence. He would do what he wanted to do, as simple as that. On cue from the ringmaster, I joined four other volunteers from the audience.

My muscles felt cold and stiff, and my ankle still hurt from my earlier slip. After a few minutes of failed volunteer attempts, the ringmaster sends me in. Kansas sees me coming.

I catch him on the run, fling my arms around his neck, and he drags me along. I jump on and get ready for the swing-around-the-other-direction bit. I let go of his mane with one hand to wave at the cheering audience and prepare myself to get thrown off towards the soft sawdust in the middle of the ring. Instead, the darn mule spins the other way! I'm thrown outward toward the wooden ring curb.

I somehow manage a frantic twist in mid-air to avoid landing on my head. The unexpected vehemence of the mule's move catches me off guard, and I land on my shoulder with a sharp pain hitting me like a punch. I continued the act as valiantly as I could, with shoulder out of place and a sprained ankle hurting, faking it in front of the audience.

Adding one final exclamation point to my initiation, Kansas chased me into the audience and bit me sharply in the butt just as I jumped over the ring. The audience loved it, and as they cheered and clapped, Karl stepped into the ring to join in the fun. I made my way back to the line of real volunteers, joking with them as we watched Karl's uproarious efforts.

This was just the first show! Day one of a long season ahead.

Back in the horse tent, I berated Kansas with my new Hungarian profanity. He stood calmly, waiting for his post-show brush down and fresh hay. Later that night, nursing my aching shoulder, I couldn't raise my arm above parallel. I had to brush my teeth by holding the toothbrush still and moving my head side to side.

★

In the American rodeo, a cowboy riding a bareback bronco attempts to stay on his bucking horse for eight seconds. In Kossmayer's act, I jumped on a bucking mule and was thrown, kicked, chased, and bitten during twelve fast-paced minutes. Twice daily.

Let me say here that the mules were trained so well for this act that no audience volunteer ever got injured. Not even close. The mules were careful to buck off to the side, missing a volunteer's leg, though in the riotous action it looked ominous. The mules knew how to act ornery, while avoiding hurting anyone.

Except me.

The shellacking I got from Kansas every day was not only a physical challenge, but a psychological vexation—what was going on here? Outside the ring, Kansas and I were buddies and bunk mates. The other three mules, rotating with Kansas to give him a break, behaved in the ring. Kansas was showing me he was the alpha-mule.

Favoring my pulled right shoulder and sprained ankle, I did the two shows a day, fetched new straw and bales of hay, mucked the stalls. I washed and brushed all four mules every morning before breakfast, again before and after every show and before bed. Then I fell into my own stall exhausted.

I also cleaned and rasped mule hooves. I was daunted at first, just cleaning the hooves: you stand behind the mule, lift and bend a hind leg to rest it on your thigh, facing your groin, while praying the mule won't kick as you scrape out muck with a pick.

Kansas never bucked. He was happily content to be groomed. As aggressive as he appeared in the ring, it was just all an act: little kids cheerfully took rides on his back outside the tent after the show.

Three days after the opening, my other shoulder got thrown out. Two pulled shoulder muscles. Kansas continued to bite my butt hard—same damned place every time—as I jumped over the ring and fell into the audience. He was supposed to pretend to chomp at my rump. He knew that. The audience, meanwhile, was loving it.

At breakfast, in the caravan with Sjouke, I appealed to Karl.

Me: (frustrated) "My butt really hurts—he gets the same spot, right cheek, every time."

Karl: (guffaw, cracking the top of his soft-boiled egg) "Hmph..."

Me: (perturbed) "How do I make him stop that?"

Karl: (scooping the egg onto a bit of toast) "You need to show him who is boss!"

Me: (stammering) "But...I...how?"

Karl: (slurping coffee) "Whack him in the snout with your elbow, just before he bites."

Me: (alarmed) "What!? I can't do that...not in front of the audience!"

Karl: (putting down his cup): "Gott im Himmel, Robin! Just do it. No one will see it."

Me: (flustered) "But...I...maybe...you..."

Karl: (while tactful Sjoukje brings a second helping of sausage) "Enough already! He's testing you—and getting away with it! Eat your potatoes!"

I began to dread facing Kansas in the ring. He was formidable. I was intimidated. I sat in the audience like an inexperienced boxer, anticipating climbing into the ring with Muhammed Ali. The other mules were smaller and courteous. They never threw me wrong or bit my butt. But Kansas—sassy and clever trickster— well, this was clearly between him and me. My immediate challenge was to do the act just once and not get hurt. And still get the audience laughing and cheering.

After weeks of bruises and pulled muscles finally healing—and sore rear cheeks—Kansas once again intentionally flung me off the wrong way. I slammed with brutal force right onto the wooden ring curb. I saw stars.

Later that night, my waist on the slammed side turned dark blue and purple and crimson, deepening like thunderclouds under my skin, alarmingly colorful. That was enough. Game on.

As I brushed Kansas down before bed that night, he nuzzled my armpit playfully. I think he sensed something was up. My mood had changed.

The next day, matinee show, he chased me, jaws chomping, and just as I leapt over the ring, arms pumping—I bopped him good on the snout with my elbow. Kansas startled for a brief moment, shook his head with a snuffle, and looked at me with newfound regard before he continued running around the ring. From then on, mutual respect. Game over.

Or so I thought...

Jackass

"The term 'jackass' derives from the male donkey's nickname, 'jack,' paired with the original donkey terminology, 'ass.' The mule is a cross between a female horse and a jack. Mules are typically calm, steady, strong-willed—and cunning."

—*Animal Husbandry* compilation

Karl had a generous spirit. He also had an eruptive temperament. He never abused the animals, but the slightest misstep from a circus roustabout, the simplest daily annoyance that anyone else would shrug off, could initiate a flurry of volcanic hollering from Karl. If the wrath was not vented directly at me, I learned just to be still at those moments and feel sorry for the other fellow.

Karl had welcomed me into his home as a colleague. I had three hearty meals in his caravan, did errands for the family, learned as much as I could about care of the animals and meeting his act's high standards. He taught me simple courtesies, like not putting my napkin on the dinner table after wiping my mouth and how to properly eat a soft-boiled egg in an egg cup.

He taught me how to speak to the animals, not in English but what I called Mulish, a verbal German-based gibberish spoken calmly but firmly. Granted, Karl could be soft-spoken at times even with humans. Luckily, he seemed amused by me and my American manners.

Nonetheless, being around Karl was unnerving. Together, Karl Kossmayer and Kansas—the Three Ks, as I referred to them privately—were a force of intimidation for me.

After several weeks of one-day towns and overnight jumps—taking the big top down after the evening show, dismantling the horse tent, loading the mules in the truck, grabbing a few hours of sleep before setting off in the early dawn, raising the tent in a new town in time for the matinee show, then doing it all again that night—it was luxury to reach Stockholm for a three-week run in one spot.

This gave Karl time to rehearse a new comedy act with all four mules in the ring. It was a revival of the old-time "Learned Horse" act. The animal counts out the solution to a mathematical problem—with stamping hoof—or finds the card a volunteer chooses from a jumbo deck, and other Amazing Feats of Animal Aptitude.

Intelligent Animal acts go far back in circus tradition. Gerry Cottle, Britain's circus impresario, gifted me an original copy of Lord George Sanger's fine memoir, *Seventy Years a Showman,* published in 1910. Written when Sanger was near eighty, it's the book that inspired me to write my own. Sanger's stories cover the same period as Charles Dickens and depict similar outrageous Victorian characters.

Author Kenneth Graham, who wrote *The Wind in the Willows,* knew Sanger, and writes in the foreword of Sanger's memoir that he was "quite the most famous showman of his day or perhaps of any day. His circuses formed a planetary system all over the Continent, and in England were almost a Milky Way."

In his book, Sanger recounts his training methods for his School for Learned Pigs act—the same way that Kossmayer was creating an act with his four mules, by discovering what an animal does naturally and encouraging this in repetitive play.

★

One morning in Stockholm, the mules were rehearsing The Learned Mule act in the ring with Karl. I wore baggy pants with bright suspenders and floppy clown shoes, playing the foil to Kossmayer's "Professor of Animalogy." Meanwhile, my job that morning was to stand at the ring entrance and fling my arms up to deter any mule from leaving the ring.

Karl was putting the mules through their routine, when he called me to bring him a small prop that sat on the ring curb.

I hesitated to leave my position. I could see Kansas eyeing me and Karl, back and forth. The other mules were docile, but Kansas, he was a smart ass.

"Robin!" Karl shouted at me, impatient.

Reluctantly, I left my post. Kansas seized the chance. In a flash, he escaped out of the ring. Both Karl and I froze. A split second later, Karl was yelling, "Go, go...GO!"

★

All show folks have stories of animals getting loose and causing hilarity or calamity. Veteran journalist A. J. Liebling profiles an old-time animal trainer, Louis Van Dycke, who tells a story of two circus chimpanzees, who liked playing billiards:

> *They was two tough customers! In San Francisco...my manager and I was riding in a motorcycle with the chimps in the sidecar and coming down a hill we skidded into a trolley. The chimps ran into a saloon and with bottles broke up the mirrors and chased the bartender and got drunk and beat up a cop, and when we woke up, we was in the hospital and the chimps was in jail.*

I wish Liebling had been around to meet Karl and Kansas. His profile of them would have made worthy reading!

★

Meanwhile, outside the tent, I saw Kansas looking over his shoulder waiting for me. I walked over with an air of nonchalance, but—zoom—off he ran!

I started running and chased the darn beast through the circus lot and onto the streets of downtown Stockholm. It's not easy running in clown shoes. To avoid tripping, you need to raise your knees up high, in Chaplinesque style. My fear was that Kansas would be lost, or worse— hit by a car. But I underestimated his cleverness. Learned Mule, indeed.

I saw him pause at a busy intersection, look both ways, and wait for his chance to cross. When a car slowed to a stop, an astonished driver gaping out his window, Kansas would buck his hind legs near the car, as if to say, "Keep your distance, Mister"—and then take off again, sometimes straight down the sidewalks, startled pedestrians jumping out of his way.

I found myself leading a parade of bemused bystanders, who took up the chase behind me. We picked up some loitering police, who began shouting and waving their arms like silly Swedish Keystone Kops.

Kansas would stop at a corner and look back, wait for the parade to catch up, then take off again when we got nearer. Stockholm was jubilant with mid-morning amusement. Two hours later, I walked back onto the lot, exhausted, leading a happy Kansas the Mule.

One jackass leading another.

The Jinx

*"There is no character, howsoever good and fine,
but it can be destroyed by ridicule, howsoever poor and
witless. Observe the ass, for instance: his character is
about perfect, he is the choicest spirit among all the
humbler animals yet see what ridicule has brought
him to. Instead of feeling complimented when we are
called an ass, we are left in doubt."*

— Mark Twain,
Pudd'nhead Wilson, 1893

By the second month on tour, I fell into what baseball players would call a slump. A more dire word, for me, is "jinx," the Latin spelling "jynx"—a spell, or fate, or a period of bad luck caused by a curse, a person, or a thing. Jynx: the word evokes a sleek, cunning jungle animal about to pounce. Or maybe a mule named Kansas.

I now think that my trials and tribulations with Kansas inside the ring coincided with my troubles outside the ring, in the same way that emotional stress can be a cause of physical illness, and vice versa.

This period of my grappling with The Jynx subsided only when Kansas and I finally came to terms. However, before negotiating our peace treaty, my life felt decidedly surreal—like a Buster Keaton film. A hurricane of havoc swirls around our hapless hero, who can only stand there in deadpan disbelief.

I awoke every morning wondering what manner of mayhem would befall me that day. Or worse—what embarrassing calamity would I cause to bring down the wrath of Kossmayer on my head? I found myself trying everything I could think of to thwart the unfolding Jynx: talking to the mules, counting an exact number of brush strokes when grooming, tossing handfuls of sawdust over my left shoulder before every show, whistling while mucking the stalls, keeping wary lookout for imminent disaster, flopping fatigued into my bunk at night.

But nothing seemed to work.

I kept a journal of mishaps, giving them titles as if they were fantasy tales, funny now. But as I write this—fifty years after they happened—I feel again the physical distress in my body and the emotional tremors in my nerves. "The Undignified Mule Chase in Stockholm" is a visceral remembrance. Here are just a few more that ensued.

★

"The Incident of the Bent Bike" involved one of Karl's prized possessions, a specially made bicycle that could fold in half, good for packing in the small caravan storage space. He would ride it on errands off the circus lot. He allowed no one to touch it, or even to speak of using it.

One fateful day, Karl needed to get a small part for his truck. He wanted it quick, before the auto garage closed, since we were jumping town that night. The garage was a mile or so away, and Karl was occupied with other business.

He unfolded his precious bike, looked at me gravely and said, "Take the bike. Stop for nothing. Get to the garage and back. You've got twenty minutes. DO NOT scratch the bike. Go!"

I had to go around a huge open-air sports stadium. Time was running out. When I got near the empty arena, I saw that I could shimmy under the wire fencing and take a shortcut through the field and save ten minutes. Done.

I rode across the arena infield, but it turned out there was no fencing to climb under on the opposite side, just stadium bleachers. Then I saw an enclosed revolving turnstile.

It was seven feet high, closed all around with heavy horizontal spikes, and a narrow iron cage. I calculated quickly. Riding back to the other side, I'd lose another ten minutes. But if I folded the bike, pushed it through the first space, then went behind in the next revolving space... Sure, that would work.

All went according to plan, until I got inside the cage, pushed forward and—CLINK! —the bike caught on the spikes and clogged the narrow one-way gate. Trapped in an iron cage, I couldn't push forward or back. It took just a moment of eerie calmness to realize I was completely alone in a vast, empty stadium, and helpless.

Panic triggers fantasy scenarios. As spectators arrived for a big soccer match, months later, I imagined being found, a skeleton with bony fingers reaching through the iron bars for some rusted contraption with wheels...

Half an hour later, through concerted effort with all my waning strength, shoulder banging rhythmically on the rotational iron bars, the bike finally crumpled enough for me to get through the gate, set free. The auto parts store was still open. I got the needed tool and walked the mile back to the circus, sweating profusely from carrying the crumpled bike and anticipating the wrath awaiting me.

I silently handed Karl the tool he had needed and set the thoroughly mangled bike on the ground in front of him. He got red in the face. Then, suppressing an internal volcano that was bubbling fiery steam but refusing to erupt, he disappeared into his caravan.

I took my dinner with the mules that night. Kansas looked at me with concerned empathy and left me alone.

★

"The Occurrence of the Runaway Caravan" happened at dawn on a jump day, in a town north of Stockholm. Except for the big top crew, gone ahead in the middle of the night, the whole Cirkus Scott—cars, trucks, trailers, caravans—lined up to leave in single file. The parade of vehicles had to climb a short incline to get off the valley lot. The two Kossmayer vehicles were in the middle of the line, our mule truck followed by Sjouke, who drove the pickup truck pulling the caravan trailer.

Always in control, Karl liked to hitch the caravan to her pickup himself, but this time we were running late. He yelled at me to hitch it up because the line was starting to move. One by one the parade of vehicles lugged up the grassy hill.

I quickly hitched up the caravan, dropping the iron pin into the holes to connect it with Sjouke's pickup. Then I ran back to the mule truck and jumped into the cab next to Karl, just as the line of caravans started moving.

Halfway up the hill, we heard shouting outside. We stopped the mule truck and jumped out to watch Sjouke's caravan, somehow unhitched, rolling by itself down the hill, bouncing and picking up speed. All the other circus folks had jumped out of their trailers to watch the imminent crash.

I stood there stupefied.

Sometimes, in the midst of an astonishing event, you feel a helpless awe at what is occurring. How the heck...? I was sure the pin had properly dropped into the hole, safety cables attached. But then I wasn't sure.

Thank the stars, the caravan careened around the other vehicles, slowed at the bottom of the hill, and came to a halt unharmed. Silently, with a taut mouth and dark frown, Karl pointed his finger at me, then at his truck. Mortified, I got in, and watched the rest of the circus pass, my Magyar friends grinning and waving. The Jynx had pounced again.

Sjouke backed the pickup downhill, and Karl hitched it to the caravan himself. We were alone in the field. Without a word, we began our slow trip back up the hill. I was feeling like Sisyphus with clown shoes.

★

"The Episode of the Retractable Roof" demonstrates that there are times in life when you are really on a roll. Good luck is on your side, everything is going great, no effort needed, you simply can do no wrong. This was not one of those times.

I felt like that man in the cartoon, walking along on a bright sunny day with a small dark cloud, raining right above his head.

Cirkus Scott had entered the Arctic Circle, approaching the far north town of Kiruna. Karl pulled the mule truck into a gas station. He asked me to jump out and signal him if there was enough space for the truck to pull under the low-hanging roof over the gas pumps. "It might be close," he said, eyeing me fixedly.

I got out, already nervous, and walked ahead, inadvertently stepping down a slight incline to get a better look. I began to mutter to myself, something I had started doing after each fiasco: "Mermin, don't fuck this up."

My mistake—that lower angle of sight. It looked like enough clearance. Heck, overhangs were designed with box trucks in mind, weren't they? I gestured to Karl with my hands "about six inches," and waved him on slowly. He inched the truck toward the gas pumps.

Suddenly there was an ear-splitting SCREECH! of metal on metal...

Before Karl had a chance to stop the rolling truck, it tore into the gas station overhang, which was stronger than our mule truck's roof, which was being curled from front to back, half of it unfolding exactly like the top of a sardine tin.

At that moment, I was literally beside myself. I had the sensation that the real me was standing alongside this other one, watching him stand there, dumbfounded with disbelief at the unfolding calamity, powerless to do anything about it. I observed myself with curiosity to see what the poor wretch would do next.

The magnitude of my ineptitude was indefensible. I felt like a hapless marionette, manipulated by some omnipotent force for a purpose beyond my comprehension. I looked up at the sky and—only in my head—shook my fists and mentally shouted: *Just...STOP it!!*

To make things more baffling, Karl didn't fire me. Exhibiting Herculean control, he didn't even yell, possibly too astonished to be mad. Maybe he was just damned curious to see what calamity I could come up with next— How can Robin top this one?

The brunt of Karl's wrath was diverted to the truck, the gas station, the universe in general. And then, in true circus fashion, we just carried on. We checked on the mules, who stood in their stalls, looking up, perplexed at the suddenly open skies. In utter silence, we finished gassing up and found a body shop.

★

I found solace with Joe Jackson, Jr. after each of these escapades. Joe was as sweet a man in person as he was in the ring. An American clown born in 1912, he was a large man whose rotundness only emphasized the comedy of his gracefully performing a break-away bicycle routine. Joe had learned the act from his famous father, Joe Jackson Sr., who had been a cycling champion.

Joe played a down-on-his-luck tramp character, who wanders through the curtain and into the ring to discover a shiny new bike. Looking around to see if anyone was watching, he sneaks a ride— but in the process the handlebars fall off, the seat collapses and the pedals drop. He attempts to put the bike back together, but he ends up with handlebars backwards and pedals where the seat used to be—and he still manages to ride it happily around the ring.

He embodied a gentle childlike clown character who only wanted out of life to have a few moments of joy riding a bike— which he does, despite the bike always falling apart.

Joe Jr. worked silently and s-l-o-w-l-y, the way his famous dad had taught him. He was especially adept at evoking giggles from little kids in the audience with his gentle pantomime and kindly, innocent demeanor. Joe Jr. became famous in circuses around the world and was especially beloved in Scandinavia. Combined, he and his father played their breakaway bike act for over a hun-dred years.

★

After "The Episode with the Retractable Roof," I found Joe and his wife, Ruth, lounging in lawn chairs under the awning outside their caravan. They listened to my woes, as always, with good-natured amusement. Joe fired up the grill.

"Joe," I moaned, holding my head in my hands. "Joe…"

"What…is something the matter?" said Joe, in his droll way, as he flipped a sizzling hamburger. Ruth, grinning, stifled a guffaw.

I stared, feeling bleak. "I don't have a smidgeon of dignity left in my aching body."

Joe turned around and looked at me for a long moment. Then he smiled. "You're paying your dues. We've all been there. Karl gets it—and despite all, he likes you. You'll be okay. You're just learning to be circus."

And that was it: I was learning "to be circus." Circus grammar—you are not "in" the circus. You either *were* circus—or not.

Joe calmed me down after each of my Kossmayer fiascos, grilling me American comfort food, hot dogs and hamburgers and toasted cheese sandwiches. But I'll always be most grateful for his guidance with the nasty Middle Eastern conflict brewing in the horse tent.

The Horse Tent

"The mule was a meek, innocent-looking creature.
The announcement was made that the management
would give five dollars to any person who could ride the
mule around the ring. Various ones were sure to come
forward and try it, but none of them got very far.
After a while, Jeremiah Backstitch would amble out
from somewhere in the audience and declare
that he could 'ride dat yere mule.'"

— George Conklin,
The Ways of the Circus, 1921

Ahmad was competent and intelligent with a tender affection for animals and decent command of English. Traveling with the Hungarian circus as a groom for the Magyar horses, he was dark in skin and shiny black hair with an imposing black mustache—and temperament.

I liked his confidence around the animals. I learned a lot from him about the care of mules: how best to use a curry comb, hoof pick, leg tape, and general fussing with ears, eyes, mane, and tail to make the best appearance in the ring.

We had many good-natured laughs about his bosses, the Magyar troupe, guys our own age, mid-twenties. They all, like us, came from outside circus: some were from a gymnastics school, another was an auto mechanic in the off season. He dreamt of running away from the circus: "Nagyon fáradt vagyok! Too much work. I want to open a garage, fix cars. More easy."

Coming from a communist state under the Soviet sphere of influence, these fellows suddenly discovered a new uninhibited world in Scandinavia. Every inch of wall and ceiling inside their caravans was covered with naked pinups from adult publications. They couldn't believe the easy accessibility of those magazines. There were lively discussions about the beauteousness of blonde Swedish women.

"Look again," I asserted. "Your Hungarian circus women, hazel-eyed brunettes, are incomparably gorgeous." That prompted raised glasses of vodka and boisterous toasts to their female compatriots.

One day all the pinups disappeared. Overnight, the caravans were spotless, the boys grim-faced. Turns out a high-ranking representative from the Hungarian circus administration in Budapest had arrived for inspection. A week later, like magic, the centerfolds were back up and the Magyars were smiling once more. Apparently, the bureaucrat departed suddenly, after being spotted at a newsstand purchasing his own stack of nudie magazines.

★

It took a while, at first, for Ahmad to loosen up to my mulish presence in his territory. The horses were magnificent animals, but clearly, in my opinion, not as clever as the mules. This was cause for some jocular debate between us.

Also cause for dispute was his blatant hatred for Jews. He would lash out against Jews with fervent hostility—completely unaware I was Jewish. This created for me a critical dilemma. We were to share the animal tent for six months.

Although his prejudice didn't often rise to the surface, anti-Semitism was always there—a seething undercurrent of emotion, surfacing now and then like hot bubbling tar.

During one of his zealous tirades against Jews, I asked if he had ever met one.

His reply, scowling while brandishing a sharp hoof pick, felt seriously unsettling: "No...and if I ever did, I would kill him without hesitation." He continued gently grooming the horses.

I never gleaned the source of his attitude. Had he a traumatic experience, as a Muslim, with racial bigotry or violence? Was his animosity a consequence of cultural indoctrination? Political tension was extremely volatile in the Middle East in 1976. The Arab-Israeli conflict in 1973, the Yom Kippur War, which took place on the holiest day in Judaism—and during the Muslim holy month of Ramadan; the Lebanon Civil War in 1975; the Entebbe Hostage Crisis occurring right then.

Ahmad was justifiably angered by events, and already a bit guarded by my being American. Never knowing what would trigger an outburst, I avoided political and religious discussion. I would shift conversations to the loftier subjects of faith, and spirituality, and the pursuit of transcendent experiences in life, like caring for these beautiful animals.

Every day I deliberated what to do. Should I confront him? Say nothing? On the one hand, I felt a moral obligation to challenge bigotry and reveal my heritage. On the other, more practical hand, I wanted to protect the mules—and my own skin. I already had enough troubles weathering each day.

I kept silent. I couldn't decide if my secrecy was cowardice or common sense. It felt like both. Meanwhile, Ahmad and I were developing an amiable friendship.

"As-salaam'alaykum, my friend," he would say, every morning.

"Wa 'alaykum salaam," I'd reply, as we tended to the animals.

Whenever I returned to the tent, panting and sweating after a contest in the ring with Kansas, he would ask, grinning, "Kayf haalik?"

"Allahu Akbar," I would answer. Between Kossmayer, Kansas, and that other annoyingly pervasive creature, The Jynx...yes, God was surely great to sustain me yet another day.

I discussed my predicament with Joe, respecting his patience and wisdom and barbecue skills.

"How are you getting along in the horse tent?" he asked.

"Joe," I groaned, "my conscience is in confusion."

"No fights, no brawls, no bruises?"

"Just from the mule," I said, rubbing my sore butt.

"Hell, then," said Joe. "Keep on following your instincts."

"My instincts have not exactly been obliging lately," I said, looking over to the shiny new roof on Kossmayer's truck.

Joe chuckled while he fired the grill. "There's no right or wrong remedy to the situation. Just let it play out. Sit. Have a hamburger."

And so it went, right up to my last day on tour, when my instincts finally determined a denouement to the dilemma.

Leaving Lapland

*"The droll and ludicrous must have its place in the
circus procession as well as the grand, the beautiful
and the imposing. So, the clowns go out to make
human beings laugh; to brighten up the faces drawn
with the cares of life; to chase away, if even for a
moment, the lines that tell of the struggle for bread,
the disappointments of ambition, and the thousands
of cares that oppress humanity."*

—*Ringling Route Book,*
Lincoln, Nebraska, 1894

The Cirkus Scott season had started in southern Sweden. Village to town to city, we had made our way slowly north until we were playing towns far above the Arctic Circle, where the highway became a two-lane road, then one lane. Our caravan of trucks finally was stopped by a fallen tree blocking the way in the forests of Lapland. We got the elephant out to move the tree.

All the while I'm wondering where the heck was the tent going up, in the middle of a forest—performing for who? Reindeer and moose?

We came to a clearing in the woods and raised the big tent in time for the eight o'clock show. At 7:45 came a rustling from the woods, and hundreds of Laplanders appeared from the forest and filled the tent. Two hours later, another rustling, and they were gone.

The energy on the lot was high-spirited as we took down the tent in the midnight sun. The sun never really set here. It seemed to almost sink below the horizon, but the sky never darkened, it just dimmed, then transformed into a pastel glow. The air shimmered with a light that crackled with energy.

No one slept. In the wee hours of the pale night, the Hungarians began a soccer game in the empty field where the tent had been.

It was nearly six months into the season, and I was leaving the show. I had let Karl know well in advance that I had to get down to Copenhagen for a special gig. A Swedish friend was learning the mule act in my place. In the middle of the forest above the Arctic Circle, the circus was heading west, and I was headed south.

The morning of my departure, as the circus prepared to move after dawn, I still had two goodbyes to make. I brushed Kansas down for the last time. It had been a grand tussle of personalities, one which inevitably forged a special bond. We were adversaries when we met, reconciled along the way, and colleagues by the end. I gently caressed his smooth muzzle.

We had been partners in making people laugh—what could be better than that? He looked at me eye-to-eye without blinking. We stared and nuzzled some more. There was a stillness, an exchange beyond words, a silent communication between two species meeting for the last time...then parting.

Circus folks are deep-rooted in superstition and ritual. (Never sit on the ring curb facing outward; the ring is your livelihood and home—you don't turn your back on it.) So I had one final ceremony: I left a little sack of sawdust in a corner for the next mule wrangler replacing me. This little burlap bag held sawdust from the beginning of the tour and would be spread with the sawdust at the last show of the season. It signified coming safely home.

★

I still felt troubled about my duplicity with Ahmad. My conscience required resolution. Our friendship had strengthened through humor, hard work, shared journey, and the loving care of animals. I knew that his prejudice was not common among circus folks. Ahmad was not circus. He had joined the Hungarians for one tour as a groom.

Circus culture—itinerant and global—was inherently inclusive. During WWII, several circuses gave shelter to Jewish families, including the Althoff Circus in Germany which hid many from the Nazis; the Mikkenie Circus in Holland had sheltered the German Strassburger circus family; the Bouglione circus dynasty of Gypsy Romani heritage harbored Jews at the Cirque d'Hiver in Paris; the Bronetts at Cirkus Scott were themselves Jewish.

That last morning, I stood with my backpack in the middle of the circle of sawdust where the ring had been, waiting for my ride south. The convoy of trucks and trailers had started leaving the site, passing me by, one by one. Then came Ahmad, standing in the back of a departing pick-up truck, waving to me, and shouting Arabic blessings.

As he passed by, I shouted back some blessings of my own—in Hebrew—then nodded and pointed to myself. His face changed, perhaps a mixture of confusion and dawning comprehension, I'm not sure.

To this day, I'm not certain I did the right thing. What went through his mind as his truck pulled away that morning? Anger? Betrayal? Conflicted revelation that despite his beliefs, he now had a Jewish friend?

I waved, shrugged my shoulders, put my hand on my heart, nodded and smiled. As his truck faded in the distance, his expression was frozen in a kind of startled shock, then he was gone. What were his immediate—and lingering—thoughts? How does he tell this story?

Fifty years later, I still wonder.

A Circle of Sawdust

"On the banks of the Mississippi, the greatest
American river, the greatest American circus closed
its most eventful pilgrimage. Here the chariot wheels
of the Ringlings rolled for the last time, and the sky
of canvas, fluttering, fell on the season of '92."

—*Ringling Route Book,*
final entry, 1892

My misadventures with Kossmayer and the Unrideable Mules, that ongoing series of mishaps, now hold a comic absurdity I didn't feel at the time. However, I don't want to leave the impression that my time with Cirkus Scott in Sweden was all misfortune. It's true that during the tribulations of that season I often lay awake at night, wondering how it was that—no matter what I did—my actions generated ridiculous outcomes. Should I just give up, surrender, and quit?

What bothered me most was a lack of personal consequence. My mishaps were inflicted on the poor Kossmayer family. I like to remember they seemed amused by me. At suppers in their caravan, Sjoukje always gave me extra helpings. I would furtively glance at Karl, but he patiently avoided mention of whatever folly I had inadvertently caused during the day. Despite all, he liked me.

But never mind. All disasters were squared with many beneficent memories of our journeys through Sweden, from the southern tip of

Malmo to the northernmost town, Kiruna, where the Sami language was heard. Those good memories include swimming with elephants and bathing with mules in the many lakes of Sweden.

What fun to ride the back of an elephant as she walks nonchalantly into the water and submerges completely like a submarine—while you sit almost floating on top—and then she emerges, joyfully spraying water like a spouting whale.

How incongruous to ride Kansas the mule into a lake and encourage him to buck me into the water, but he wouldn't—despite my pulling his mane, thumping his sides, daring him to throw me. I would finally get down and stand waist high in the lake and wash him down. He loved that.

And how exciting, and scary, to join the hurtling, trick-riding Magyars when one of them got injured. The leader of the troupe had insisted I knew how to ride—after all, friend, you can trick-ride the mules, so c'mon, quick, put on this costume!—as he joyfully pushed me into the ring with resounding "Hup-HEYs!" from mustachioed Magyars.

They sprang onto galloping horses, and as they rode upside down, hanging on their horses' bridles with one hand, I frantically handed them props, then hopped from one crossed ankle to another in a Hungarian jig, flinging my arms in the air, adding my "Hup-HEY!" to theirs, always a bit off the beat, before it was my turn to madly dash across the ring and run two steps up a small inclined platform and jump upon the rear end of a running horse who already had three riders, but of course there is no room, the gag being for me to slide down the rump and fall into the sawdust and jump up with another "Hup-Hey!" to the delight of the crowd, hoping they won't recognize me from the mule act.

★

I recall the wonderful cookouts and laughter and reminiscing with Ruth and Joe Jackson, Jr; the circus tales at campfires with Karl and Sjoukje and their baby under the shimmering aurora borealis; and gathering with the Hungarians around a small portable TV to watch the 1976 Olympics. A few had been on the gymnastics team in the last Olympic games, and it was a delight to pull stories from

Sjoukje about her experience as the 1960 Olympic silver medalist, a three-time World champion (1962–1964), five-time European champion (1960–1964), six-time Dutch national champion (1959–1964), and the 1964 Olympic Gold Medalist in ladies' singles.

Like many world champions, and star circus artistes, she had nothing to prove. She was proud of her accomplishments—years of hard work and high pressure—yet modest about retelling them, humble and always ready with a smile, especially with kids. She cheerfully gave them rides on the mules between shows.

I remember giving magic tricks and trumpet lessons to the young Bronett boys, Henry and Robert, the sons of Francois, Cirkus Scott's owner and ringmaster. Francois was kindly and soft-spoken, known for his ringmaster phrase: "Får jag be om största möjliga tystnad." (May I ask for the greatest possible silence!)

Familiar with Kossmayer's act, he had helped by standing in the middle of the ring to direct the action between audience volunteers and the mules, keeping the action fast paced. His sons Henry and Robert later produced Cirkus Scott together until 2003.

The professional animal trainers displayed a rapport between human and animal kingdoms that was beautiful to witness that season. The Donnert horse acts carried on the legacy of a six-generation Donnert Hungarian equestrian dynasty, begun in 1820 when Adolf Donnert created a legendary performance using forty horses.

After our mule act was over and mules were fed and groomed, I would return to the big top to watch one of the Donnert acts. A single rider, wearing a gray tuxedo and gray top hat, would enter the ring on a large gray horse, followed by one gray elephant. The circus band began a smooth waltz number as the man, the horse, and the elephant trotted around the ring in time to the music. Then the man was gently let down by the horse bending her front legs, and he left the ring, leaving the horse and elephant completely alone.

The elephant, with her trunk, picked up the horse's reins and led her in small circles in waltz time. It was mesmerizing. After a while, they switched roles and the horse led the elephant, who grasped the horse's tail. They circled each other in their waltz around the ring. There was no human presence, no voice cues. At length, the man reentered the ring, the elephant carefully lifted him onto her back, and the mellow waltz continued until they and the horse pranced and danced their way out. It was a stunning exhibition of silent communication and harmony between three species of the animal kingdom.

★

Another astonishing elephant image comes to mind, from the circus winter quarters in Scandinavia. Snow covers the ground, the circus trucks, tents, equipment all packed away, hibernating in barns until spring. An elephant pokes her head through the tall wooden doors of the animal barn, opened to the cold of the day. She carefully steps out onto the plowed driveway, slippery with packed snow and ice.

Slowly making her way to the end of the drive, the elephant starts frolicking in the snow drifts by the side of the path, her trunk playfully tossing powdery snow onto her back, misting the air with snowflakes. She turns toward the barn, fifty yards away, and starts running—no, galumphing—a good twenty yards, braces her front legs on the ice and joyfully slides into the barn!

★

There's an old saying that refers to the first elephants brought to America in the early 1800s. People were struck with astonishment. To say "I've been to see the elephant" meant more than a visit to the circus. It became a catchphrase for gaining experience of the world, for encountering the impossible, often at a significant cost. During the Civil War, returning soldiers used the phrase to describe going off to fight.

After Hoffman, Benneweis, and Kossmayer, I can truthfully say, "I've been to see that damned elephant!" I got the experience I needed, absorbing everything about tenting circus, following my intention of someday going out under canvas with my own itinerant company. As it turned out, I was closer to my goal than I knew. When I stood in that circle of sawdust in Lapland and waved farewell to the show that early morning, I didn't know it was my last appearance in a European circus ring.

Years later, I watched the wonderful Charlie Chaplin silent feature film, *The Circus,* impressed by the authenticity of the circus scenes. I clapped and laughed out loud with déjà vu when Chaplin is stalked by a mischievous midnight-dark mule, who chases him out of the ring and into the laughing audience! He also got it right in the last image of the film.

Charlie stands in the middle of a circle of sawdust, where the ring had been, and he gives a little wave to departing horse-drawn caravans disappearing in the distance. He, too, had "been to see the elephant." Alone, once again, after a dream-like circus adventure, he picks up a piece of paper on the ground—the last vestige of the circus—a painted star. He rolls the paper into a wad, tosses it in the air, and gracefully kicks it from behind. With a shrug and a little skip, The Little Tramp, no longer the circus clown, sets off for further unknown adventures.

The end-of-season *Ringling Route Book* put it so eloquently in 1892:

> *"Farewell! We have been as one great family. We have learned to like each other well, and now it is sad to part. To most of us there comes this consolation, like scissor-blades, we 'part to meet again.' To all the ladies and gentlemen connected with this show, wherever the great future finds them dwelling...may you have success and happiness unbounded. And now, with grasping hands: farewell—a word that must be and hath been...a word that makes us linger yet—FAREWELL!"*

Act IV

Rufus in Denmark

Rufus in Denmark

Top: "Three Mimes on a Couch," Marcel Marceau, Rufus, Mermin, Burlington, Vermont, 1996.

Bottom left, Rob and Rufus perform on the green, New Haven, Connecticut, 1986. Bottom right, R-and-R in front of the Circus Barn the year Rob started Circus Smirkus, 1987. Facing page, Rob and Rufus, 1986, publicity head shot.

The Pantomime Pup

*"The Grecian shepherd, tending his flocks, saw with
no more wonder the passing of the Athenian hordes
during the time of Pericles than that with which
the boy of to-day watches the coming and going of
the Ringling Brothers' Shows."*

—*Ringling Route Book,*
Hutchinson, Kansas, 1894

My years-long apprenticeship in the world of traditional European circus and clowning with the Hoffman brothers, the Benneweis circus, and Kossmayer's tour made a strong imprint on my character and worldview. Looking back, I can see I was there to learn but not stay forever. It's as if I were on an extended George Plimpton-esque mission of participatory journalism, enduring odd indignities and clutching momentary triumphs, to write about them in the future.

I left the European circus behind, still wanting to leverage my experiences into my dream of a circus company back in the States. But I was out of work, needed to find a job, and felt discouraged by my failed attempts to find anyone who understood my stories of the European circus world and the dream of starting my own company.

By then I had found a new performing partner: Rufus, a small terrier pup, white with large brown spots, a dog pound mutt barely two months old when found. He was carefree, easygoing in human society, a charmer—courteous to women, indifferent to men—a born performer, a canine con artist, a gentleman rascal. I sensed his special character but had no clue he would eventually bring me back to Europe with his unique canine celebrity style.

★

I took Rufus up to Toronto, where I had found work as a mime with my old friend Paul Gaulin and his Canadian mime troupe. Paul had been a fellow student of Marceau in Paris and was a master of the Marceau/Decroux school of mime technique. I joined Paul for a couple of years as a charter member of his company.

Rufus came on tour with us when he was six months old. He curled up, snoozing on a blanket backstage, as the troupe performed. When our show finished and we took our bows, the applause would wake him up, and he'd poke his head through the back curtain to see what was going on. The first time this happened, it got a big laugh.

We came to expect that reaction every night. So, when he poked his head out, I'd call him over, and as we all took our bows, Rufus stood by me, yawned, and stretched. With his front legs extending, head down, rump sticking up in the air, he looked for all the world like he was bowing. I whispered, "Stay!" and he froze in that bow position—and got more laughs.

It became a standard part of the show's finale. He soon took his bows without any cue from me. Then Rufus started to do pantomime in the show.

I had discovered his talent one day when I was practicing mime-eating an invisible feast: drinking glasses of wine, biting a juicy apple, cutting a steak, munching on cakes, stuffing my mouth, chewing, chomping, swallowing, wiping juice from my lips.

As I was feasting, Rufus—who had been keenly watching from his bed in the corner—got up, walked right beside me, and sat down without taking his eyes off me. I stopped and looked down at him, an invisible piece of food in my hand. Then he surprised me and sat up with front paws in the air, asking for a piece; he even licked his lips.

This was unusual in itself—I had never taught him to beg like that! We stared at each other for a moment, then I slowly mimed breaking off a piece of invisible cake, reached down and offered it to him—and he took it in his mouth, chewed a couple of times—then swallowed! He sat down, licked his lips, and stared intently at me as if wanting more.

Well, this routine became part of my act with Rufus the Pantomime Pup.

My only explanation for this development is our companionable understanding of each other, and our shared visceral language, the power of imagery—or mime. I'd had other dogs in the past, but Rufus was different.

You can gauge an animal's intelligence by how they look at you. If the eyes are wandering, or focused only on getting some food, or asking to go outside, or sizing up your defenses, that is instinctual. If the gaze of your canine companion is solid, it is nonverbal communication of intention, imparting what they want. The silence carries information.

That communication can become a two-way path. Though Rufus did comprehend a few dozen words, he didn't speak English, and I didn't bark Dog-lish. Our common link was visualization. Our minds met halfway in a universal language of imagery.

My thought-intention, doing mime, is translated as a physical image in space, both in body language and strong visualization—you "see" my intention when, as my mentor Marcel Marceau liked to say, I use mime to make "the invisible become visible."

I believe Rufus and I communicated nonverbally through mime. I had to let go of the typical pretense of my human prominence of intellect and learn from Rufus to grasp his intention to communicate an image to me.

Distance didn't seem to matter. For example, once Rufus had been gone all morning somewhere in the forest beyond my old farmhouse. I had an appointment and needed to find him. I closed my eyes for a minute and projected a focused mental image: I saw him way back in the woods by our favorite waterfall. I mentally called to him to come home. For a couple of minutes, I pictured him hearing my call, raising his ears, and trotting back along the path.

When I opened my eyes, sure enough, there was Rufus coming out of the woods, rounding the corner of the house to jump into my waiting car.

Another time I was visiting my mother in suburban Connecticut. I always took Rufus for a walk on a leash on those streets. He didn't like the leash, as he was used to running free in the Vermont countryside. I tried an experiment. I took him out to my mother's small front yard. I sat him down on the grass and asked him to stay put. I released the leash. Then I slowly walked to the edge of the yard and carefully mimed an invisible wall bordering the yard. Rufus watched intently.

Then I turned my back to him and took a dozen steps down the road away from the yard. I turned around and called out loud for Rufus to come. I called verbally and made a joyful gesture. "Come on, Let's Go!"

Rufus stood up and took a few tentative steps. When he reached the edge of the yard he just stood there, then sat down, looking at me, in what I took to be a slightly confused way. I mentally erased the thought-formed wall and gestured again, "C'mon!"—and he got up and trotted right after me.

What do I make of this? Our intraspecies communication was surely unusual, something I had not experienced with previous dogs. People who knew Rufus or saw him perform remember him fondly, surprising me with their memories forty years later. Fortunately, I have some footage of Rufus and the "mime eating" routine. People see it and their jaws drop, having not believed me at first when I told them about his unusual talents.

The Danish television show that filmed that routine was another unexpected adventure that came about only because of my partnership with the character, intelligence, and personality of Rufus the Pantomime Pup. I loved touring Canada with the Paul Gaulin Mime Company, but always in the back of my mind was that bothersome itch of a dream—I knew there was more for me to accomplish, and only one way to find out.

I decided it was time to get back into the circus world. Could I run off to join the circus a fourth time? I booked a flight for Rufus and me on SAS—Scandinavian Airlines— from New York's JFK to

Copenhagen. I figured I'd get to familiar territory, look up a show business agent I knew over there, and see if he could find me a job in some circus.

It had been four years since leaving Circus Scott and the mules in Scandinavia. I wasn't sure of contacts there anymore and, without cell phones and the internet, had no way of finding people or circuses I knew. With nothing to lose, I would try my luck once again. I knew by then that whatever plans you make, fate has other ideas in store— and luckily not always bad ones. I was counting on that...

Kennedy airport, spring, 1980. Rufus was a calm fellow, a small dog and a very good traveler. So, I naively figured he would be allowed to stay with me, on the floor by my seat. We arrived at the airport in plenty of time, no lines yet at the ticket counter. I approached with Rufus on his leash. The ticket lady was a blonde Scandinavian. She smiled at me, then at Rufus.

I smiled back and addressed her with a Swedish greeting. Curious about my speaking Swedish as she perused my American passport, she spoke with a lilting accent. Hoping to raise the level of small talk, I answered: "Ah, well...a few years ago I toured Sweden with Cirkus Scott—maybe you know it?"

She looked up at me, smiling: "Ja, of course! We always went to the circus when I was a child."

"I'm a clown with the circus. I'm headed back there to work...with my partner here." I pointed to Rufus, who wagged his tail helpfully and stared up at her with ears folded back, eyes bright.

"Oh, he's very handsome...aren't you, little fellow?!" She forgot about me and spoke directly to the dog. "Hello, I'm Inger," she said, bending down to scratch his neck at just the perfect spot behind his ear. Rufus melted and looked at her with liquid eyes, clearly in love. I caught myself thinking if she scratched my ear, I, too, would be in love.

"Do you have his cage here?" She looked around, seeing my one suitcase.

"Cage?" I gulped. "No...I...I thought he would just sit with me. He's very well-behaved. I could buy an extra seat..."

"He must have a cage to go in the baggage compartment. Really, sir, it's the only way."

My heart sank. No way would I let Rufus be caged up inside the belly of the plane. I tried for ten minutes to work some charm with her, but it was hopeless. Dejected, I sat on a bench by the wall facing the ticket counter, Rufus looking up at me.

If I refused to fly, where to go now? Somehow, I'd get back to Vermont, with no money, no job, no plan. I was at a loss.

I sat and watched travelers happily checking in at the counter, with Inger occasionally glancing over at us. Final boarding was called, only thirty minutes until takeoff. The ticket counter cleared again, when suddenly Inger called out to Rufus. He quickly ran over to her, wagging and wriggling in her arms like a long-lost lover.

I went over then, and she said: "Let me try something." She got on the phone to her floor manager. He came over and they spoke confidentially. Then he looked at me and said: "He's really a circus dog? What does he do—could he jump through my arms?"

The manager came forward and bent down to make a circle with his arms. Rufus looked at me, then to him, then back at me. I was about to say, "No, he doesn't actually do tricks, he's an actor..." when Rufus made his own decision, ran up to the guy—and jumped through his arms! He had never done that before, not even with me.

The guy was delighted, and Rufus then jumped through Inger's arms! I was amazed. He was a charmer, the rascal, and took control of the situation, bless his heart.

It was fifteen minutes until take-off by then. The gate was closing. The manager got on the phone and spoke with the bursar, the chief flight attendant on board. The manager covered the phone with his hand for a second while saying to me: "He's asking if you have a self-contained receptacle for the dog?"

Without waiting for an answer, Inger reached under the counter and threw a black trash bag at me. "Yes sir, he does," said the manager to the flight attendant. Meanwhile, Inger was frantically clicking away at the computer. Then she took the phone and said: "Yes, there's an empty row available, 5-A." She had moved some passengers to other empty seats, freeing up a whole row. She hung up, grinning prettily, took Rufus by the leash and called out, "Follow me!"

They held the plane for us as Inger ran across the tarmac, leading Rufus—with me trailing behind like an afterthought. The crew lowered the steps, and we ran up into the plane, Inger leaving us with a quick hug from me and licks from Rufus. Two happy stewardesses led us to our seats past astonished passengers, kids reaching out to pat the dog as we went by, and within minutes we took off for Copenhagen.

I had the window seat. Rufus spread out over the other two seats as if he owned them. Over the speaker we heard: "This is your captain speaking. On behalf of the flight crew, I'd like to welcome you to SAS flight direct to Copenhagen. And a special welcome to Rufus, the circus pup!" There was scattered clapping, and, hearing his name and applause, Rufus sat up.

Throughout the flight Rufus was treated royally; I was merely his sidekick. When it was dinnertime—those were the days when airline food meant pretty good and free hot meals—I was served a simple chicken sandwich. But the dog? A broiled steak and mashed potatoes in gravy. The chef from first class presented the tray for Rufus, who sat politely and watched the stewardess cut his steak into bite-sized pieces, mix in the potatoes, and charmingly blow on the food to cool it down.

I observed this charade with envy and was about to ask if I could exchange my dish for a steak, hoping the stewardess would blow on my food also, but they had already patted Rufus on the head, made mock bows, and departed.

★

In hindsight, it is always more than remarkable when you play the game of retracing the numerous and seemingly inconsequential incidents leading up to some major event in your life. Because a sympathetic ticket lady in New York was charmed by a dog and called her manager...who loved the circus...who called the bursar...who held the flight at the very last minute and escorted the pup onto the plane to the delight of everyone who witnessed the unexpected good will and humor of it all—because of that rare kindness of a few people in positions of authority, my career took a turn I never in my daydreams could have written into my life's script.

TV i Teltet

In Copenhagen I looked up an agent I knew. I had a comedy dog act, I explained as I introduced Rufus—did he know any circus needing another act? I knew it was a long shot—it was the beginning of summer and shows were already on the road, as the agent explained. What was I thinking? It was 1981—four years since I was last in Denmark. I started to feel foolish, sensing an oncoming discouragement and the insecurity that comes with getting older, all of thirty-one! Adventures didn't automatically happen like they did when you were just nineteen. Being young and foolish is, well, appropriate, I thought. But now...I was starting to lose faith in the efficacy of adventuring.

No job, no money, in a foreign land, with a dog that looked at me quizzically. No, I told him mentally, I don't know what I'm doing.

★

The agent called around. He found a circus in Finland that was interested in my clowning, on the strength of my years with

Benneweis. But when they heard I had a dog, that was that: there was a six-week quarantine on the animal. I no longer knew anyone at Benneweis, and besides, I didn't want to step backwards into that world.

Forlorn, I wandered the streets of Copenhagen. I ate one meal a day at the fabulous buffet at the central train station, stuffing extra meats in a bag for Rufus. Finally, I put up signs at Copenhagen University offering a weekly mime class, hoping to earn a bit of pocket money.

Three people showed up for the class. It was a bust, so I canceled class, and we all went out for lunch instead. One of the girls mentioned her father was a TV producer, and he loved dogs. Later she called me and said her dad wanted to meet with me.

We met in a room with four other people, all sitting in a row of chairs behind a table, studying me and Rufus. I didn't know what was going on. When they asked, I showed them a bit of mime... they seemed mildly amused. Then Rufus did his pantomime eating routine and the room burst into exclamations. What I didn't know? I was auditioning for Denmark's hit TV show.

Niels Hovgaard was the producer and the on-screen host of a popular weekly television show called *TV i Teltet,* or "TV in the Tent." Only two major stations existed in Denmark at the time, and the Saturday night variety show Niels had created was hugely successful. It was broadcast live to the whole country, ninety minutes with no commercials.

Niels said to me, in perfect English: "I need to fill five minutes in the show this week. Could you perform this Saturday with Rufus?"

I answered: "I'll have to ask the dog," and went to a corner to whisper gibberish to Rufus, whose ears lifted straight up. We went back to Niels, and I said, "Yup! He'll do it!"

The show was based in Aarhus, the second largest city in Denmark, on the east coast of the Jutland peninsula on the Kattegat Sea. The premise of the show blended *Saturday Night Live* comedy skits performed by a small cast of regulars, with *The Ed Sullivan Show*'s musical guests and other variety acts, and *The Late Show with Johnny Carson,* with Niels playing the host. He introduced the acts and did interviews with special guests seated on a couch.

The unique feature of his program was filming the show, not in a studio, but in a round circus tent! Right up my alley! The traveling TV-studio-in-a-tent would set up in a new town every week, spanning the Danish countryside like a circus.

The theme each week was based on something unique about the locality and perhaps would include interviews with a local celebrity and guest performers. The three regular cast members, my age, were actor Donald Anderson, dancer Sandy Grant, and singer/actress Kit Eichler.

Also appearing regularly was Denmark's hottest phenomenon, Linie Tre. This was a trio of young guys who were a singing/comedy sensation, Denmark's version of The Smother Brothers. They sold out their appearances in theaters around the country and were a formidable reason for the huge success of the *TV i Teltet* program.

Niels himself, besides producer/director, was a wonderfully amiable TV host. A slight man with silver hair and gray goatee, Niels was very affable and warm on camera, wearing an open collar shirt with rolled up sleeves. Even on live TV, the Danes were easygoing.

I knew none of this at the audition. All I knew was that I should report to the tent studio the next day and have a quick rehearsal to get ready for the show that night. The little circus tent was a familiar sight for me. Inside was a stage set with a large performing area and curtains for backstage, a platform for the live band—a jazz combo— and a three-camera set-up for closeup, mid- and long-shots. The live audience numbered maybe a hundred people.

Stage left featured the couch and a table, with a vase of flowers and glasses for the ubiquitous schnapps or akvavit—Denmark's national drink along with Carlsberg beer. Niels would offer a drink to his interview guests on live TV, displaying Danish hospitality, called hygge, meaning a mood of coziness and conviviality with comfortable feelings of wellness and contentment.

Taping in front of a live audience was a throwback to the 1950s era of live American television, with a live audience and a live broadcast to the nation: no chance for editing out mistakes. Denmark saw what was happening in real time. A ninety-minute variety show with no commercial breaks must have been nerve-wracking for Niels; he was boss of the whole shebang. Anything can happen, once the red light of the camera turned on.

Everyone seemed nervous the night Rufus and I first performed. We were scheduled to go on after the ventriloquist, and just before a local troupe of tap-dancing girls in blue leotards and pink miniskirts. Of course, I was nervous too, but I was in a What-the-Heck-Nothing-to-lose-Except-Dignity mood, as well as Another-Fine-Mess-You've-Got-Yourself-Into-Mermin state of mind.

The technicians with headphones were nervous, performers backstage were solemn-faced, the audience could be heard murmuring with expectation, Niels was pacing, studying last minute notes for the show...and poor Rufus!

His ears were flat out horizontal, a sure signal that he was not happy, not happy at all. He was very sensitive to the human condition and reflected the emotions around him. The atmosphere created by humans in that tent buzzed, fraught with tension.

The show started and appeared to go smoothly. One act after another finished their routine and performers could be seen walking offstage, smiling broadly with exaggerated relief. I still was worried about Rufus. Did he need to go pee? Would he just stand onstage, frozen in front of the bright lights and camera?

I frantically imagined scenarios I would need to improvise. The ventriloquist was nearly finished. We were up next. One minute to go.

I picked Rufus up in my arms, and he promptly threw up.

I panicked. Waving frantically for a stagehand to clean up the floor before the amateur tap dancers in short skirts were due to run out and slipped backstage into a pile of bare legs and limbs, I whispered to Rufus just to do whatever he wanted, we'll fake it, and as Niels introduced us, I walked out onstage, followed slowly by the Pantomime Pup.

I was doing "mime," so I didn't speak. I walked over to the couch and sat down. Rufus just stood, frozen mid-stage. Niels looked at me, then the dog, acted surprised, and said something to the effect that he expected a mime number, what was that stray dog doing there?

I shrugged. Niels started to call over a stagehand to remove the dog, but I interrupted and pantomimed that maybe he's smart, let's find out.

Niels said: "Okay, if you think you can train him, go ahead, we've got time." He got the audience to agree, so I went over to Rufus, while the band played some nice background music, and we did our "Dog Training" bit.

I mimed sitting down to show him how, but Rufus just stared at the audience. His ears were still horizontal. I tried pushing his rear down to the floor, but instead he put his head down to his paws in his "bow" position. The audience loved it.

I tried to get him to jump through a hoop, but he just stood there, unblinking. I lowered the hoop. Still nothing. Lower again, until finally I was lying on the floor, looking frustrated, the hoop touching the ground. Then Rufus ever so slowly walked through it and stared at the audience. Everything I tried, he did wrong, which was perfect.

I searched my pockets for a dog treat to give him but had none. So I mimed a piece of food, which he mimed eating, which really got delighted applause, which Rufus acknowledged, deadpan, by lifting one ear in the way a human would lift one eyebrow.

Finally, I tried to get him to jump through a circle of my arms, like he did at the airport for the pretty ticket lady! He refused. I walked over to Niels, acted sorry, he just won't jump...so Niels went over to him and said to the audience: "He just needs a little love and encouragement!"

The band played faster music, the audience clapped for Rufus and yes!—he jumped through Niels arms, not once but twice, and they both took bows to loud applause, and we were done.

Such was the debut of the dog, who would become famous in Denmark as Rufus the Pantomimehund.

Niels

*"Some trouble getting rooms, and some had to put up
with small rooms in a little hotel adjoining. By the
way, the largest room in the world is said to be 'room
for improvement.' By another way, there is room for
improvement in getting our Sunday rooms."*

—Ringling Route Book,
Hot Springs, Arkansas, 1891

Niels and Rufus became fast friends. Later the next week, I got a call: would I come back again for that week's show...and bring the dog? Well, sure! I needed the work. They wanted me to join in some comedy skits with the three regular cast members, as well as do a mime bit and encore with Rufus.

Afterword, I was happy to have had two weeks of interesting work. But now what? Pack my bag and hit the road again? Meanwhile, I had met a lovely girl of auburn hair and hazel eyes who recognized me from the TV show. We arranged a date at the beach the following Saturday, so I stuck around a while, waiting for inspiration on what to do.

I liked the area around Aarhus. Everything felt cozy and friendly, even the air felt different, a lightness, like walking around a garden of fresh spring flowers. After a visit to the Viking Museum, I had daydreams of raucous Viking feasts on the shores of Danish beaches, a weird foreshadowing of bizarre events to come.

Saturday came. I met with the lovely Danish girl of auburn hair and hazel eyes, and we rode our bikes toward the beach for a picnic lunch. I had left Rufus in the hotel room. We were about fifteen minutes out on our bike ride when we stopped for a moment. I said: "You know, it's such a beautiful day, I feel bad keeping Rufus inside. Why don't we make a full day of it? I'll ride back and pick him up—he can ride in the basket—and you go ahead, and we'll meet you at the beach. I won't be long." She agreed to pick up some food on the way. I was excited: a day at the beach with a beautiful girl, the dog happily running along the shore, chasing the waves, a pleasant ride back at twilight to her place for...well, who knows? Things were looking up.

★

Back at the room, I grabbed Rufus' leash. He started wiggling with excitement, and we were about to run out the door when the phone rang. It was a landline of course, well before cell phones. I hesitated, thinking to ignore it. But then again...no one ever calls me here. Who even knows this number? I picked it up. "Hello?"

There was crowd noise in the background and then Niels' frantic voice: "Robin?! Thank god, we found you. What are you doing? Drop everything, whatever it is. Where are you?"

I said: "In my room, in Aarhus. But not for long! I got a hot date waiting at the beach, a girl with auburn..."

"Never mind that! We need you to get down here right away. We'll have just enough time before the show tonight...if you get moving NOW!"

"Wha...? What are you talking about?" I suddenly had a bad thought that I had totally forgotten we had a job that night, and broken a contract, and I'd be deported and forever banned from working in Denmark again...

"Sorry, Robin—we need you to fill in one of the skits with the troupe again, and... Can you do another mime bit? And maybe... you said you do some magic tricks, right?"

"But Niels! Is this a joke? Where...the tent...I mean...how... the girl, auburn..."

"Listen carefully, Robin," said Niels, out of breath. "The show needs to fill another six minutes, and the skits need another actor.

The tent is down south of Aarhus. If you start now, it will take you three hours, two and a half if you drive fast. We will have an hour before showtime to get you ready."

"Niels—I don't have a car, how..."

"Take a taxi, right now. Bring Rufus. Here is the address, you'll see the tent as you arrive in town. Tell the taxi driver the bill will be paid by Danmarks' Radio & TV. Quickly, please! Great! See you soon!" And he hung up.

★

I thought fast, my heart racing, Rufus could tell something was up. He stopped wiggling and sat down, looking at me with his head cocked to the side. There was no way to reach the girl with auburn hair and hazel eyes. The beach was north, in the wrong direction—I was headed south. My heart sank—so much for that budding affair. She would be furious at being stood up. Danish women were wonderful, but not to be crossed.

Handsome Danish men looked like they might rule the roost, but no. In my experience the women were more clear-eyed, straightforward, no nonsense, uncomplicatedly candid

and upfront, whether about sex, personal intentions, or relationships in general. It was refreshing, no games—and here I was, seemingly playing a very woeful game with her. I had a lot to think about on the long taxi drive.

I made it in time for the show. It was fun to see everyone again. They gave me a room for the night. I thought about the girl on the beach. No doubt she had gone home, angry at being rejected, turned on the tube and watched TV i Teltet like everyone in Denmark—and there I was, clowning around, with Rufus, on live TV! An insult on top of a mystery.

As it turned out, nothing happened with the girl—I had lost her number and I never saw her again. Ah well.

The show that night went fine, and Niels asked me to stay on as a regular member of the cast for the rest of the season, and the next one, 1981-82. For a long time whenever I showed up for rehearsals the joke would inevitably arise: "Hey, Robin: been to the beach with anyone lately?"

The experience of being a cast member on weekly TV in Denmark was, to put it mildly, interesting. By the second year of *TV i Teltet,* I was a celebrity. That's what being a regular on a hit TV show will do. I couldn't walk down the street without folks stopping and pointing, with the usual courtesy of a handshake and thanks. Really, though, it was all about Rufus! He was the famous pantomimehund and kids wanted his pawtograph.

It was wonderful to be recognized, but it got to be confusing. I knew as soon as I stepped out of my room onto the street, my private world was gone. People would stop me and say, "Thanks for the show!" It was a very polite, Danish way of being well-known.

If I walked down the street and people did not stop and stare and point and smile, I felt invisible and somehow embarrassed. Why didn't they say hello? Had I already lost popularity? It was not easy to shake my discomfiture: awkward if I were being constantly stared at; my ego was pleased, but modesty made me self-conscious. And a different kind of unease arose if I were ignored; my self-esteem, wounded.

I could feel relief for two things: a) I was able to analyze celebrity from an inside experience, thankfully in a small and courteous country, and b) all I had to do was cross the border of Denmark and I'd be an anonymous private citizen again, free of the burden of fame! How great was that!?

★

Meanwhile, Rufus took his fame in stride, happy to be cooed over and petted by kids, tolerant with amused adults, nobly indifferent to reporters taking his photo. Once, outside the TV tent, I was walking with Rufus when he stopped at a small wooden sign temporarily posted in the ground a couple of feet high. On it was the word "Toilet," with an arrow pointing to the portable outhouse nearby.

Rufus ambled over to the sign and lifted his leg. His business done, he sauntered away.

A small crowd of people had witnessed this act, including several reporters who wanted a photo. One photographer called out: "Hey, Rufus! Come back! Do that again!" Hearing his name, Rufus stopped, looked at the guy, then at me.

I looked at the reporter, thinking he was joking. I just waved, smiling, "C'mon Ruf, let's go." The guy ran up to us and said, "No, really—get him to raise his leg again. Great photo for tonight's paper!" I said, "You're not serious..."

"Of course, I'm serious!" he said. "What a great image! Wait, the sun is behind, let's move the sign this way..." and he turned the sign. "Come here, pupdog...over here, Rufus...come on, boy."

"Listen," I said, "that's just embarrassing. Even if I wanted him to pose like that, there's no way. He doesn't lift a leg on command!" Rufus just stood there watching, wondering what the fuss was all about. The small crowd was amused.

The man wouldn't give up. "Come on, be a sport, make him do it."

I couldn't believe this guy. Suddenly, he walked over to the sign, unzipped, and peed on the sign, motioning for Rufus to watch. I was aghast. Even Rufi was ashamed for the guy.

Enough was enough. We silently walked away. I pondered the public insanity real celebrities in America must endure and once again I felt grateful for this comparably minor insanity in Denmark.

Vikings

"Notorious pickpocket 'Oyster Jim' was caught at the show and brought into the ring for public ridicule by Pinkerton Detective Henderson, who was employed by The Great Forepaugh Circus. Fact: the arrest was faked. Oyster Jim was later spotted on the circus train and admitted employment by 4-Paw."

—Burlington Free Press,
Vermont, July 28, 1883

One week the studio circus tent was set up at the Roskilde Fjord, near a Viking Museum and several reconstructed Viking longboats. Or was it in the town of Trelleborg, near Slagelse, on the island of West Zealand? Trelleborg was one of the great Viking fortresses constructed around the year 980 by King Harald Bluetooth Gormsson, son of King Gorm. Legend has it that King Harald had a very conspicuous blue-black decaying tooth.

The name Bluetooth, for a wireless technology allowing mobile devices to communicate with computers, was first suggested by an American Intel employee, Jim Kardach, in 1997. He figured its technology would unite devices the way King Harald Bluetooth had united the tribes of Denmark into a single kingdom.

Kardach had apparently been reading the historical novel, *The Long Ships*, about King Harald and the Vikings of the tenth century. The wireless Bluetooth company logo is a bind rune, merging the rune signs of Harald's initials.

In any case, the TV tent that week had been set up in a town known for its Viking festivals, where scores of folks reenact the Viking era, in much the same way modern Renaissance Faires operate in the States. Our show that week, naturally, had the theme of local Viking history.

Gathering one morning for a rehearsal with the usual round of schnapps to jumpstart the day—orange juice for me—someone mentioned the Viking party we were invited to after the show. I'm not one for partying, and after the tension of our broadcasts, I was always pretty tired. So I begged off.

There was a lot of joking about that. I was encouraged by all of the company to at least check it out. It would be worth my while. However, I was warned to be wary, "just in case someone offers," of the Viking drink called Dansk Mjød, a kind of mead the Vikings considered a drink of the gods. It made anyone who partook of it a poet or a scholar. It was a drink much older than the Viking era, they said, made from honey, wine, yeast, sour apples, and sweet berries.

Laughing at the idea of me being drunk, my friends told me that I should taste it "for a real Danish experience," but if I partook, to take just a sip. It was very sweet, deceptively so, they cautioned. Drinking it, you don't feel a thing, until "WHAM!" Twenty minutes later, you are slammed, like you've taken a blow to the head with the blunt end of a Viking axe.

★

After the show that night, there was some food and drink. I may have had a beer, but it was already late, after midnight, so I wandered away from the trailers surrounding the tent and took Rufus for a walk in the woods before retiring. It was a beautiful night with a full moon, and a relaxed feeling of relief and satisfaction washed over me. We'd had a successful broadcast. I felt good. A little walk down a path in the woods would be great.

With the bright moon. I could follow the path easily by following moon shadows through the treetops. What a great feeling! Alive in Denmark on a midsummer's night, fresh air, thoughts meandering to the events of the day. That afternoon we had gone down to the shore to witness the disembarking of "Vikings" from a reconstructed longship. It was quite a sight. Men dressed in tenth century Norse leather helmets and spears came ashore, followed by a procession of women and children who carried bundles of hay on their backs, herding sheep and goats and geese and donkeys. They sang in some Old Norse language, while setting up tents and wooden structures for their "village" on the coast. Some of them had later appeared on our show that night.

I walked with Rufus farther into the forest than I had planned, trying to recall the way back. The woods were dark with spruce and fir, and beautiful with streams of moonlight flowing through the gnarled branches.

It began to feel more than possible that we were being silently observed by mythic creatures captured wonderfully in the drawings of Swedish artist John Bauer, a contemporary of Arthur Rackham. Bauer's Scandinavian Forest held unseen elves and gnomes and trolls and tomte—the mischievous spirits responsible for the protection of farmsteads—hidden near isolated boulders and caves.

The woods' eerie silence had been broken only once, by a flutter of dark wings I took to be an owl on the hunt for small prey. I saw a light through the dark woods, off in the distance. Rufus and I made our way toward it and came to a huge wooden structure, an ancient barn, planted in a clearing in the forest. There was muffled music behind the majestic wooden doors. They were very high, very wide doors that opened in the middle with huge wooden handles.

I grabbed these and slowly swung the heavy doors outward, immediately bathed in bright beams of yellow light. We had stumbled upon a world of uproar and noise and wild commotion...

★

If this were a movie, it would be like a scene from Fellini's *The Clowns*. A little boy is awakened in the middle of the night and wanders over in the dark to the entrance of a newly raised circus tent, the camera at his back looking in at the lighted activity in the ring. Or maybe a Spielberg film of a boy entranced by wondrous light, shining on him from an alien ship.

Rufus and I stood in the entrance of the barn, staring like a little lost boy and his pup. The dark woods behind us must have silhouetted our bodies. Streams of golden light from burning torches and thick wax candles of huge wooden chandeliers engulfed us.

We saw a vast, open Viking Hall with earthen floor, filled with long oak tables piled with food on wooden plates and carved bowls: red fruits and goblets of wine and burned meats and round loaves of bread pulled hot from stone ovens, and massive rounds of smelly cheese, big as wheels of ancient wagons.

In the center of the hall was a fire pit, where a pig slowly turned on a spit overseen by two huge Viking men in tunics and greasy beards and leather boots. There must have been two hundred Vikings carousing: dirty, long-haired men gnawing at bones with hands dripping bloodred meat juice; buxom women outfitted in dresses of wool and flax, carrying wooden trays with goblets of wine and mead, laughing and filling cattle horns with drink; deafening noise of song and toasts and laughter and shouting; sheep and goats wandering between the tables, picking up scraps of food thrown down to them; music and song coming from musicians somewhere in the tumult.

★

Dumbstruck, I stood there as if enchanted by a strong medieval spell. I was inside some time-travel hallucination in a *Twilight Zone* fantasy. Rufus stood by me, tongue hanging out.

Someone noticed us and called out: "Hey, it's RUFUS!" Suddenly a dozen arms took us into the hall and someone from the TV show recognized me and cleared a seat by sweeping his arms across the massive table in front of him, knocking plates to the ground—and a goat appeared from under the table, eagerly gulping the scraps.

I could hardly hear my voice for all the noise, but I accepted some food, a huge shank of lamb which I tore apart by hand to give to Rufus. I was offered some wine but declined. Then the mead was brought over by a bosomy woman, suggestively leaning forward with the flask.

I had noticed every table was served by uninhibited females in wide skirts and with ample cleavage, laughing and sitting on laps and spilling the drink right from the flask to the open mouths of the heavily bearded men. It was all overwhelming.

My friend suggested I at least taste the mead, so I did. It was overly sweet, like a thick liquid made from very sweet honey and blackberry jam. I tasted no alcohol. Its sweetness made me thirsty, so I gulped some more. Someone poured a bowl for Rufus, too, who eagerly lapped it up. After waiting a while with no inkling of dizziness, I felt safely sober.

I figured it was probably a sweet fruit punch of some sort, and I would stay away from the hard stuff. I was shy in crowds like this, happy to be just an observer of the bawdy riot all around me. About twenty minutes later—BAM!—I was laughing as hard as anyone, at everything and nothing in particular.

Somehow, I found myself standing on top of the table, which someone had cleared for me, I don't know when, and I was dancing a little jig and singing something about "the flagon with the dragon / and the vessel with the pestle / and the chalice from the palace / has the brew that is true..."

And someone placed Rufus with me and we both danced up and down the table, stepping lightly between plates and platters of food, Rufus munching as we went, me waving a leg of lamb, Vikings playing fiddles and drumming and clapping with delight and swearing and cussing and singing, and goats wandering wide-eyed, and firelight, and swords clanking, and before I knew it I was led outside and Vikings were waving and shouting me goodnight and turned back to their carousing, and Rufus and I were suddenly outside in the dark, quiet forest once more.

An owl hooted. I had no idea how much time had passed.

I looked around—the path was ahead, the barn behind me. I glanced at Rufus; he looked back at me. We agreed we both needed to pee. I said, "OK, little fellow...see that tree over there? Let's see if we can walk in a straight line over to it. I'm a professional mime, I can do it, I'll go first..."

It was only about twenty feet away, but it took all my dizzy concentration to walk over, with many unsteady steps. I tried hard to control my movement, but I just laughed: I simply could not walk a straight line.

I remembered Marcel Marceau once asked our class to give a demonstration of a drunk person. Some students staggered around, grossly out of balance, and he stopped them, saying "Non! A drunk tries to show that he is NOT drunk. Your movements must be subtle: you must try to act sober...but you fail. Only the occasional off-balance catch of a step, then nobly try to hide it, unsuccessfully."

When I reached the tree, I called Rufus, who had been sitting, watching me. He stood up...and wobbled over. It was hilarious. I tried not to embarrass him by laughing. He walked a few steps slowly, head down, lost balance and caught himself. He stood still, then took another couple steps, and stopped. Finally, he made it to the tree and lifted his leg to pee...but on just three legs, he lost balance again. Confused, he looked slightly ashamed with ears at half-mast, and I told him, never mind, we were both in the same shape.

I have only been really drunk like that with the Vikings in Denmark. Sure, I have been a little tipsy, relaxed with an occasional cold beer on a hot day. But I don't really care for drink. The taste of alcohol just doesn't suit me. The next morning when I came in for breakfast with the TV gang, they all looked at me with amusement. On the table was a toy Viking helmet and a large pitcher of orange juice with a sign that said: "Do Not Touch—Medicine for Robin Only."

Jonas, the one who had sat with me in the Viking Hall, said that I had a good singing voice. "What?" I said, confused. "Ja," he said. "Something about a dragon with a flagon...?"

God, I thought to myself, me singing? I tried to explain how Danny Kaye had sung this in the classic comedy film, *The Court Jester,* but even when sober I could never get the words right: "castle with a pestle...pestle with a vessel...?" "It's a great film," I told them. "One of my all-time favorites. Check it out."

I confessed I must have had a lot to drink, but surprisingly I didn't have a headache and felt no nausea or even much of a hang-over, just some fatigue.

"That's about right," said Niels. "That was a special Danish mead. Our own combination of sweet wine, beer, schnapps, honey, berries, and spices. Now you are really one of us: an honorary Viking!"

They all raised their glasses of schnapps, I raised my glass of orange juice, and there was a general clinking of glasses and "Skal!" all around. Rufus, looking a little sad, drank a full bowl of water.

The Blond Girl
on the Red Bike

"The circus was everything,
everything else we knew wasn't."

— William Saroyan,
My Name Is Aram, 1940

After the first season was wrapped, I flew back to the States on SAS with a letter in hand from the Danish TV producers addressed to the bursar of the airlines, introducing Rufus, TV star, and requesting a row of seats as before. To my amazement and pride, it was a successful petition. Rufus, of course, took it in stride as if to say, "Really, I expect nothing less."

I returned to Denmark for the second season, innocent of any expectations. The first season felt like a marvel of luck, a surprise gift from fate, the kind of unexpected adventure one feels upon falling in love at first sight. This second year felt like the security of returning to a well-paid job.

As rehearsals began, I found a room in Aarhus, a city I'd become very fond of. I took a temporary side job, directing a mime show for actors in a local theater. One of the actors was an attractive, petite blond with sky blues eyes and a shy feminine smile of a kind that made me wonder: was she purposefully alluring, or simply charming in personality?

As so often happens, flirtation is commonplace and even inevitable when actors work on a show. Rehearsing together—whether for stage, film, or circus, but especially for theater—creates a kind of intense intimacy, a magnetic pull generated by the electricity of mutual physical and emotional work. That's a roundabout way of explaining inevitable sexual attraction.

It is true that the nature of theater work—emotions on display—exposes you more quickly than normal social interactions do. The girl and I were rehearsing a Love Duet—an improv exercise that was part of my training in mime school. The idea was to create an abstract movement piece, expressing attraction in lyrical form without our two bodies touching. We decided to play two statues in a wax museum, standing close but apart, in classical poses.

A janitor comes by and raises the thermostat. The heat is turned up, literally and figuratively, as our two wax statues very, very slowly melt, wax dripping from fingertips, limbs bending and twisting in slow-motion melting, bodies dripping on each other but not touching, until finally we melt together, embracing, in a motionless puddle of wax on the floor.

One night after a long day in the TV studio and a late evening rehearsal in the theater, I was getting on my bike to ride home, and I offered the girl a lift to her place. She sat in the basket on the handlebars. It was around midnight. The streets were quiet, and the ride was slightly bumpy, going slow on the cobblestone street.

Suddenly a parked car turned on its headlights and gave a short BLEEP! to make us stop. Two police got out and shone flashlights on us.

Thinking they wanted to ask if we were lost or needed some help, I said, "Officer? Everything's fine, we're just going home." I figured they would recognize me from the TV show. Maybe I could autograph something for their kids.

One of them shone his light on the girl, the other knelt and pointed his flashlight at the back of the bike. "You are not Danish?" he said in English in a not unfriendly way.

"No, but I work here," I said. "We were just going home from rehearsal."

The girl, who had hopped off the handlebars, started to explain in Danish about the theater troupe. The cop asked for my papers. "Excuse me?" I said, patting my empty pockets. "I don't carry papers, I didn't know it was necessary in Denmark," I explained.

"I need to see your identification," he said patiently but firmly, his flashlight roaming over my body. The second officer stood up, holding a note with some numbers copied from the rear fender of the bike. "This is your bike?"

"Yes, sir. I mean...I found it."

"So, you do not own the bike?"

"Nooo...I mean, yes. I found it in the bushes." I went on to explain how the bike was abandoned, the front wheel bent out of shape. I had taken it to a shop and got it fixed, so...yes, I figured it was mine now.

"Did you register it?" asked the second cop, showing me the registration number he had found on the bike. "Did you try to find the owner?"

I said I didn't know bikes needed to be registered in Denmark. I didn't know they had numbers...

The first cop said: "So here is the situation: It is not your bike. It is not legal to have a person ride the handlebars. You are working but have no work papers. And you have no identification." He paused, adding, "We need to go to the station and take down your information."

For the next ten minutes the girl and I tried to reason with them. I talked about the show, *TV i Teltet,* and my companion smiled her dimpled smile. They remained friendly but firm. They let us go, but I had to promise to bring my passport and work permit the next morning to the Office of Foreign Affairs downtown. And they took away my bike.

There was nothing amusing about the incident. So much for a romantic evening. We walked into the night, both silent. She went her way, and I went back to my place.

The next morning at the TV studio there were many jokes: "Ah, Robin—first a girl on a beach. Now a girl on a bike...what will happen to the next poor girl?" Niels agreed to drive me to the Foreign Office.

The clerk at the Foreign Office looked at the policeman's report, looked at me vacantly as if she had better things to do and in a flat voice asked for my papers. I handed her my passport. She looked at my photo, then at me and back at the photo.

I shifted my gaze involuntarily, feeling like I was at a customs border trying to illegally cross into the Soviet Union. She pushed the passport aside and, sounding officially bored, asked for my working ID card. I said: "Which one?"

There was a charged silence. She looked up at me. I looked at Niels. I took out my ID cards. "Here's the one from Danmarks TV..." I pushed it forward and fumbled for the second card. "And here's the one from the Aarhus Theater Company."

Everything in order—two jobs, two working permits. I even showed her my signed contracts. Surely, she knew Niels from the TV, and maybe me too.

She was staring at the cards without expression. Still nervous, I smiled and shifted my weight to the other foot. Niels kept staring at the cards. "All in order?" I asked innocently.

Niels and the clerk conversed for a couple of minutes in Danish, then she called over her supervisor. He stared at the ID numbers, then at me. He held up the cards and said: "Who gave you these?" I looked at Niels. There was more incomprehensible discussion in Danish. Niels tried to be jovial—unsuccessfully—and then some serious conversation ensued with Niels holding up the ID card from TV, the supervisor waving the theater ID, and the clerk calling someone on the telephone.

This went on for ten minutes with shaking of heads, stern looks at me, Niels looking very uncomfortable. I felt like a toddler at day school called into the principal's office—now what had I done?

The supervisor took my passport and papers and walked away. Niels explained that I was not to leave the country—What? I had no intention of leaving!—and I would need to come to the Foreign Office every morning for the next month to sign in, to show I had not tried to leave—How could I leave without my passport?—and that Niels had agreed to act as my supervisor, responsible for my cooperation.

I signed something and we left, the clerk staring at me blankly.

Niels took me out for coffee and a Danish and explained the situation. The ID number he had given to me with my TV contract was my tax number, equivalent to a US Social Security number. It was my personal identification number, not easy for a foreigner to acquire. It is only issued once, and you must be registered with the Civil Registration System.

The number is an integral part of Danish society. It is virtually impossible without one to receive any form of government service, free health care, education, childcare, or pension. There were multiple tax codes for the state and the municipality where you lived. With his government contacts, Niels had somehow managed to rush through the process of getting me a card. That, in itself, had raised the eyebrows of the official at the Foreign Office.

But the red flags began fluttering briskly when I presented two different ID cards, one from the TV show and a different number registered to the Aarhus Theater Company. How did they get me an ID number? But even more disconcerting to the officials was why, how, and who in the Tax Bureau had authorized these cards? What bureaucratic office unknowingly certified two cards—and to a foreigner?!

So, I reported to the Foreign Office every morning. Sometimes I brought pastries for the clerk. Niels was off the hook and the Aarhus Theater folks were reprimanded but found blameless. It turns out the Tax Office didn't bother with us; we were small fish. They combed through local office files, all the way up the chain to higher Tax Bureaus in Copenhagen, trying to find the flaw in the system and who was at fault.

Niels showed me articles in the papers over the next few months, dealing with shakeups in the way the tax system gave out ID numbers, and the government officials blamed, and the tax code itself discussed and argued by politicians at the highest levels of the nation's capital.

The Danish Tax Scandal eventually blew over. I never did find out the political ramifications. The morning jokes from the crew in the TV studio became more elaborate at each telling. Niels especially enjoyed leaving souvenirs for me in the studio.

A little Barbie doll in a bikini sitting in a bowl of sand was labeled, "The Legend of the Girl on the Beach." A little toy bike made of wire and another doll in a small basket had a sign: "The Scandal of the Blond Girl on the Red Bike."

"The Viking Tale of the Drunken Dog" named a toy dog lapping from a small bowl, with his rear leg lifted. "The Nefarious Plot of the Clown to Bring Down the Social Welfare System in the Kingdom of Denmark" displayed a fake visa and forged working card stamped over my picture.

I appreciated their not-so-subtle sense of humor. They all wondered out loud: "What, Robin, is next?" What indeed...?

Rufus on the Beach

*"I belonged to one of the oldest of societies:
the society of those who, at one time or another, have
surrendered, without even a show of resistance,
to the bedazzlement of a circus rider."*

— E. B. White,
The Ring of Time, 1956

Near the end of the second *TV i Teltet* season, I sensed a change coming. I was no closer to my dream of a little tent show. I was also unfulfilled, tired of being known just as the mime guy. It was an odd situation: I was making good money. I was a well-known celebrity. Job offers were coming in from TV, theaters, film. Rufus and I were invited to perform on the Tivoli stage in Copenhagen.

It seemed my career was set—but only so long as I stayed in Denmark. Maybe, I thought, if I could just fall in love and marry a sweet Danish girl—maybe a circus bareback rider—maybe start a family, a new circus family dynasty, maybe grow old in Scandinavia.

★

Meanwhile, Rufus had become even more renowned. The TV studios wanted to make a half-hour children's film called The Rufus Story—a biopic portraying his life from dog pound pup to star of stage, circus, and TV, all before deciding to give up showbiz and become a regular dog. My idea for this was to have no dialogue, just a soundtrack, like an old silent movie, and to film it from the dog's point of view.

I set to work creating a storyboard, a visual outline of every shot and angle through images showing everything that would happen in the film. It would be great: Niels Hovgaard as producer/director seemed perfect. Rufus loved him, and he had the right sense of humor and fun. We prepared for a two-week shooting schedule all around Denmark.

And then everything fell apart.

Niels was pulled from the project at the last moment for some other TV business. He was replaced by a programming director, a woman who clearly didn't want the job and showed it. When we met her, Rufus had no wag. He just sat, looking at her and then walked away; I knew we were in for trouble.

Then she told us we had only a week for the shoot, she couldn't spare more time. The process became ever more nerve-wracking.

I had written a comedy piece, with Rufus the star and me his hapless sidekick. We had already lined up shots at the Benneweis circus building, the Benneweis traveling show, the TV studios, the Tivoli, the airport, and other locations around the country. It was a one-camera shoot and to save time with all the traveling, the new director wanted to film everything in one take—and just forget the complications of shooting from the dog's point of view.

At least I convinced the director to have no dialogue, simply a soundtrack.

We managed to pull it off in a week, and friends tell me it is a charming little film. But for me, it's a reminder of how a creative vision can be sabotaged by bureaucratic decisions and sullied by uninspired directors. I grasped more deeply how Chaplin and Keaton could pull off inspired gag after gag by being their own creative boss, both of them their own silent film writers/actors/directors.

Here are some examples of comedy opportunities abandoned in *The Rufus Story:*

In the scene at the airport when Rufus first charms his way onto the plane, my script called for the dog to jump through the attendant's arms, then the arms of the manager, all of us then running through the busy airport at the last minute to escort him onto the plane, "where two lovely stewardesses and a first-class chef would fuss over him—just as it happened in real life. This crowd of excited people fussing over the dog and disregarding me becomes a comedy motif throughout the film."

When it was time for the shoot at the airport, the director had only arranged to have one ticket lady there. She raised her eyebrows at the dog and walked us to the plane, where she gave him some food on a tray, and left. That's about it.

Another scene was shot at the TV studio where I had planned and written in my script: "In the dressing room before our first TV appearance, Rufus sits in a highchair before the makeup mirror, while four or five pretty girls, smitten with Rufus, are giggling and excited as they brush him, polish his paws, and generally make a fuss. I sit in another chair watching this commotion, anticipating the girls fussing over me next. But they ignore me, and I'm left to brush my hair alone."

I imagined some comedy with the girls: they would try different ribbons, bow ties, a little outfit on the dog, with me trying to get their attention until one girl sees me and quickly powders my face with a cloud of talcum powder, hands me a brush and returns to fuss over Rufus, who sits there like a gallant prince with his entourage of ladies-in-waiting. I envisioned a fast-paced scene with me sitting alone, deadpan, in the middle of a swirl of action by a bevy of beautiful young ladies.

What actually happened? When we got to the studio dressing room, the director had arranged no crowd of pretty girls, in fact, no one. So the camera assistant went to find a girl in the building. Since there was "no time except for one quick take," the girl brushed Rufus and tried to fuss while I watched mournfully, and she handed me another brush, no powder—and that was that. The lack of comedic chaos to contrast with my quiet scenes gave the film a one-tone mood.

Rufus was clearly wondering what in the world we were trying to do. Before each scene he looked at me and seemed to say: "Where is Niels?" His body language implied all he wanted was to go outside and find a tree to pee on. Me too.

I was resigned to walk through the paces of the filming, glad to at least have the dog on film for posterity. Watching the short film now, I can see how Rufus still projected intelligence and charm, though I can tell he looks rather sad. The film captures him chewing mime food, jumping into the Benneweis circus ring, nonchalantly taking everything in stride. The final scene is priceless, his acting and presence Oscar-worthy:

Scene: We arrive at our cottage on the shore after a long busy period, performing on stage, circus, and TV. Rufus runs around happily on the beach, eyes smiling, ears up. A messenger arrives with a telegram. I open it and read: "Hollywood wants Rufus for Gala Show!"

I get excited, the music swells, I wave for Rufus to come, and we'll pack our bags again and head out! The camera has a close-up of Rufus standing still, watching me jump around. His ears are straight up, eyes now focused, looking worried.

Mid shot of me continuing to call him. Rufus takes one step towards me, then stops. (Believe it or not, off-camera before the shot, I had told him, "Act hesitant when I call you.")

I call him again, waving. With his ears flapping at half-mast, he comes forward a few tentative steps, slows down, gives a Chaplinesque skip with a back leg, then comes to sit by me. I look down at him, concerned. Close-up on his face: eyes sad, his ears are flat-out straight. (When his ears are up, he is happy and alert; half bent, he is hesitant; flat out, he is unwilling. His ears have more expression than his tail.)

The camera holds on his face: his eyes are half lowered, clearly unhappy; he glances back to the beach, his head tilted as if to say to me, "Please, my friend...I just want to be a normal dog, no more show biz, at least for a while, let's just have fun on the beach."

And so ends the film, with me about to tear up the telegram. Will I? Who knows, maybe there could be a sequel, *Rufus Goes to Hollywood!*—and then Rufus and I chase each other down the beach, laughing, our ears all straight up, very happy the filming is over.

Katja

*"Large tracks of feet are painted all over the wooden
sidewalks, all leading to a prominent saloon.
Some of our gang are seen surveying these tracks,
with a look like that on Robinson Crusoe's face
when staring Friday's foot-step in the sand."*

—*Ringling Route Book,*
Oklahoma City, Oklahoma,
May 23, 1892

While in Copenhagen, I spent some time visiting the artists at the Benneweis Cirkusbygningen. Some of the Bulgarian acrobats had seen me on *TV i Teltet,* the night when we four regulars were singing and dancing and doing gags to the Cole Porter song, "Be a Clown." The day of the broadcast, the choreographer/actor Sandy Grant said to me: "There's a perfect spot in the song when the band kicks in between choruses—you can flip me in the air!"

He then described the trick: I was to crouch forward and put my hands together on my lap to form a step. He would run to me and place one foot in my hands as I quickly lifted up to throw him in the air into a back tuck—and he'd land on his feet. Easy airborne, assisted somersault.

We tried it once for the timing. Then we went over the song, and he said: "Here's the downbeat where you flip me. Then the next beat right after me, you do a standing back tuck, then run and jump into my waiting arms."

I hesitated. Sandy said: "You can do a standing back tuck on your own, right?"

I shrugged, taken aback. "You worked in the circus, right?" I nodded. "Great! It will be fabulous. No one will expect it—let's not tell Donald or Kit, or Niels. We'll just do it!"

I raised one index finger and started to say, "But, there's just one thing…" but Sandy had already walked away to choreograph the rest of the number with the others.

A standing back tuck goes like this: you stand straight, then suddenly bend your knees, begin to lean back and spring into the air backwards as high as you can, tucking your knees to your chest as you somersault mid-air and straighten out in time to land on your feet into your original standing position. It happens in a blink if you do it right.

When learning to do this, you always have a strong spotter holding your belt or your lunge in one hand and with the other hand helping to flip you. This provides a safer momentum as you jump backwards into space. When learning this trick, in the beginning you invariably land either on your hands and knees, or you don't make it all the way around in mid-air and land on your head, spared a broken neck only by the good grace of god and your spotter.

The thing was, I had only done a standing back tuck on my own a few times, and that was many years ago in my youth. Now I was an elderly thirty-two years old. I knew the technique of how you do a back tuck, but I was not sure I could do a back tuck for real now… with no warmup…while dancing on stage…in the middle of a song… on live TV.

I tried to find Sandy to back out of it, but he was nowhere to be seen. Everyone was running around, nervous, the show getting ready, the audience coming in soon. I thought to myself, maybe I could do it. But just the thought of breaking my neck on live TV gave me cold sweats.

I'll just flip Sandy on the downbeat, I thought, and then fake jumping in air, just mime it. No… if I concentrate I can surely do it. I was good at imagining an action mentally, in every detail—and then doing it physically. Like a basketball player at the free throw line, tied game, two seconds left on the clock, thousands of eyes focused on him: he doesn't just toss the ball to the basket.

First, he'll slowly bounce the ball a couple of times to steady the nerves, then hold the ball up in position and stare at the net, unmoving. During those motionless moments, he visualizes the image of tossing the ball as it flies slowly in air and—swish—a perfect aim to the net. Then he does it for real. The motor of imagery fires the body's mirror neurons, which trigger the muscle memory to do the action in real time. Piece of cake.

I can do this, I told myself again. I'm just not sure if I have the guts, or the nerves, or the stupidity. No, what the hell am I thinking? I'm gonna break my neck! Who will take care of Rufus? And yet... what the hell—what a great moment it would be, maybe I could do this...but...

Now I was damned curious to see what I was going to do when the moment arrived. I sleep-walked the other routines that night, nervous as hell for the musical number.

The video of the act shows me flipping Sandy, pausing for a very brief moment—visualizing perhaps?—and then I leap up and back, spin in mid-air and land on my feet in a sort of crouch but I quickly stand up straight and throw my arms up in colossal relief, shaking like a leaf as we continue the song.

The Bulgarian acrobats later said to me, laughing, "Not a perfect standing back tuck...but you made it all the way round. We weren't sure you would!"

With some chagrin, I said: "Me too," keeping private the insanity of my fears that day. One of the guys said, "Well, you might want to stick with clowning."

I asked him if he had been in circus all his life.

"No, no... gymnastic school," he said. He waved to the other guys. "Most of us, they took from gymnastic school. I'll do this for a while, get to travel. But really what I want is to be an auto mechanic and have my own garage. One day, I will, maybe soon, maybe in a nice place like Belgium or Denmark."

It struck me then that this was the opposite of what my dream had been. I wanted to run off to the circus. He wanted

to run away from the circus. I was used to working with circus traditionalists, performers who were fifth or sixth generation in circus. I figured it was natural for them to carry on the family business forever. I can't think of another vocation where it is so easily assumed the younger generation will naturally carry on the family profession.

I wondered what kind of dreams I would have if I had been born into a circus family. But I wasn't, and neither were those young Bulgarian acrobats. I understood why they would have dreams of being something other than circus in the modern world.

My dreams were still viable, I told myself. I knew I would get there, when the time was right, when I was ready, when the stars aligned. I would straddle both worlds—circus and non-circus—as I had been doing all my young adult life. I'd create something new: a circus format as a home for combining all my interests in music, athletics, literature, science, even metaphysics. A place where magic could occur because of the magical environment of circus. A circus that enacted the great adventure stories...a Story Circus.

But...Just how do you create a tenting circus from scratch with no money and no partner? How do you make magic in this modern world?

★

The end of the second season with *TV i Teltet* was fast approaching. But first, I had the chance to catch Cirkus Schumann, which was touring the countryside, in 1980, in classic circus style. I visited Katja Schumann, who was fifth generation of the Cirkus Schumann dynasty, performing with her horses in the family circus.

Katja is the quintessential circus equestrienne: assured, creative, competent, beautiful in the ring with the horses, quick to flash a brilliant smile perfectly matching her quick Danish sense of humor. I didn't know her well. I was certainly impressed by her.

I had Rufus with me, so while I watched the show, Katja put him in her caravan, a beautiful old-style European wooden caravan, the kind with a curved roof, etched glass windows, and a carved wood door at one end with removable steps leading up to a porch. Upon entering, you find yourself in the living area with a small kitchen, fold-down table, couch, Oriental rugs, everything in its place for traveling.

The built-in bed was at the other end behind floor length curtains. Rufus immediately made himself at home on the bed. After the show, Katja showed me a letter from Paul Binder, co-founder of The Big Apple Circus in New York, and asked me what I thought of the invitation to perform with them next season.

I replied: "Well, it's not yet comparable to the shows over here, but I'll say it's the closest to a traditional European circus you'll find in the States. One ring, nice tent, Paul is quite knowledgeable of circus culture. If you want to get to the States with your horses, it might be your best bet."

I didn't know Paul at the time; I told him this story years later. He just smiled.

The upshot to this, of course, is that not only did Katja take the contract in 1981, but she married and had two children with Paul. Circus historian and author, Dominique Jando, who was associate artistic director of the Big Apple Circus from 1983–2002, writes in the online Circopedia:

Schumann has two children with Paul Binder, Katherine (b. 1985) and Max (b. 1987). Max was born in her family's RV, without a doctor or midwife present, after Schumann performed two shows

earlier that day, experiencing "a couple of contractions during
the act." Said Schumann at the time, "I caught him before he hit
the floor. He quacked and snorted a little, and I thought, 'This
boy looks just fine to me!' so I tucked him in with me under my
bathrobe and waited for the midwives to arrive." Max was born
on a Wednesday, and Schumann took off the Thursday morning
circus show before returning to perform that evening.

★

After the show at Cirkus Schumann, I gathered Rufus from Katja's caravan, but not without a humorous bit of struggle. Katja was reluctant to let him go. "He's perfectly fine here," she said. "Look at him."

True, Rufus was pulling one of his charm routines, reluctant to leave the bed, ears at half-mast, eyes moist. I hesitated but resisted both their arguments and charms. Dammit. I think I was a bit intimidated around Katja.

On my way home with Rufus I had a flash of imagery that almost made me turn around to the lot and run back to her caravan. I imagined Katja keeping both Rufus and me happily living in the caravan, performing together an act where the forlorn clown falls deeply in love with the beautiful equestrian. He attempts to woo her by trying to ride the horses in a comedy routine, reminiscent of Kossmayer's mules.

Rufus would have a litter of Little Rufi pups running around and we'd have a comedy dog act with the Rufus dynasty performing all around the world, and Katja adding our litter of kids to the dogs and horses, training them as sixth generation artistes. Circus Rufus...

Ah, well, I chickened out. I fell into the doleful habit of berating myself on the ride back to the city. As happens many times in a long career, that boat left without me. I decided it was time to leave Denmark behind, move on, and finally pursue my old dreams with dedicated fervor. Hesitancy be damned.

NYC

*"One woman looks long and earnestly at
the zebra, and then raises a laugh by inquiring
'where they got that striped mule.'"*

—*Ringling Route Book,*
Florence, Alabama,
November 1895

For the final show of the TV season, I pulled one last stunt on Niels, who was always a good-natured sport. At the end of each broadcast, he would sit in his spot on the couch and, while holding the microphone, say goodnight to the audience in Danish: "Thanks for tonight...and we'll see you next week!" Only this time it would be "we'll see you next year."

I had warned the cameramen to be ready, and my partners were in on the joke. As Niels began his farewell, I sneaked up behind the couch and in the final twenty seconds, I grabbed the mic out of his hands, and as he turned around, startled, I said in Danish—the first time the mime had spoken on camera in the two whole seasons—"Finally! I get to say a few words! Tak for i aften...og vi ses naeste ar!"

We all converged on the couch then, tossing confetti as the credits rolled and the band kicked in, and the audience happily applauded, and even Rufus jumped up on the couch getting the last word with some barks. And that was my last appearance on Danish television.

It was also the last season for the show, as it turned out, ending on a high note. We all moved on. Niels had other projects and I, well... I still had to figure out how to conceive a little circus, out of thin air.

★

I had already made up my mind to forego performing for a while. I wanted just to have a normal job while figuring out the next phase of my life. What better place to be anonymous than in New York City! There I could settle in, plan a course of action, and make contacts for creating my circus.

In New York I stayed briefly with my cousin Laura Ann and her boyfriend Simeon. "You're really looking for any kind of regular work, eh?" he said.

I had told him no acting, nothing to do with show business. "Go to this address," he advised me, scribbling something on a scrap of paper, "and ask for the job."

I said, "The job?"

"Right," he said, "I can't explain. Just go and ask for The Job."

The address was downtown Manhattan. I made my way to an office building. I said to the receptionist, "I'm here for...the job." She looked me over, pressed a button on the phone, and said, "Go right in."

I entered a large, spartan office with big bay windows overlooking the cityscape. I walked across the open space to a man sitting behind a wide desk in front of the windows. The desk was conspicuously empty of papers or any kind of clutter.

The man watched me as I made my way to him in an awkward silence. He looked me over. "You here for the job?"

"That's right," I said. I was very curious. What did I have to lose?

"You sure you want it?" He reached into his desk drawer.

I imagined him pushing a gun toward me and handing over an address. Dick Tracy came to mind, and tall redheads with long legs— I would need a pin-striped suit and a fedora hat and speak out of the corner of my mouth, a seedy habit acquired from too many years of smoking cheap cigars and drinking too much Danish mead...

He held up a jangle of keys on a chain. "I own twenty-six buildings downtown. By law I'm responsible for keeping the sidewalks clean in front of the buildings. I pay ten dollars per building to pick up any trash and sweep the steps inside the buildings."

I cocked my head, filled with visions of taking elevators up ninety floors and sweeping down, down, down...

"No building is higher than five floors. This must be done twice a week. Another ten dollars for mopping the steps every two weeks." He stared at me, still holding up the keys.

My mind was frantically calculating: twenty-six buildings @ ten dollars = two-hundred-sixty...twice a week = five-hundred-fifty bucks...plus two-hundred-sixty for washing...let's see... Jingle jangle.

"You are on your own time, I don't care when you do it, morning or midnight, as long as it gets done."

I smiled. "Okay, boss" I said. "When do I start?" He pushed a paper toward me with addresses. We shook hands, I took the jangle of keys, and that was that.

★

I got myself a bike with a basket for Rufus and saddlebags to carry trash bags and paraphernalia, a broom and mop to sling over my shoulders, and a cap and coveralls for my outfit. I started out on my tour: the buildings were all fairly close. Up Spring Street, down lower Broadway, across Houston to the Village.

When I got the feel for how to best map the tour, I timed myself. The sidewalk area in front of a building was nominal and usually pretty clean; dash up five flights of stairs, sweep down: ten minutes. That's four hours of work, twice a week, say Mondays and Fridays. Enough in one week to pay a month's rent on a small room.

Sometimes on a cool summer night, I would put on the coveralls and cap, ride out, waving to deli managers, busy putting out fruit on tables near the buildings. Sometimes I'd sweep their sidewalk and they'd toss me an apple. What a great NYC job! Plenty of time during the days to do whatever I wanted. I had learned it was a job passed down from actor to actor, so they'd be free to make auditions.

One day I was on the job with Rufus in the basket. I liked to walk him around Washington Square Park. He enjoyed meeting other dogs there and I enjoyed meeting the girls who had those other dogs.

Rufus and I stopped at a corner near Chelsea and waited for the lights to change. Diagonally across the street some people were pointing in my direction. I looked around to see what they were pointing at—a fire? A movie star, incognito? There was no one around us.

They kept pointing. It was a young family: all very good-looking and very blonde and smiling, two little kids, a boy and a girl, looking like twins.

The lights changed. Starting to feel a little uncomfortable—did I know these people? I stayed where I was. They crossed over to me and started talking excitedly:

"Is that Roofoos? Ja, surely, it is ROOfoos!" The two kids were petting him and talking to him in Danish. The father said: "Robin? It is you, right? The kids recognized you—well, actually, Rufus first."

We all shook hands. They knew us from *TV i Teltet,* of course, and they were on holiday in New York. Go figure. I came to New York City to be anonymous, and here I was signing autographs again.

The family couldn't stop grinning and exclaiming how it was a good story to tell when they got back home. They took photos of the kids with me and Rufus, and we parted ways, waving and laughing.

What incongruous fun! I felt a little silly in my overalls and brooms, imagining them sharing the photos back in Denmark. Ah, but what the heck, that's show business. I felt light-hearted the rest of the day. Yes, I had to admit, it is nice to be recognized, a wonderful, remarkable feeling.

I stayed in The Job through the winter. I was getting restless in the city. It was becoming harder to imagine life outside New York. The whole world was here, I felt the pull of the city, like being in a maelstrom swirling nonstop, spiraling down, down…to what?

And that bothered me. I knew I had to escape, or I would be transformed into a city dweller, absorbed into the splendor and squalor of the place.

I had these thoughts as I walked Rufus to the abandoned lot near the water. There was a hole in the wire fence surrounding the overgrown weeds and trash, where he did his "business." I took off his leash and he went in. Suddenly there was a short BLEEP!

BLEEP! siren and a policeman stepped out of his unmarked car. He had been waiting.

"It's against the law to have a dog unleashed in the city," he said, taking out a pad and starting to write me a ticket.

"Yes, sir, I know. It's just that he won't do his stuff when he's leashed. It's only for a minute."

The officer was unmoved. "Is that supposed to be an excuse?"

"No, not an excuse...well, yes, in the sense of it being a factual kind of..."

He tore the ticket off the pad and handed it over. "Pay the ticket. Or appear in court." Then he waited until Rufus came back and was leashed again. Not even a warning first. I looked at the ticket: seventy-five-bucks!

Rufus looked at me as if to say, "So what? That poop was worth every bit of it."

I decided to appear in court and plead my case. I would show irrefutable evidence that the dog would not perform when leashed. In front of the judge and jury, I would command the leashed dog to jump through my arms, or sit, or do anything. I knew he would just stand there, staring blankly. Once unleashed, Rufus would come to life, even jump through the arms of the judge, who would be so charmed that not only would she tear up the ticket, but she'd take us out for lunch.

A week later I appeared at the courthouse with Rufus. I went up to the clerk's desk and asked where I was to go. I showed him the ticket.

"Room 203, second floor," he said. "But the dog is not allowed in the courtroom."

I said: "He's not 'the dog'—he's my case." The clerk said: "Sorry, no dogs allowed." And he went back to his papers, ignoring us.

I was indignant. I knew now that I would probably have to pay the ticket even if I saw the judge. And here I had thought Rufus would provide a little fun and a good story for everyone. After a bit more haggling with the clerk, we left in a huff. I had shown up and been denied a chance to plead my case. I'm outta here.

As it turned out, it was the last straw that convinced me of where I already subconsciously knew I was headed: out of New York City and back to the wilds of Vermont, where both the dog and I could run free. Soon after, I turned in the jangle of keys to The Boss with The Job and headed north to a cabin in the woods in Vermont.

There, I got a forwarded letter from New York City: "Your Fine Is Now $150. Pay or Appear in Court." Every few weeks another letter came: "Your Fine is Now $225...$300...$375."

By the time the letters reached $1,570, I had visions of a plain-clothes detective in black suit and dark glasses knocking on my cabin door. "I've been tracking your whereabouts for five months—Gotcha!" he'd say, handcuffing me to a radiator, as he put a locked collar on Rufus and dragged him out the door.

The letters, though, finally stopped arriving. It was time to stop gallivanting around the world and get serious. It had been fifteen years since—itchy for adventure—I first got it into my head to run off and learn the circus business. It was already 1984, and I wasn't getting any younger. I was a grand old thirty-four by then.

My vision for a small country circus was still clear in my head—clearly stuck in there. Little did I know the biggest adventure was yet ahead. It would be the birth of a persistent dream I would name Circus Smirkus, a story that sometimes reads like a movie script and just as often feels like fiction.

But heck. What could sound more like fiction than the very real Hoffman gang, and an ornery camel in Wales, and rampant Vikings, and a wire-walking Spanish dwarf in Denmark, and those runaway mules in Lapland?

Act V

Circus Smirkus

Circus Smirkus

The troupe climbs the trees of Sherwood Forest. The perch pole act of the Robin Hood Tour, 1999.

The Smikus Big Top set up in the hills of Vermont, 1999.

Above left, Robbo atop five stacked rola bolas, 1996. Above right, Circus troupe "Flying High."

Above, the Smikus troupe arriving in Red Square, Moscow, 1990. Right, Alla Youdina and Rob, Russia, 1990.

Facing page, top, Marcel Marceau, Alla, Rob with troupers in the Smirkus ring, Middlebury, Vermont, 1999. Bottom, Marceau as Bip, Mermin as Robin Hood, 1999 Big Top Tour.

Marcel Marceau

The Smirkus
Chronicles

*"The circus saw fit to come parading into our
quiet little village on the last Sabbath. Legislative
enactments are needed to guard the community
against these baleful influences."*

—*The Farmer's Herald,*
St. Johnsbury, Vermont, 1831

When I founded The Circus Barn, Inc., in 1987, doing
business in Vermont as Circus Smirkus, the circus world in
America was not in great shape. There were no circus camps, after-
school circus activities, social circuses, or circus schools dotting
the American landscape as they do today. In the year Circus
Smirkus began, no one-ring show featuring talented kids from
around the country, and touring the rural countryside under a big
top, existed anywhere.

Circus here in the United States has a grand and checkered
history. The late 1800s was a Golden Era. Touring tent circuses, large
and small, were abundant and generated excitement everywhere.
Towns shut down on Circus Day to fill tents that could hold eighteen
thousand customers, eager to experience an exotic world of glamorous
performers and glimpse animals they had only read about in books.

But by the time I arrived in rural Vermont, circus people were suffering from an unsavory aura, associated with carnival transients. Why I chose northern Vermont as a home base for my circus is still a mystery to me. The town of Greensboro had a population of six hundred, a single general store, a lake, and a deserted farmhouse with rundown outbuildings. In the most rural county of what is dubbed the Northeast Kingdom, Greensboro sat in one of the most rural states, without so much as a whiff of circus among its rugged farmers and maple syrup growers.

At my first Town Meeting after moving to the village, I stood up and announced that I needed volunteers, preferably kids, to help pound three thousand twenty penny nails to create a bed of nails for the first Greensboro Village Circus. I sat down and heard murmurs, "That must be the carny fellow moved into the old Richardson place."

Townsfolk warmed up to me that summer when we had that first outdoor circus with town selectmen as roustabouts, the town clerk and sewing circle as costumers, Tim the Town Meeting moderator as ringmaster, and various town personalities showing off whatever non-circus talent they might have.

Rufus stole the show. The event introduced me to the town, and the town to me. I knew I needed to convince the public that having a circus in town was not a threatening notion.

Historically, an element of Vermont society shunned what was considered the sinfulness of circus and theater worlds. An 1873 letter from an English tourist in Vermont reads: "The transients or chance customers of a wayside inn are of all occupations: minstrels, tumblers, equestrian performers, strolling lecturers, musicians, jugglers, rope dancers, and traveling dwarfs."

The Vermont Legislature of 1836 introduced a law that stipulated "All circus riding, theatrical exhibitions, juggling or sleight of hand, ventriloquism and magic acts shall be, and are, declared to be common and public nuisances and offenses against this state." Transgressors were to be fined two-hundred dollars.

American differences were also noted. "All sorts of amusements, which among Europeans are considered innocent relaxations, are here proscribed as immoral pleasures." I venture to guess the phrase "immoral pleasures" was a useful marketing tool used by unscrupulous mud show owners to entice a curious public. In those days, "a glimpse of stocking" may have been shocking, but male and female aerialists performing together in tights was acceptable at the circus!

By 1880, Vermont law had added to the list of sinful frivolity, "a company of persons who exhibit tragedies, comedies, farces, pantomimes, or other theatrical shows for money." Ignoring the law, however, Vermonters began building ornate Opera Houses around the state that featured all kinds of circus and vaudeville acts that filled the halls and circus tents, too.

Finally, Governor Richard Snelling, in 1991, issued a proclamation "to wipe out any lingering remnant of Vermont as an anti-circus state." Circus Smirkus was thereby officially recognized by the Vermont General Assembly as the only tenting circus based in Vermont, the "unofficial state circus."

I had sought recognition as the "official" state circus, which would have made Vermont the only such state. But I was told only something permanent, like a flower or tree, could acquire the "official" status. I took what we could get. The *Boston Globe* wrote: "Smirkus is the first Vermont-based circus in over a hundred years."

★

I have written origin stories of Circus Smirkus in two books published by The Circus Barn, Inc.: *Smirkus: A True Story of High Adventure & Low Comedy,* a tenth-anniversary book, published in 1997, with a foreword by Marcel Marceau; and *Circus Smirkus: Twenty-Five Years of Running Home to the Circus,* co-authored with journalist Rob Gurwitt in 2012. The latter is a comprehensive coffee-table history of the company, with a hundred gorgeous color photographs and anecdotes from coaches and troupers who lived the adventure.

I won't reiterate here that formidable history, now spanning over thirty-five years and still on the road. But I will include a sampling of haps and mishaps from the archives, and personal episodes that shaped the evolution of the company. In telling these stories, it becomes clearer in my mind how the much-loved style, spirit, and traditions of Smirkus were infused with my early escapades.

Smirkus has an unconventional, rough-and-ready, do-it-yourself mud show style, much like the Hoffmans. Smirkus has a Joke Show every season, just like Benneweis. And like Kossmayer, Smirkus has always had animal partners—if not mules, then dogs, horses, miniature donkeys, llamas, racoons, and a tightrope-walking boa constrictor.

In my two earlier books, the stories abound of Smirkus putting up the big top in thunderstorms, on muddy lots, with teenage troupers digging trenches around the tent in costume between acts. Smirkus never missed a show, even after a small tornado hit the lot. We improvised as needed. For a couple of years, I even wrote occasional reviews of the show for a national circus magazine, under a pseudonym, to get the company noticed outside New England. The company still uses quotes—unknowingly!—from those reviews.

Smirkus was born only after a long stressful period of pain and spasms and near-devastating miscarriage of the dream. The idea still seemed simple enough in my head: a traveling circus based in an idyllic country setting; a company run by artists touring small villages in the old-fashioned style; a modern show where artists could try out new ideas in a traditional big top setting; a young troupe composed mostly of talented teens, working as colleagues with adults; an international organization with a philanthropic intention and a social heart; a company whose very existence symbolized the idealistic spirit of having a dream and overcoming obstacles to make it happen.

Okay, maybe it wasn't such a simple idea after all. For over a decade I looked everywhere for a spark of interest to help me. I constantly promoted the idea to other artists, managers of arts organizations, business leaders, philanthropists, executive directors of state arts councils, but everyone listened to me with amused eyes and nodding of heads and the shaking of my hand, wishing me good luck.

I had even made brazen attempts to garner support in some unusual corners. I wrote two letters asking for a meeting: one to the executive director of UNICEF in New York with a proposal outlining the creation of an international company of young circus performers—children of professional circus artists—who would tour the world, performing as circus ambassadors promoting the work and ideals of the United Nations Children's Emergency Fund.

At the same time, I wrote a letter to Theodor Geisel, better known as Dr. Seuss, also proposing the idea of an international children's circus. In 1956, Dr. Seuss had published *If I Ran the Circus*. In the book, a young lad leans on a fence staring at the overgrown backlot behind Sneelock's General Store.

He daydreams of erecting a huge Big Top right there as ringmaster of his own circus. "Why, ladies and gentlemen, youngsters and oldsters, your heads will quite likely spin right off your shouldsters!"

Reading this as a six-year-old, of course I also imagined creating my own fantastical circus. How fitting that thirty years later, I would set up my own big top, not far from Willey's General Store in an abandoned dairy farmhouse, which became the Smirkus World Headquarters.

Once back in the US, I figured if I could garner the patronage of Dr. Seuss by promoting the connection with UNICEF, and the sponsorship of UNICEF through the connection with Dr. Seuss, together there might be the kind of impressive symbiotic authority that would attract national attention and open some eyes to the idea of assisting me in such a nervy endeavor.

I hopped in my car and drove from the East Coast to Southern California to find myself knocking on the door of Theodor Seuss Geisel's beautiful hilltop home in La Jolla. A tall man with glasses and salt and pepper hair and beard, Seuss answered the door. Apparently, he had never received my letter, which I had hoped would be forwarded by his publisher.

Nevertheless, he invited me in, and we sat outside in deck chairs by his swimming pool in the sunshine, as his wife brought out tall glasses of lemonade. He seemed amused by my European circus escapades—kicked by mules, knocked out by a camel, running amok with clown dwarfs. I'm not sure he believed my stories, a common reaction from folks without any real connection with the circus world. Besides, my quiet, somewhat reserved demeanor didn't fit the image people typically had of circus rogues.

Geisel was like an irascible but kindly uncle who, inspecting you sternly, finally ascertained you were an interesting enough young person to scrutinize further. When I shifted the conversation to the children's circus idea and UNICEF, he asked polite questions. But I was woefully inept at answering queries about how all this would actually be organized and funded.

I had what I thought was a great idea. Surely these more experienced worldly folks would see the value and, if not immediately jump on board, at least give me contacts who could tell me how to make it happen. But I had no properly composed budget, no financial graphs, no five-year strategic plan on paper in a clear binder with duplicate copies. I'm sure I appeared as the idealist I was—a big dreamer with no plan.

He said when I was ready, to send him a strategic plan and formal proposal. We chatted some more, then he shook my hand and offered good luck. And that was that. Ten years later, after I had started Circus Smirkus and begun international cultural exchanges with circus kids in 1990, I was ready to contact Mr. Geisel again with something real to show—but he died in 1991 before I had the chance.

As for my subsequent meeting with the director of UNICEF in New York, the results were similar to those I'd just gotten in La Jolla—though the story he most wanted to hear was about Dr. Seuss. The UNICEF meeting was cut short because, the director apologized, he had to deal with some issues that had just come up concerning an event happening a few hours later: a UNICEF benefit concert by The Bee Gees.

We shook hands and he wished me the usual good luck. It was a polite dismissal that had become all too familiar. I was still not ready, and my idealism was wavering.

Ever since, whenever young idealists approach me with an idea to start their own circus company, I see myself in their faces and feel complicated feelings: a desire to lend support and encouragement, mixed with a sad smile for knowing what they will have to go through, harboring implausible dreams.

The Green Mountain Circus

"Circus Smirkus can in one swift moment touch your heart and bring tears. Unforgettable circus experience: the unabashed and as yet unspoiled professionalism kicks you in the pants."

—*Circus Report* magazine, 1996

I was sitting on the porch of the old farmhouse, with my canine partner Rufus sitting calmly next to me. Both of us stared at the cows wandering in my fields. They periodically got loose from my neighbor's farm a mile down the dirt road. For some reason they liked to amble around my place.

"How the hell do I start a circus out here?" I said out loud. "With performing cows?"

This was not such a bad idea. I daydreamed of touring the Vermont countryside in a small tent. I daydreamt of wide-eyed farm kids sitting on piles of straw right up to the ring—the ring fence made of bales of hay too—gazing at a half dozen cows circling the ring, encouraged by a barefooted Diana Benneweis.

She's no longer in her usual Parisian gown, but dressed as Daisy Mae in cut-off dungaree shorts, straw hat tilted on her head, long, dark hair tied in pigtails. A dozen fluffy Vermont sheep waltz around the ring, stepping gingerly through hoops made of wool, and led by Rufus, who guides them with short barks and ears standing straight

★

In the winter of 1986, I had planned the first appearance of The Green Mountain Circus, under "the little big top" in towns around Vermont. My plan was to tour a small show with a handful of professional acts, build a reputation, and in a few years get around to my long-held dream of an international children's circus.

I had designed a small two-mast, round-end circus tent made by a company in Florida. It had a heavy vinyl blue top representing the blue sky, green sidewalls like the Green Mountains of Vermont, and a sunny yellow valance. The tent measured fifty by seventy feet and its top came in three sections, which needed to be spread on the ground and laced together at each site. Rickety steel bleacher frames supported hard-on-the-butt wooden stringers.

The whole structure could seat a couple of hundred folks at best, but we had straw spread up to the ring for kids to sit up close, and we often filled the tent with squeezed-in audiences of five hundred.

I contracted a few acts and booked the show through local nonprofit organizations. These groups—fire departments, playground managers, school boards—would arrange our site, fix local permits, hang our posters, sell tickets, and get a percentage of the sales.

"Vermont's Own Homegrown Country Circus!" said the posters illustrated by a Vermont artist. It featured a circus ring containing a cow, a goose, a pig, and Daisy Mae—yes, I had even found a real "Daisy Mae's Barnyard Animals" act! Posters were put up, concession supplies bought, lighting and sound system equipment rented, trucks leased, and million-dollar public liability insurance acquired.

And then the dung hit the fan. Nationwide. The insurance industry, after years of mismanagement, exploded in our faces. The *New York Times* told the story:

> During 1985 and 1986, the cost of liability coverage for busi-
> nesses, municipal governments, and non-profits rose rapidly. The
> industry also reduced the availability of coverage; the resulting
> shortages further boosted prices. Now the pool of available

insurance has contracted, and most insurers can get all the premiums they need writing only the lowest-risk business. The legacy is being felt in many ways. For consumers, it is in sky-rocketing rates and the inability of many even to find insurance.

A new circus did not qualify as low risk. We were suddenly denied liability insurance, our policies canceled.

The effect of the insurance crisis was to swing a sledgehammer to my dream. With only a month to go before the circus was to begin its maiden voyage, I started to get calls from all the town sponsors, as well as unwanted notices from the insurance carrier.

First came the cancellation of our insurance policy. It was not even a matter of forking over a huge price increase to the industry. We would see a fee hike, as much as a one-thousand percent increase for less insurance coverage. I could find no company that would even negotiate a public liability policy for a) a new circus; b) large public gatherings under a tent; c) circus performers liability; d) liability for child performers; e) liability for "tightwire, trapeze, acrobats or other dangerous circus activities," etc.

Even worse, the local sponsors—the fire departments, summer schools, playground sites, nonprofit youth groups—all called to cancel the circus booking on two understandable grounds: either they had lost their own insurance and shut down the playgrounds and public spaces, or they could not sponsor the circus unless we could provide a new policy guaranteeing a huge increase in coverage. And of course, we could not.

I had to cancel the tour.

I had debts to pay off. I felt a duty first to all my local creditors. I showed up to their offices in person, hoping to preserve future relationships. Some places I would send five or ten dollars cash weekly, to show good faith and that I was still there. Then I felt a special obligation to pay off the performers whatever I could manage, at least a portion of their canceled contracts. As a self-employed artist, I knew the last-minute booking cancellation meant not only loss of immediate income, but missed opportunities of other gigs.

Some of the performers, in support of my efforts, would not accept payment. Others were grateful for the gesture. All this pay-off came from emptying my pockets. Basically, I lost not only my shirt and socks and any foreseeable means of income, but something that hurt more deeply, an internal wound that would fester. I had lost my dream.

I rolled up the tent into sacks and stashed it away in the barn for good. I sat outside the barn and fell into deep melancholy.

Sucker Day

*"Circus Smirkus: the name says it all.
Irreverent, impudent, amusing, ironic.
Circus Smirkus is all those things and more.
Smirkus is, above all a circus with a heart."*

—Ernest Albrecht, *Spectacle, A Quarterly
Journal of the Circus Arts,* Fall 1998

I felt swindled by the insurance industry. Scammed, conned, suckered.

I thought of Wetumka, Oklahoma, when the entire town was suckered by the flim-flam man, J. Bam Morrison, who arrived in town in 1950, posing as an advance man for a circus supposedly enroute, just three weeks away. Morrison persuaded residents to put up money to bring the non-existent circus to town.

People would be coming from miles around to attend this circus, he promised, presenting Wetumka merchants with the potential to make lots of money. Pretty soon all the advertising space in town was sold, as well as advance tickets, with cash paid directly to Morrison, of course. Meanwhile town merchants prepared for expected crowds, stocking up with tons of food, beverages, and souvenirs.

Then Morrison disappeared. On the morning the circus parade was scheduled to march down Main Street, the citizens of Wetumka lined the streets. Nothing happened. So, the town council, realizing they'd been taken for a ride, decided to hold their own celebration anyway, with a parade and street fair. They had plenty of food ready after all.

Thus, the annual Sucker Day tradition was born. Instead of resigning themselves to the misery of a swindle, Wetumka enthusiastically turned disillusionment into amusement.

Like Wetumka, I had cartons of popcorn ready to pop, a cotton candy machine, boxes of tickets, and a circus tent all packed up in the barn, and no circus—it was my own personal Sucker Day. But I lacked the enthusiasm for turning disaster into celebration.

The life of a creative artist is fickle. You were always hustling for work, promoting yourself. Flush periods were followed by drought, and always doubt clouded the future. I was thirty-six years old. What else could I do with my life, besides circus?

I was broke, out of ideas, out of luck, and worse: out of a dream. At least my shoulders felt lighter. I no longer felt the burden of carrying around a complicated vision, a load which had only gotten heavier over the years from the increasing strain of constant frustration. Maybe I could learn a real trade and have a normal, easier life. What other careers were available to me? Bread baker? Schoolteacher? Open a school for training trick dogs?

That summer I wandered the woods and sank into apathy, despondency, depression. A fellow performer from New York City came to visit. Michael Moschen is an extraordinarily gifted creative artist, innovator, master of object manipulation, and juggler. He arrived at the farmhouse in much the same mood as me—a disillusioned and derailed dreamer.

I had lost my circus. Michael had lost his bearings. He had been up for a huge grant award, which would have enabled him to create a visionary one-man theater production, a long-held project, which had consumed him. That was something I understood.

We took a canoe out on Caspian Lake. Depression seemed to follow us like a dreary cloud. We rowed in silence and stopped in the middle of the water. Without a word, we looked over the boat sides, down into the depths of the lake, dark and inviting.

Then we looked at each other. Alarmed by the same dismal thoughts, we solemnly rowed back to shore, went home, and made ourselves some dinner.

As things turned out, Michael would go on to receive the prestigious MacArthur Fellowship award, astounding the world with his unique solo theatrical performances. But I didn't know that then.

For over fifteen years, I had nurtured a vision of having my own touring tent circus. Through my European apprentice years, I'd suffered bouts of insecurity, periods of loneliness, long stretches of self-doubts—a near universal disposition fairly common to young idealists and creative artists. But this blow had really knocked me to my knees, and I began to question the dream itself.

All the strange looks and knowing smiles and shaking heads from people over the years came flooding into my brain, and I felt shame at my naïveté. Disillusionment sank into depression like quicksand. What had I been thinking all these years? I had finally put everything I had on the line...and come out absolutely beaten, with nothing left.

I tired of always thinking, planning, dreaming about the future. The philosophers say don't live in the past or the future—embrace the present. What if the present cannot hold the imagination's visions? Was it nonsense to have big dreams? To carry them so long?

A dream not realized becomes a solitary worm eating you up inside, especially when you see it in all its detail, and know it can be real. Hoffman, Benneweis, Kossmayer—sitting in the Vermont farmland it all began to seem like a made-up fantasy. In my head, I heard the Yiddishism my mother spoke years ago, when I first said that I wanted to go off to find a circus. "Circus, Shmirkus," she said. "Go get a real job, like in a bank."

I suffered alone that summer, wondering what was next. That October, I was in New York City, and it so happened I met with Jay Craven, a Vermont arts producer, over a breakfast of blueberry blintzes and coffee in a Ukrainian restaurant in the East Village. That breakfast changed the course of my life and put the original steadfast dream back in its rightful place: my heart.

★

It took a political radical from New York to see my dream had potential. Jay, later to become a successful independent filmmaker, at the time had founded Catamount Arts, a nonprofit producer of major arts events in Vermont's Northeast Kingdom. During that fateful blueberry breakfast in the autumn of 1986, I bemoaned the Fiasco of The Green Mountain Circus, decried conventional people's failure of imagination, and disparaged my own woeful ignorance.

"I give up, I'm done, the dream is gone," I said. I looked down at my plate. "I can't even pay for these Ukrainian pancakes."

Jay asked what my dream really was. Was it a little show with trained geese, a cow, and a few professionals? "That was just meant to be a start," I said, a build-up to a bigger vision. I explained my long-held dream of a children's circus, a showcase for exceptional young talent, an international company run by and performed by kids, all under canvas, and traveling with the style and traditions of a European circus.

There was no model for this dream. Nothing like it existed. Well-meaning friends, sympathetic to my passion, suggested I just start a local school program and perform in the high school gym. I shook my head at the thought, protesting: "It's in a one-ring, European tent...or nothing. A place of magic...or no place. Certainly not a high school gym. With kids from around the globe. And it's a traditional touring circus—not a day camp. The kids would be committed to joining a unique family away from home, like an apprenticeship, performing with professionals in the ring."

Jay took out a pen and started making a list on a napkin: "What do you need?"

I groaned. "Oh, god...a truck to carry the tent and seats, a bus for the kids, parents crazy enough to drop off their kids with circus folks, vans for the crew, a cotton candy machine...ticket booth, props, costumes...liability insurance..."

Jay kept scribbling numbers on the napkin. When I was done fantasizing, he showed me the napkin. "One hundred thousand dollars. That's doable. You already have the tent. We can produce it under the insurance policy of Catamount Arts. We can finagle that."

I was unconvinced. "One hundred thousand dollars?!" Being in debt, I could not even fathom that amount. But he was serious, and we shook hands.

Back in Vermont, with Jay as the producer and me as founding artistic director, we recruited a few professional friends to jump on board as coaches, performers, and founding members: Stewart Lippe, Donny Osman, Karen Gersch, Irina Gold. I insisted from the start that we have a live band with original music, which we got with Vermont composer Peter Tavalin and his three-piece band.

It was a daunting task, to establish not only a circus in the backwoods, but a training ground for kids, all before summer. The details involved administrative setup, contract negotiations, insurance, fundraising, property acquisition, recruiting kids and holding auditions, staffing, housing, trucks, touring logistics, marketing, bookings, sponsors, and a veritable nightmare of legal codes and artistic considerations for everything concerning kids, tents, and circuses.

I called it Circus Smirkus, recalling my mom's wry comment. Smirkus had a Seussian ring to it—as well as hidden meaning. I once, only half-jokingly, defined Smirkus as: "an old Yiddish word signifying irreverent humor; a scent for adventure; an attitude of cheerful nonconformity."

The young troupers, ages ten to eighteen, were immersed in a world they had not imagined. Seven days a week, twelve-hour workdays, three months away from the comfort and confines of home and the rigid structure of school. Circus life is not for everyone. For those not born in the circus, it is a hard life, requiring dedication to craft, long hours, and close-knit community. Many adults, long set in their ways, cannot adapt to the irregular and intense communal lifestyle as easily as youth can.

All winter the team mobilized and by June, Smirkus was born, after training the kids, rehearsing a full show, and hitting the road. The biggest lesson for me, which I always encourage young dreamers to remember, was this: Don't Compromise the Dream!

Be bold, I would tell them, and don't concede to disbelievers when negotiating your creative vision. I had for so long tried to get to the big dream, I felt worn down by lack of success. Discouragement compelled me to pare down my ideals and be less ambitious. In retrospect, the insurance debacle of 1986 was, in a way, a successful fiasco: I had survived.

I had succeeded at failure! As if fate had winked at me, smirked, and allowed me to fail so completely, my truer, deeper vision could bubble back to the surface past my doubts. The freedom to follow an unknown fate is awesome in its possibilities, but the discomfort of unpredictability can be terrifying as well, kicking you out of complacency.

Ha! I thought—maybe Kansas the Mule was a fitting metaphor for beating yourself up until you get it right.

Illustration by Ed Koren

The Circus Barn, Inc.

*"The larger feeling of Circus Smirkus is joyful,
exuberant. Mostly, one remembers the applause
echoing off the tent walls: loud, happy,
foot-stomping applause."*

—New York Times, 1987

I ran off to join the circus as a young fellow with the goal of learning the trade and with the dream of one day creating a circus of my own. I wanted to expand my artistic vision and share with others the unconventional lifestyle of the circus. I wanted Vermont's Circus Smirkus to be a place where, like me, kids could follow their own dreams right into the circus ring, and embody their capacity to enact, with imagination and perseverance and collaboration, their own creative vision.

It became my livelihood, as well as my life's work. We created a life-changing experience for thousands of kids, with all their heart and soul immersed in the three-months-long program. We were doing something new, and everyone felt that magic. Whenever I see the eager, bright-eyed, talented youth who show up at The Circus Barn, itchy for circus adventure, I see myself and my youthful dreams.

Everyone took personal pride in the accomplishments and unique experiences we created with Smirkus. In time, the company grew into a huge itinerant creature, with the Big Top Tour arriving in a new town every two or three days, a seasonal traveling entity of seventy people. There were thirty teens, three cooks, five coaches, ten tent crew and three technicians. We had musicians, drivers, administrative staff, directors, a dressing room tent, a concession tent, a four-mast Big Top, and twenty-five trucks, bunkhouse trailers, vans, and cars.

Happily, one essential part of our creation has lasted through the trials of growth—the style and spirit of Smirkus. Our energy was described by everyone with one word: magical. Our participants experienced a vibrant knowledge that together we were creating a magical event through hard-won effort.

In the early years, whenever I received letters from parents after the end of a season and our teen performers had returned home, I would hesitate before opening them—what had we done wrong now? Then I would read: *What did you do to my child? He is not the same person. He makes his bed, does his own laundry, volunteers for extra chores around the house, no longer fights with his younger sibling... What, pray tell, what did you do to my child?!*

I thought of all the hazards I had experienced in my struggle to climb up and hold onto a dream, like sitting atop an out-of-control bucking camel. I've often been asked to describe the Smirkus experience. As I tried to explain in the first Smirkus book:

> *There is a palpable magical aura stepping into the circus ring or the first time every spring. It is entering a world of enchantment with an expectation of things to come. But it is no secret that magic can be painful as well as beautiful. Some people are suspicious of what they don't understand—the mystical, the magical—and can unwittingly sabotage good intentions. Any enterprise involving hard work, long hours, and close living quarters will brew a clash of personalities and adult egos. Any dream may only be a nightmare in sunshine. Read the fairy tales.*
>
> *Smirkus has an aura of magic, but all of us here know the frustrations and challenges that flow as undercurrents under the big top and make this fairy tale a trial of imagination, an enduring lesson in magic realism. That transcendent meeting point of fantasy and reality: maybe that's where magic—and circus—happens.*

There are stages to having big dreams. First comes the striving to reach it, taking many years of frustration and mistakes. Next comes the creation of the dream and this involves administrative resistance, in direct conflict with the creative process. It is always easier to say no—"no time, no funds, no staff, too risky"—to impossible-sounding initiatives. But the very existence of Smirkus repudiates that attitude.

Then comes maintenance of the dream. Once the dream is firmly established, expect a periodic struggle with those who want to take over and remold it in their image. Finally comes stage four, passing on its traditions, working to ensure the vision is strong enough to endure beyond your term. There is joy in this stage, watching new generations carrying on the legacy and living their own adventures "happily ever—after all."

Like every young corporate life, early Smirkus experienced the emotional thunderstorms of personal conflicts, egos, internal politics, societal conventions, and power manipulations occasionally surfacing within the organization's culture. It was another fascinating lesson: the conflicts were generated mainly by grownups, not the kids and teens as one might have expected. Nonetheless, the wonders and adventures and satisfactions continue to change lives and by now the company has grown and thrived for three and a half decades.

My Uncle Harry, upon attending the opening night of the first season in 1987, waited until all the well-wishers had left after the show and the tear-down of the tent had begun before moving on to the next town. Over the years, he had witnessed my trials and tribulations, struggling to create this entity. He looked me in the eye, shook my hand, and in his solemn stentorian voice declared, "'Tis comparable to the miracles that Moses wrought!"

'Tis not untrue, I thought—then put on my work gloves and went back to overseeing the tear-down. There were still hours of work ahead after the happy audience went home. The real work of circus had only just begun.

Horizons

"Audiences are always amazed by the
professionalism of Mermin's tenderfoot troupe.
The circus camp is one of the few of its kind,
and quickly gaining a reputation."

—*People,* 1989

Momentous events change the orbit of our lives. The happier occasions—choosing a college; getting married; having children—are made by us. More tragically fateful events happen to us. They may grow over time as long ordeals, or they can hit like a bolt of lightning to the heart. In either case, your world is never the same again.

Marÿn was twenty-six years old when she came from Holland to join us at Smirkus, the spring of 1989, the third Smirkus season. I was still a bachelor at age thirty-nine, when I got a very unusual off-season call from founding Smirkus coach, Stewart Lippe, who was now down in Tampa, Florida.

"Hey, Robbo," he announced without any preamble, "I'm sending you your future wife!" He had encountered Marÿn on her travels. She was looking for a circus job in the states.

"Sure," I joked, "Why not."

When Marÿn showed up at the farmhouse and our eyes met, I felt an electric shock and the trajectory of my life—and Smirkus history—changed.

Besides her loveliness—green eyes, long wavy auburn hair, starbright smile—her infectious enthusiasm and love of children made her an instantly beloved member of the Smirkus family. She became a counselor and confidante for the troupers. The young girls flocked to her like ducklings. Even Rufus took to following her around. She had an authentic charm with kids and a forthright manner with adults that bridged her inner worlds of child and woman.

I once saw her take aside one of the male staff, who had been ineptly flirting with her for a couple of days. "Listen," she said plainly, "if you like me, just say so. I like you, but in my own way—there's no need to play games." The abashed coach was not used to such frankness, and the way was cleared for a respectful friendship.

Her open sincerity prompted the same honesty from others. About a week later, she approached me: "Why are you avoiding me?"

It was true. I had avoided being alone with her. I was nonstop busy during the rehearsal period, and though we couldn't avoid the magnetic staring at each other, I hesitated to show my attraction to her around the kids. I acknowledged her comment and apologized, thanking her for waking me up to the truth we shared.

From then on, we enjoyed secretly passing little notes to each other throughout the day, like teenagers in the blush of love, spending quiet nights together in my caravan. That initial electric spark only grew in intensity, until there was just no concealing the romantic aura around us.

★

It was a rare day off in the middle of the circus tour. The company was back at headquarters in Greensboro, Vermont. That afternoon, Marÿn and I borrowed an old car—so old it was unequipped with safety airbags—and went skinny dipping in a secluded wilderness lake down a dirt road. Drying off back on shore, we talked gently and deeply about matters of life and renewal of spirit.

Our conversation turned to dreams of our future together. She listened to my hopes and plans. She said she was happy and profoundly content for the first time in her life. Then she stopped. "It's strange," she said. "I always have a vision of the future, or at least a plan, but right now it's just...blank. I see nothing, beyond this moment with you."

We silently walked back to the car, both of us lost in mutual feelings of acceptance and calm readiness for whatever lay ahead...

★

Later that afternoon, the police arrived at The Circus Barn with the news of a freakish accident. On a washed-out, downhill curve of the dirt road, Marÿn had lost control of the wheel, and the old, borrowed car had veered off into a tree. She died instantly. I had somehow fallen out onto the road and had tried to crawl for help—but finally lay there broken, unconscious, my life dangling by a thread. An old farmer eventually found us and called the rescue squad.

I recall nothing of the moments leading up to the accident. Totally blank. Lying on that road, I seemed to hover in darkness between hard earth and eerie fog. There was extreme quietude. No birds. Nothing. Like all sound had forever departed the world.

And no pain: why doesn't the body feel pain when you're in shock? A defense mechanism to override extreme despair? Maybe there is a quality of mercy, as Shakespeare put it, when approaching Death.

I must have been lying there on my side for, I don't know, maybe twenty minutes, sinking in and out of consciousness, with extreme effort struggling and failing to push myself up with one arm—when the first vision came.

I'm lying on my side high above the earth on an ocean of thick white clouds. I look up and see Marÿn, beautiful in a simple white dress, standing over me. I struggle with one arm pushing to get up but I can't. Then I hear her words mentally, her lips don't move: *You can't come.* I struggle some more. She smiles a gentle smile. *You have to stay.* Then all is dark again.

A second vision: I'm still lying on the dirt road, confused. I don't see anything, everything is dark...but I can hear disembodied voices. They are discussing my body, casually, as if they were perusing a menu.

How about his leg, what do you think?

Hmmm. Let's leave it like that.

What about his neck...maybe his spine?

Anyone for ribs?

I desperately try to say, *I can hear you!* But I have no voice, it's just in my head. I lose awareness again. Everything goes black.

The rescue squad arrives. I become aware of being lifted. They take me to a small rural hospital. There, I'm on my back in a small room, barely conscious. I can only move my eyes. Donny and Stewart, coaches from the circus, stand by the left side of the bed, looking scared. My eyes shift to the right and I see a doctor standing over me, white in the face, gripping a sharp knife like he's about to stab me through the heart. A nurse in white, staring at me intensely, stands behind the doctor in the corner.

I say, "Doctor...?"

He says, "Good. You're awake. I need your permission—"

"—For? What?"

"You may be bleeding internally. We need to open your chest to find out. If you are hemorrhaging, it could be fatal if we don't operate...now."

"Options?" I can hardly speak the question.

"I suggest we operate immediately...or...we put you back in the ambulance to the hospital in Burlington. They have more equipment. But it's a forty-five-minute drive. I can't guarantee you'll survive it." He paused, then said: "You need to make a decision. Now."

I shift my eyes to Donny and Stewart, who stand there in dismay—no help there. I see the nurse behind the doctor slowly, firmly, shaking her head. It seems I can hear her thoughts: *No, get out of here...go...right now!*

I go. In the second hospital—I survive the ride—doctors hover over me. I say, "Go ahead, I'm ready, cut me open."

The doctor in charge looks puzzled. He says: "Why would we do that?!"

★

Deep wounds create raw emotions. Every feeling floats on the surface and time is given over to profound reflection. Dreams, memories, exquisite visions, and piercing emotion all flow, windblown, through a heart broken open. What is called a near-death experience is really a new-life experience. It is hugely sobering and enlightening and returns in dreams.

Two shows were scheduled for the circus the next day after our accident. Troupers and staff gathered for an emergency council meeting, I was later told, standing in a circle around the large crystal boulder in the woods, across the field from the farmhouse, a shared sacred spot, a place to go when one needed solitude from the world.

The young troupers made the decision. Their love and anguish and prayers and courage and strength must have been over-whelming: they wanted to perform in tribute to Marÿn and to keep the circus alive for me. When I heard that, my emotions—they simply can't be written.

★

I spent ten days in the hospital, barely moving, meditating, trying to get back to those visions, trying to see Marÿn in the clouds again. But every day the clarity of those visions was fading, slipping away. It was breaking my heart.

Stewart and Donny visit, and I say to them: "Guys, find out the name of that nurse at that first hospital. I want to send her some flowers. And chocolates. She saved my life!"

They look at each other, flustered. Finally, Donny says: "What nurse?"

I say: "The one standing behind the doctor."

They stare at me, frowning. Stewart says slowly: "Rob, it was just us and the doctor. There was no nurse in that room..."

But there was.

★

After ten days, the hospital sent me home. There had been visits downstairs, by wheelchair, down to the physical therapy room where they tried to loosen my rigid limbs, especially my neck. They massaged my head and shoulders, but I still moved my trunk like a wooden marionette.

They had stitched up wounds in my arm, leg, head. Several broken ribs. It was a university teaching hospital—the doctor made his rounds early in the morning, followed by a gaggle of interns.

By the third morning I was fed up with all the interrupted sleep. So, I put on a red foam clown nose, delivered by visitors from the circus, and I feigned sleep. The hospital crew arrived on schedule.

The doctor went right to my chart at the foot of the bed and read out loud for the benefit of students: "Five broken ribs, lacerations on the knee..." He had not once looked at me, the patient. The interns were trying their best to stifle giggles.

The doctor finally glanced up at me. Without missing a beat, poker-faced, he continued "...and there is pronounced swelling along the nasal passages, resulting in severe red discoloration of the proboscis."

During that first week, barely moving, my emotions astonished me. I felt enveloped in sadness, wearing grief like warm flannel pajamas. At the same time, I felt a transcendent calmness, especially when alone at night, having private communion with Marÿn, and feeling in my soul that everything was as it must be.

In poignant irony, a nurse brought me that week's issue of *People*, happily showing me a three-page spread on the joys of Vermont's Circus Smirkus, featuring photos taken just a couple of weeks before the accident.

★

A month after my release, I drove back to the hospital to have stitches taken out of my arm. The doctor saw me sitting there, my head and trunk still moving in a block, like a robot. "Why still so stiff?" he said. "Let's take more x-rays."

When that was done, he came sliding into the room, waving his arms, white-faced like a ghost, shouting, "Don't move! Don't move, Rob! You broke your neck!"

Turns out it was a fracture of C-2—the Hangman's Bone—the vertebrae that breaks when...well, you get the picture. I can only surmise that the body's intelligence knew how to keep me alive after the accident, by holding me rigid while I bumped around in pickup trucks and got hugs and physical therapy—neck massages! Some compassionate higher power really had been looking out for me.

Before discovering the broken neck—the fracture had somehow avoided detection the first time—I had been sent home in time to make it to the last show of the circus season. I sat very rigid in an aisle seat. After each act, the troupers styled to the audience, then jumped the ring curb to give me a hug. I sat there and sobbed.

Journalist, and trouper parent, Rob Gurwitt wrote: "The first show after the accident was in Montpelier, Vermont. The tent was filled with parents, friends of the circus, and a few others who knew what had happened. We were heart-struck watching the young troupers' devotion. The general public had no idea of tragedy, only that they seemed to be witnessing an especially radiant show."

The effect on the company was profound. Now more than a circus project for youth, it became about growing up. All our hearts were broken open. I changed overnight. I was more vulnerable, more sensitive to emotional expression, more in need of meaningful connection, and I saw the same need in others. The troupers were more emotionally honest and supportive with each other and empathetic with adults. The adults truly respected the kids as colleagues.

From then on, I would get hugs, not polite hugs-at-distance, but hugs-as-embrace, full body squeezes with compassion. Physical affection was more easily accepted and became an integral function of what made Smirkus a "family," as it was so often called by participants.

The bonding between coaches and kids from that early era became lifelong. To this day, the kindness, compassion, and honest affection of Marÿn's joyous spirit lives on in all of us. That sense of experience as magic has become a mandate for the troupers: absorb the magic, make it part of yourself, then go out into the world and spread it around.

Soviet/American Youth Circus

*"The Soviet/American Youth Circus was, even one
year ago, totally unthinkable. But it did happen
here in Yaroslval in the circus building... Without
any tension or rivalry, but instead pure joy and
friendliness, a deep connection happened here."*

— *Yaroslavl News,* Russia, 1990

During my slow return to health after the car accident, I
had time to think. I once again envisioned a dream I had
shared with Marÿn—and Dr. Seuss—of an international youth
circus. I wanted the company to always grow—not in size, but in
artistic standards and innovation. We had won national attention
from the *New York Times,* the *Boston Globe,* and *People.* We were
recognized for our spirit and charm, a reputation based more
on youthful enthusiasm and the magical circus setting than on
circus skills.

After the grief of the accident, my ambitions were rekindled. We
had established Smirkus as more than an educational program: it was
an apprenticeship in the experience of circus as a lifestyle. Now we
could use a boost in skills training. We needed an infusion of circus
discipline and new coaching talent, and I wanted the best.

The Moscow Circus produced the best circus performers in the world at the time. In 1919, Lenin had nationalized the circus as a cultural institution on a par with ballet and opera, calling circus, "The People's Art." With the creation of The Moscow Circus School in 1929, the circus officially became a cultural treasure respected around the world. By 1957, the Centralized Circus Administration—Soyuzgostsirk—governed a huge bureaucracy overseeing training facilities, circus hotels for twelve thousand circus performers, and seventy permanent circus buildings, scattered around the vast expanse of the Soviet Union.

I had seen the Moscow Circus on their US tour and noted in the program listing the Director, a Mr. Sirotkin. In 1989, still a naive idealist, I composed a letter to Mr. Sirotkin, proposing a cultural exchange with joint performances bringing together Soviet and American circus kids.

Project Harmony, based in Waitsfield, Vermont, had been founded in 1985 for the purpose of cultural and educational exchanges between Soviet Union and American high school students. I contacted them and arranged for one of their staff, David K., who was headed over there shortly, to please take my letter and find someone from Soyuzgostsirk. This was still the era before the internet, cell phones, laptops—what else could I do?

Rob Gurwitt later described the effort: "A letter from a tiny kids' circus in an obscure corner of the United States didn't stand a chance...like sticking a message in a bottle, tossing it in the Atlantic Ocean and hoping it got to Moscow's Red Square."

I wrote the letter only two months after the car accident. After sending it through Project Harmony, I forgot about it and continued focusing on healing. What happened next, I still think of in terms of "The Implausible, the Improbable, and the Impossible."

As I sat alone in the old farmhouse in Vermont tending my wounds, Alevtina Anatolievna Youdina, a top official in Soyuzgostsirk, sat in her office in Moscow. Alla was head of a division of the organization that oversaw the design and creation of new acts throughout the vast network of theater and circus in the USSR. Before taking up her role as an important official in the circus bureaucracy, she had an impressive career as a select member, at age sixteen, in the original Moscow Circus on Ice. She performed trapeze, web, dance, and all on skates—as well as earning a degree in technical engineering for rigging and architectural design.

The Moscow Circus on Ice was the first of its kind and stunned the world with its tours. I could not conceive of making a connection with this woman. I did not know she existed.

As Alla tells the story, she was at her friend Yuri's apartment for a birthday dinner party for his wife. The seat next to Alla was empty. Yuri was expecting a new American friend, a David K., who, when he arrived, sat next to her. Their conversation turned to work.

"He asked me what I did. I said circus. He jumped out of his seat... 'What? Circus?! I have a letter for you in my pocket! It's from a circus director in America for a Mr. Sirotkin. Do you know him?'

"I smiled and said, 'Yes, his office is next to mine.' Then I explained the KGB always had a man who traveled with the circus, officially as 'director'— but he really had nothing to do with it. If I had delivered Rob's letter, it would have ended up in the garbage."

Alla decided to take up the initiative herself, as a personal project, and sent a fax inviting me to Moscow to discuss bringing American kids to Moscow. This was in the fall of 1989. It was a marvel of technology at the time that a piece of paper with scribbling on it could be fed into the slot of a machine in Moscow and appear simultaneously in Vermont.

But the fax machine didn't always work: a telephone line was required and a good connection between the US and the USSR was haphazard at best. It often took days of repeated dialing trying to connect. All this was exacerbated by the impending breakup of the USSR, already underway, and the general failure of Soviet communication systems.

That Alla Youdina, a high ranking official in the Soviet circus world, would privately take on my project was "implausible." That my letter had even come to rest in her hands at a dinner party was highly "improbable." What occurred in the next chain of events fits the "impossible" category, on a par with my stepping out of the rain, right into the ring of the circus building in Copenhagen.

Sometimes when you place yourself in improbable circumstances, the unexpected happens, and you find yourself in an adventure. When you are in an impossible situation, things are taken out of your hands completely, and extraordinary events must transpire through the guiding will of some bemused higher power. That's the only way I can think about it. On my own, I felt quite hapless.

The Impossible: when I got Alla's invitation to come in February, I booked a flight to Moscow, unaware that she had meant February

a year later, not a couple of months later. New initiatives took a long time to happen in the Soviet Union, and our communications were usually misread in awkward mistranslations. My mistaken response was to jump while the iron was hot: Let's do this!

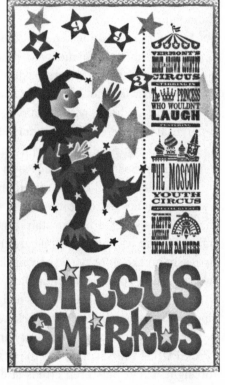

I set out to get a visa, then waited. And waited. As the time for my flight approached, I put in panicked calls to my two US Senators, but they had no luck in Washington. The day of the flight arrived. I was nervous, and still stiff from only a few months of healing after the accident. But I was determined to go forward. I couldn't miss this opportunity to meet someone from the Moscow Circus office.

I had no way of contacting Alla Youdina personally. No phone number or home address. I was expecting David, the Project Harmony guy in Moscow, to meet me at the airport. I'd deal with it then. So, I flew off to Moscow with no visa.

It was February and very cold. I flew from New York to Helsinki, and that's where I first ran into trouble. When I checked in at the gate for the flight to Moscow, the man at the Helsinki desk was appalled that I had no visa.

He told me it was impossible to get into the Soviet Union without a visa. "When you get there," he said, "they're just going to send you back. Or worse."

I shrugged and asked if it was a problem to get on the Finnair plane. He sighed and waved me on. "Either they will send you to Siberia, or I'll see you back here tonight."

On the Finnair flight from Helsinki, I befriended a young Canadian couple going to Moscow with teaching jobs. When we got to the long customs line in Moscow, they looked back, waved sorrowfully, and wished me luck.

"Passport!" said the expressionless guard. I slapped it down. "Visa," he growled, not looking up. I waited. "VISA!" He looked up.

I shook my head, with an apologetic smile. There was a blissful momentary pause of silence when I felt my world was balanced on a ledge and could fall one way, or another. He called over another guard, who repeated the same "Passport! Visa!" charade with me.

A puzzled argument between them ensued. This was beyond their experience. After some heated discussion, two armed soldiers marched me away, up some stairs to the Airport Security Director's office. On the way, we treaded carefully over a row of people sitting listlessly on the floor with their backpacks against the walls. That's where I'll end up shortly, I thought.

The Director of Security was a big man with a barrel chest and a thick neck being choked by a dark necktie. He looked annoyed and bored at the same time. We went through the familiar pantomime: "PASSPORT! VISA!" I pointed to my suitcase on which, with shrewd foresight, I had plastered circus stickers, including one with large Cyrillic letters: TSIRK!

"Tsirk?" he said.

"Da! Da! Da!" I said. "Klown!" I added, pointing to myself. I knew clowns were respected artistes in the USSR.

"Prove it!" he pantomimed.

I picked up a stapler, an ashtray, and a cigar from his desk and juggled. He liked that. I started to hand back his cigar, but made it disappear. The soldiers with rifles liked that. The director sat back and folded his arms. I wrote Project Harmony guy's phone number on a slip of paper and pushed it forward.

He had one of the soldiers dial the number, but there was no answer. (I found out later he was out of town in St. Petersburg!) I began to feel desperate.

The director turned over the slip of paper and wrote a figure—50—and pushed the paper toward me.

"Rubles?" I asked hopefully.

"Doll-ar!" he said firmly, slapping the desk.

I handed over fifty bucks. He stamped a visa and that was that. The soldiers escorted me past the listless folks sitting on the floor... and I was out on the street.

Now what?! Alone in a city of eleven million people, unable to read the signs, unable to speak the language, and utterly exhausted in the dead of a Moscow winter night. Was this how it felt to be a poor, cold, shivering immigrant, lost in the vastness of a foreign metropolis?

My mind raced back to a vision of my ancestry, when my father's father had left Ukraine and stood in New York City, a young man with his suitcase and no English, lost in the swirl of...America!

Years later, I would recreate the young Russian immigrant and his suitcase in the first and only Soviet/American Youth Circus-on-Ice, touring ice arenas in New England, produced by Alla and me. But that night, I stood outside in the snow, paralyzed with indecision. I heard a shout. I turned and saw the Canadian couple waving to me, about to get in a car.

I went over and they took me in for the ride downtown—maybe I could find some cheap hotel? It was already getting late, ten o'clock, and everyone was exhausted from the flights. Their driver dropped the Canadian couple off.

He spoke some English. His name was Yuri. I told him my plight, how my contact never showed up. He said, "Nyet problem. Come to my apartment. It is not far. You need vodka, then we figure out something."

Over vodka I related my efforts trying to find someone from the circus, a lady named Alla Youdina... He interrupted my tale of woe: "Alla? She's my neighbor!" he shouted happily, pouring some more vodka.

Alla tells of that moment: "I was at home that evening when the telephone rang. It was my friend Yuri, the friend in whose apartment I had met David K. from America. Rob's letter had come in December, and it was only February—I hadn't expected him to come for a year!

"So, I went to Yuri's house, right around the corner. He opened the door and Rob appeared. He said, simply, 'Hi, I'm Rob Mermin from Circus Smirkus.' I held out his letter. We stared at each other, and the world seemed to swirl in spirals. What does all this say? It says it was meant to be—it was in the stars."

We walked in the snow to her house and stayed up half the night, drinking vodka with her family, talking, singing, laughing. The next day we wrote a contract of agreement to bring Smirkus to Moscow that spring and then bring Russian circus kids to America for the Smirkus summer tour—the first ever "Soviet/American Youth Circus" joint program.

All this was exhilarating, and improbable, and impossible. Ten days later, on my flight home from Moscow, once again the connecting flight was through Helsinki. The same agent I'd met on the way over was standing at the gate. He did a double take when he saw me. "You're back!" he exclaimed. "I've been wondering what happened to you. You got in?"

"Yes!" I said, enthusiastically. "Siberia was lovely!"

Multicultural Hodgepodge

"Watching them, it is hard to say who gives more to the show: the very professional Russian circus kids, or the young Americans with their enthusiasm and charming desire to give the best of themselves. It is like watching young flowers blossoming— together they are the heart and soul of the future."

—Yuri Nikulen, beloved clown and
director of The Moscow Circus

Barely three months later, after my no-visa adventure, I returned to Moscow in the spring of 1990, this time with visas and a company of a dozen Smirkus teenagers and coaches and chaperones.

Three weeks of rehearsing with Moscow Circus artists ended in joint youth performances in a two-thousand-seat circus building in Yaroslavl by the Volga River, and at The International Youth Performance Festival in Anapa on the Black Sea (with Best Director Awards to Alla and me), and a showcase event for Yuri Nikulen, a Soviet icon, cinema star, clown and director of the famous Moscow Circus on Tsvetnoi Boulevard, in Moscow.

Completing the first cultural exchange, that summer the Russian coaches and kids came to Vermont to tour with Smirkus in the initial joint program between American and Russian circus kids.

That all of this transpired in a single year—first connecting with Alla in February, then going to the Soviet Union during the breakup of the USSR with Smirkus kids that spring, and then touring the Soviet/American Youth Circus from July through September in New England—and all before the internet—seems barely conceivable today.

As Alla would put it: "Those two hoops that we were able to jump through—USA and USSR—came together in history only once like that. Before perestroika, it was ideologically impossible. Then history changed again, and it became commercially impossible. One very small window of history opened up for us, and we jumped in."

Alongside the practical goals of expanding the training methods and worldview of American kids, I wanted to recreate the traditional circus atmosphere under canvas. It was meant to be an education in real-world, multicultural experiences. That goal was reached.

That first international program in 1990 initiated a decade of Smirkus cultural exchanges, bringing to Vermont coaches and circus kids from Russia, Latvia, Ukraine, Mongolia, Kazakhstan, Hungary, Georgia, Moldova, Canada, China, Cuba, Brazil, Indonesia, Israel, Palestine, Ethiopia, Great Britain, New Zealand, states from all around the US, as well as ten First Nation tribes, the Sioux, Yakama, Hunkpapa, Cree, Santee, Dakota, Oglala, Navaho, Azteca, and Cherokee.

The predicaments were constant. In 2000, Smirkus was dubbed "The United Nations of the Youth Circus World" at the International Festival at Wolf Trap Performing Park outside Washington, D.C. In those days, like the United Nations, we were a good example of how multicultural relations are simultaneously fascinating in action, and fraught with cultural misunderstanding, daily negotiations, and diplomatic folly, passion, goodwill, and humor.

For example, in 1994, the Russian coaches, Zina and Vladimir Auvgustov, Genne Totukhov, and director Alla Youdina sat in the Smirkus farmhouse living room, stone faced, avoiding eye contact with the Latvian delegation of a dozen coaches and teenagers. As the Smirkus season ended in late August and the American kids went home, the Latvians and Russians were stuck for another three weeks at the farm when all flights were canceled. We sat glued to CNN, watching the attempted coup in Moscow against Gorbachev, while Latvia struggled for independence from the Soviet Union. World political history was enacted at the Smirkus dinner table.

In 1994, we also invited a delegation of Palestinian and Israeli circus youth to join our show in mid-tour, under the auspices of Alan Slivka's Abraham Fund Initiatives, which fostered coexistence between Israel's Arab and Jewish populations. I was backstage getting ready for the afternoon matinee. The audience was already seated, fifteen minutes before showtime, when someone came running up to me with news: "Rob, you better come quick. The Israeli group has finally arrived, and already there is a fight."

I found two scowling Arab and Israeli boys, held apart from a fistfight. Apparently one of them had picked up the other's juggling ball. I had no patience for this. I asked their coach if she still had the return airline tickets in hand? "Good. The easiest thing to do is get you all on the bus back to the airport. Simple as that. I have a show to do. You work it out yourselves, if you can, while the bus waits. I'll be back in fifteen minutes."

The Smirkus magic did its work—thanks to the young Smirkus troupers, who knew how to handle things by then. It was fabulous to see those same two boys, a couple of days later, one standing on the shoulders of the other, smiling and joyfully tossing clubs to another two-high pyramid in the group juggling act.

On a lighter diplomatic note, you can imagine the surprise and ensuing hilarity during the Smirkus Joke Show in 1993, when the ten teenage performers from First Nation tribes came dancing into the ring in full Native American ceremonial regalia with feathered headdresses—and Groucho Marx glasses.

★

Those who participated in those eventful years still shake their heads in wonder at it all. But little is known of the other side, namely how Alla managed to create all these improbable foreign relations through her vast network of circus contacts.

For while she was signed on to work every summer as Smirkus head coach and new act creator, she was also being courted by Ringling Bros. and Barnum & Bailey owner/producer Kenneth Feld, and Vice President of Talent Tim Holst, to accept the role as Creator of New Acts for both the Blue and Red units of the Big Show every winter.

Kenneth, owner of the biggest show on earth, seemed always puzzled why Alla insisted that her summers would be occupied in Vermont with the smallest show. "What is this Smirkus?" Whenever I encountered Kenneth after that, he would ask, "So Rob, how's business?"

I always replied, "Just fine, Kenneth. How's yours?"

And we both just smiled.

★

Alla pulled some amazing strings in Moscow, in order to fund our cultural exchanges. Smirkus agreed to pay for all expenses on American soil for the Russian group, and Alla independently found funding for the Soviet groups to get here. How she arranged funding while the Soviet Union was breaking apart is evidence of her remarkable ingenuity and impressive scheming. This led to an episode I refer to as Mermin Meets the Mafia in Moscow.

On one winter visit to Moscow to make arrangements for our cultural exchange, I found myself being escorted to a restaurant near the Kremlin by an uncharacteristically pensive and nervous Alla. She had suggested I dress in my best clothes for a luncheon meeting with potential sponsors. I only had jeans and a jacket.

We arrived at a swanky eatery with a nightclub-style dance floor. It was midday, yet I was puzzled to notice that it was empty of customers. The doormen and waiters dressed in black were bustling around us as we were escorted to the dance floor where a long table had been set up with candles, white tablecloth, and platters of expensive food. Seated around the table waiting for us were a dozen men dressed in black suits, black shirts, and white ties.

Alla nervously brought me to the table and sat me down next to the heavyset man at the head, who was adorned with gold rings and a diamond wristwatch. What the hell was going on here? Alla's translation of the ensuing conversation seemed hesitant.

I was still getting to know Alla personally, but I had already seen her in action. She usually commanded a room unintentionally. Her presence was impressive: smart, cultured, competent, highly attractive, charismatic, aristocratic, a singular force. She seemed always in control of a situation. This was different. Later she told me she was as confused and anxious as I was at the time.

The dozen lackeys around the table sat in silence. This was clearly meant to be between Alla, the Boss in Black, and me. The vodka started flowing, and for a nondrinker, I did my best to keep up appearances. While the Russian public had to line up outside stores just to find basics like soap and eggs, the seven-course lunch in the emptied restaurant began. The conversation, as best I could piece together from Alla's nervous translation—which seemed to be hiding most of what the Boss was saying—focused on money and commercial business.

I began sweating. I knocked down the vodka as nonchalantly as I could and sat back in the chair in a vain attempt to look sophisticated.

The Boss in Black slugged down the drinks, imitated at once by his dozen henchmen, while the waiters scurried about and hurriedly refilled the glasses. All eyes were on me to watch how I would keep up. After an interminable meal of seafood, borscht, meats, delicacies, and desserts, all drowned in vodka, we got up to leave.

It was not until Alla and I were ushered into black cars with dark tinted windows, flanked by three other long black cars, that I became really agitated. We silently drove to the outskirts of Moscow into some wooded park, and down a dirt road. By now it was dark. The imagination takes over at times like this.

I imagined we were being taken out to be shot, after our final glorious meal. How would the papers back home report my sudden unexplained demise by the Boss in Black on the dark soil of the Russian Motherland, over some incomprehensible negotiations in the dead of winter? At least my last meal had been impressive.

Through the snow, we entered a wooden building. I was directed to take off my clothes and hang them up on the wooden hooks. It was a sauna building, the famous Russian banya! I joined the men in black, now clothed only in white towels, in a large steam room. There were several visits to the sauna, with intermissions in the ante room—where we were served pickles, caviar, and more vodka, then back to the sauna—followed by dips into the ice-cold water-filled hole in the ground. We duly thrashed each other with birch twigs brought to us by sturdy Russian babushkas.

After this bizarre day with the Russian mafia—still inexplicable to my mind, I just wanted to get out of this alive—we got back into the cars and drove farther into the dark woods. Our black caravan of vehicles stopped in front of a huge building to shine our headlights on some enormous warehouse doors. We entered in silence, and I stood there in amazement.

The massive space was filled with spanking new circus equipment, immaculately piled high to the rafters. All along one wall were shiny steel cages for wild animals. Over there were rows and rows of props for horses and equipment for lions and elephants, and rigging, and huge poles for the tent, with enormous exquisitely designed murals and circus banners and signage, ring curbs and carpets and painted circus wagons.

Finally, it dawned on me: they were trying to sell me a completely brand-new circus. This was Russian-style circus: huge, beautiful, millions of dollars' worth of stuff. They were courting me, believing I was a big rich American circus director, coming to Russia to buy a new circus. Such a deal!

Of course, I must be such a filthy rich American! I could afford to dress casually in jeans, which at that time in Moscow were very expensive and coveted.

Now my dilemma was how to turn them down, without being taken outside and shot for fraudulent impersonation and wasting their vodka. I made a big show of inspecting each piece of equipment, asking for paper to take down a few notes. I nodded appreciatively to whatever they were saying and said I would take this information back to my partners in America. They really thought I was a Kenneth Feld or a Tim Holst, some big shot impresario.

More toasts and backslapping all around. Eventually we made it back to the city, and I collapsed into bed. Alla got her funding for the cultural exchange, which in those days was called a "joint venture." Smirkus got the Russian circus kids, coaches from The Moscow Circus, and a couple of mafia guys as "chaperones" of the exchange. I imagine all that sophisticated circus equipment still sits untouched in the dark Russian woods on the outskirts of Moscow, awaiting the notice of some hotshot impresario wearing jeans. You know—someone just like me.

When Alla brought to Vermont the first Russian circus kids and several Moscow Circus stars to be Smirkus coaches, I experienced a keen moment I had been dreading: the moment these world-class artistes would arrive at our headquarters in Greensboro village and stand in front of our little Smirkus tent, then a meager two-mast affair with a small ring, rickety bleachers and straw spread around the outside of the ring for kids to sit on.

The famous Russian stars stood with their mouths open in front of the tent. I was sure they were mortified, upset at the predicament in which they found themselves. There were exclamations and heated discussion in Russian between them and Alla. Then they rushed inside the tent, leaving me standing outside with her. "Well?" I said tentatively, wondering if we had their return tickets to Moscow available.

"They can't believe it!" Alla said. "It's like the little traveling circuses of Russia a hundred and fifty years ago—they love it! They are so happy! They were never in a tent...they only know the fancy circus buildings and pressures of Soyuzgotsirk bureaucracy to be the best. Here: the smell of straw, the intimacy, the freedom to improvise in a new mood! Unbelievable!"

She went inside to join them, and I stayed a moment outside, almost weeping with relief.

★

The next year, a new Russian delegation was coming over to Vermont after the successful first cultural exchange. Alla was again seeking sponsorship from the Russian side to pay for the venture. This time her sponsor turned out to be a major transport company, dealing with aircraft, ships, and the trucking industries. They were in import/export and saw Smirkus as a possible cover operation— an innocent nonprofit children's charity—for making inroads into American corporate activities.

Little did they know.

So along with the Russian circus kids and coaches, we got a boss from the Russian sponsor and two suspicious looking officials, supposedly from the Soviet circus federation bureaucracy. They turned out to be KGB, of course, the Soviet equivalent to our CIA. Were they here to oversee the activities of Smirkus, posing as a front for illegal import/export business?

So long as they stayed out of the way, and we got our exchange, well, I had no time for politicking. They were in my territory now. In the backwoods of Vermont, speaking no English, they were fish out of water. On with it: I had a show to produce.

One o'clock in the morning, during our rehearsal period. The Russians had been here barely two weeks. I'm asleep, exhausted from a long day. I get a knock on my door. It's the police of Hardwick Village (population 2,750). They want to know what to do with two drunken Russians, who don't speak English and are mumbling about "Seer-kus Shmeer-kus."

I go down to the police station, and there are the KGB guys, handcuffed to a radiator. I smiled. This would be good. Apparently, they had gotten drunk, stolen my car, and had been driving across the cow fields and smashed into a haystack.

I said to the officers, "Okay, you just locked up the Russian KGB. Play along with me. I'll act outraged, and we'll keep them hand-cuffed for a while. Let's give them a show."

I yelled at the cops, pointing back and forth to the worried prisoners, sometimes pleading, then shouting and gesticulating madly, until the officers threatened to take out their pistols. This went on for a while. Finally, we shared some doughnuts, and I motioned to take out my wallet. With my back to the prisoners, I pretended to bribe the officials, who then smiled and uncuffed the Russians.

I nodded to them and said, in Russian, "Let's go. Everything okay," and suddenly I was a bigshot with the KGB.

The upshot of this story, of course, is history. The KGB men returned to Russia, probably told this story of the American penal system, which struck terror into the hearts of the KGB bureaucracy and six months later, the Soviet Union collapsed.

Highlights

"One of New England's most treasured educational
and cultural resources, Circus Smirkus will be
in the annals of American circus history.
With its artistic acts, zany humor, and celebratory
cultural atmosphere, adults enjoy Circus Smirkus
as much as kids do!"

—*Boston Globe,* 1993

The Smirkus big top travels only for a short summer season exclusively throughout New England. It stays just two or three days in each town, so you have to seek it out to catch the show. One of the pleasures I most enjoyed was observing first-time adult attendees exiting a Smirkus performance after a show. Oftentimes this was a grownup, maybe a grandparent, who had been dragged unwillingly to the tent.

"I'm not in the least interested, haven't been to a circus since I was a kid, don't care for them, and especially not an amateur kiddie circus."

Sometimes these jaded grownups would approach me outside the tent after the show. Sometimes I would just overhear conversations. But invariably the reactions were the same: a face transformed with joy and amazement and an exclamation, "I had no idea!" and a new yearly attendee.

It was also gratifying to see the delight on the faces of professional circus directors—from Ringling, Cirque du Soleil, and Big Apple Circus—visiting the show, and who often would later hire Smirkus graduates.

★

Once, during the Smirkus tour, I saw three kids trying to sneak under the tent fifteen minutes before showtime. I came up behind them and said, "Hey! What are you doing?"

They were startled into submission, like kids standing at the principal's office for some schoolboy prank, heads looking at their feet. The apparent leader made up some hollow excuse about not having any money, but I cut him off short.

"Look, you're doing it all wrong," I said. "If you're gonna do something, do it with confidence and style. Here's how you do it." I looked around to see if anyone was watching, then walked them over to the side and held up the tent flap for them.

"One acts as lookout, ten feet away, ready with a signal. Got one?" One kid gave me a low whistle. "That'll do," I said. "You, number two, repeat the signal for the third, who is ready to slip under the tent flap. When he slips under, the lookout checks and, if all is clear, gives the signal to number two, who gets ready to hold the tent flap up for the lookout to quickly slip under, followed last by number two. Meanwhile number one has scouted out some good seats sitting on the straw right up to the ring fence. Okay...ready? Quick! Now!"

And following strategic instructions, in they went.

Rapscallions! They had no idea who I was, until fifteen minutes later they saw me enter the ring in costume with the microphone to welcome the crowd. I winked at their surprised faces. Now they had a story to tell all the rest of their lives. Oh, I enjoyed doing that!

I also had a habit of looking around for an elderly couple. They would stay in their seats during intermission when it was too hot outside, and they couldn't fight the crowds in line at the concession tent. I would send a trouper over with free popcorn and cold lemonades, with a smile and tip of the hat, "Compliments of the House." Troupers loved doing that.

When I saw a family at the ticket booth who had driven two hours to find us, but we were sold out and they were turned away, and the kids had a look of dismay, about to cry—why, I'd just walk them in free, against the disapproving looks of executive management if they saw me. (There goes the founder again, he can't do that!) The money counters had the job of making the company run, and they frown on such stuff. But which is the greater value: the price of a few tickets or a life-time of goodwill?

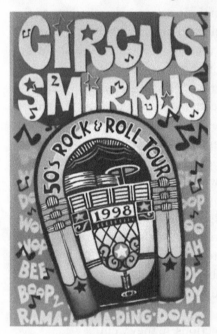

Some of the priceless moments occur after a show, when the young Smirkus troupers mingle with the audience in the ring signing autographs. One can see the parents of young kids watch their child stare, star-struck, at the troupers barely a few years older. You can almost visibly see their young minds spinning, "Someday, I want to do this too, someday...!" and the parents' minds next to them, thinking, "Uh, oh...!"

The fact is, the troupers signing autographs had themselves, not long ago, been those star-struck kids in the audience. It is simply amazing, and poignant, to watch dreams forming in little kids' heads, right in front of you.

★

The show gained a reputation for integrity, youthful spirit, surprising professionalism, charm, and style. Our Vermont shows were periodically visited by well-known personalities, some of whom graciously joined our Honorary Board.

Lottie Brun (1925–2008), sister of the phenomenal juggler Francis Brunn, herself a world-famous legendary artiste, is generally regarded as the fastest female juggler of all time. What a pleasure to have her visit the Smirkus headquarters in the off-season and to see her relaxing in a rocking chair on the porch of the old farmhouse, completely at ease watching the cows amble in the field.

★

Julia Child, *The French Chef,* hosted a Smirkus board meeting in the dining room of her Cambridge, Massachusetts home, where she also filmed her famous television show. Unfortunately, she didn't cook for the board; it was catered!

When she came to visit Smirkus, she was delighted to join us for dinner from our cookhouse. She was served outside on a picnic table dressed up with a tablecloth and small bouquet of wildflowers picked by a few troupers. Our cooks were extremely nervous, but they did well with a chicken couscous dish. Julia, in her sing-song falsetto: "Oh, my! Couscous is SO underrated!"

Over dessert, a Boston cream pie, I unwittingly asked if, being a celebrity, she had ever been pied in the face? She glanced around quickly and then looked directly at me and said quite sternly, "Never—and if anyone ever tried it, I would chase him down and kick him in the nuts!" Startled, I shut up and watched her calmly finish her piece of pie. What a lady!

★

Norman Lear, radical Hollywood TV creator/producer/writer of *All in the Family,* and other hugely influential sitcoms in the 1960s and 70s, came to the Smirkus big top in southern Vermont in 1999 to celebrate his seventy-eighth birthday with his family and close friend, actor/comedian Dom DeLuise. The circus that year presented The Adventures of Robin Hood.

There was a moment in the show when, as Robin Hood, I would rob from some "rich" spectator to give to the poor, calling on a member of the audience to "Stand, and show your purse!" I boldly pointed to Dom DeLuise. He begrudgingly rose to his feet, felt in his pockets, pulled out his wallet and said, plaintively, "Do you take plastic?"

At the end of the show, I introduced our special guests to the audience and Norman Lear shocked us all by bending down and doing a forward roll and standing back up with arms out in a

Ta-Daaa! pose, to great audience applause. Forever young and active, surrounded by his extended family and friends, Mr. Lear said, "Laughter extends life."

Ed Koren, the prolific cartoonist for the *New Yorker,* Vermont neighbor and board member, designed a wonderful Smirkus tee-shirt with his recognizable fuzzy creature drawings. Playwright David Mamet would show up with his wife, actress Rebecca Pidgeon, who always sported a friendly smile of anticipation, in contrast to her husband's habitual dour demeanor.

Michael J. Fox came to shows in Woodstock, Vermont, and again on Martha's Vineyard with his young family, his kids going home with Smirkus tee-shirts. Two of our young troupers, Chris Grabher and Dan Brown, who idolized Michael, later became actors and stuntmen in Los Angeles. At the Hollywood Thirtieth Anniversary celebration of the *Back to the Future* films, Chris and Dan were thrilled to be chosen to recreate the famous clocktower-and-lightning scene, with Chris playing the Michael J. Fox character Marty, and Dan playing Doc.

A visit to the show in Maine by former Republican President George H. Bush and First Lady Barbara—with a small secret service detail that reminded me vividly of the Greek bodyguards in Benneweis—was balanced by those of Vermont's Democratic US Senators Patrick Leahy and Bernie Sanders and Independent Jim Jeffords, all of whose support, during the early years of the Smirkus cultural exchanges, were of invaluable assistance in procuring visas and other necessary documents, whenever we ran into the inevitable international bureaucratic obstacles.

★

In other Vermont connections, I had a humorous discussion with Ben Cohen, cofounder of Ben & Jerry's Ice Cream. I created the Smirkus nonprofit organization on a circular "everyone benefits" business model. The company negotiates a fee with a local nonprofit youth organization in each town on the tour—schools, children's museums, youth services, etc.—who then use the circus as a fund-raiser for their organization through ticket sales and program ads, while in turn helping to promote the circus.

In Ben's Vermont office, I proposed what I figured was a win-win-win idea for social-minded businesses like Ben & Jerry's and Smirkus. "Ben," I said, "both our organizations are renowned as 'Homegrown' Vermont companies, am I right?"

"That's right," said Ben, sitting back with his boyish grin.

"Both our companies serve the public with our own unique brands of joy and fun."

"That we do..."

"Your Ben & Jerry's Foundation donates funds to local charities and nonprofits in Vermont and beyond. Smirkus helps dozens of local nonprofits raise money and aware-ness of their programs. If your Foundation sponsored the whole Smirkus tour through generous funding, in one fell 'scoop,' you would reach all our local sponsors, through us. Everyone wins: Ben & Jerry's fulfills its philanthropic mission, Smirkus gets essential financial support, local nonprofits raise needed funds, and there is goodwill and good PR all around!"

Ben's eyes lit up. "I like it!" he said. "Ben & Jerry's Ice Cream Circus!"

"Uh, no..." I said. "Ben & Jerry's presents Circus Smirkus..."

"RIGHT! I can just see it: Ben & Jerry's Ice Cream Circus!

"Um, no, Ben..." And so it went.

No true organizational partnership developed, but Ben did donate free tubs of ice cream for our use seasonally, as well as the Ben & Jerry's touring bus for the troupers one season. As Cirque du Soleil became ever more ubiquitous, I did propose, unsuccessfully, a new Ben & Jerry's flavor.

I thought it was a natural: "Smirque du Sorbet!"

Many actors and writers with Vermont connections came to the Smirkus tent, including Luiz Guzman and Grace Paley. Peter and Elka Schumann, founders of the Bread & Puppet Theater, were long established in Glover, Vermont, just twenty minutes away from Smirkus headquarters in Greensboro. Bread & Puppet became world-famous for their politically radical themes, featuring forty-foot-high puppet figures. Their appearances at protest rallies and demonstrations have become legendary.

When I first moved to Greensboro, I had dinner with Peter and Elka in their cabin. I mentioned my idea to create a small traveling tent circus in the traditional European format and told them stories of my follies with the Hoffman show in Wales. That tickled Peter's mischievous sense of humor. His eyes lit up as he fondly recalled the itinerant circuses of his childhood in Germany. Peter listened to my dreams of a future tent circus in Vermont and with grinning encouragement said, "This is good! We do the Dark side and you do the Light side—we'll have everything covered!"

The 1999 tour capped the first Smirkus decade. It was a milestone season in the history of the company, consolidating our international reputation and bringing together all the principles of what made the company singular. It was a showcase for my original intentions to recreate the traditional one-ring tent circus, make scripted theatrical productions, include animal partners in the ring, invite circus legends to tour with us, compose original music, and engage Smirkus alumni in the creation and production.

In the "Story Circus" productions, I had played a pirate captain, an astronaut, a silent film director, rock 'n roll star, and in 1999, the outlaw of Sherwood Forest. The Robin Hood tour included many highlights.

Circus legend Alberto Zoppe joined us with daughter Tosca—seventh-generation member of the Zoppe Family Circus, established in 1842— and her horses. In just three weeks of rehearsal, Tosca had the Smirkus troupe forming three-high pyramids atop three trotting Percherons.

Tosca writes: "We absolutely loved coaching and performing at Smirkus! It teaches the fundamentals of what circus really is—the charm and beauty and passion you need to be a circus artist. You're not just learning a circus skill but learning to be a performer from the heart."

Alberto Zoppe—at age seventy-seven, still agile with comedic physicality and timing—brought down the house with his famous comedy horseback riding act. In 1948, Alberto was visited by his friend the actor Orson Wells, along with John Ringling North of Ringling Bros. and Barnum & Bailey Circus, and producer/director Cecil B. DeMille, who was soon to begin filming his then-new Hollywood epic movie, *The Greatest Show on Earth*.

Each of these gentlemen, relates his wife Sandra Zoppe, tried to convince Alberto to come to America, not only to be featured in Mr. DeMille's movie, but to also be "a center-ring star with Ringling Bros. and Barnum & Bailey." Not wanting to leave his Italian family circus behind without a star for their show, Alberto decided that he would need a grand attraction to take his place. Since there were no elephants left in Italy after WWII, he negotiated a deal with Mr. North to send one to his circus in Italy...and so Circus Zoppe got its first elephant!

The Robin Hood Tour also featured our first scripted show with dialogue; an original score by Vermont musicians under the direction of Pete Sutherland and the Merrie Greenwood Band; a sold-out benefit show performed by Marcel Marceau in the ring alongside troupers; and Hollywood producer Norman Lear gracing our big top.

The Disney Channel filmed the entire summer tour for a documentary TV series, *Totally Circus* and Ringling Vice President Tim Holst was seen happily mowing the front lawn at Smirkus headquarters.

Tim was at first frantic when he learned there was no cell phone service in Greensboro. But he soon relaxed, possibly for the first time ever, truly away from the stress of managing The Greatest Show On Earth. He was, said Alla, actually envious of Smirkus.

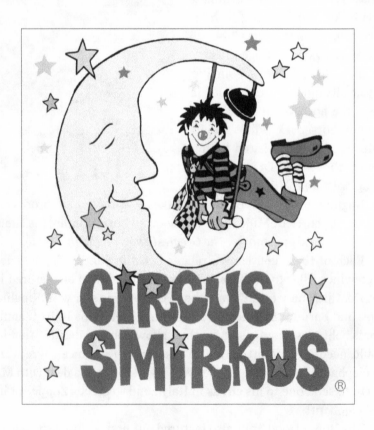

Happily Ever Laughter

"Smirkus has provided a great training ground;
I sent two of my kids there. And now I'm pleased
to have several Smirkus troupers as members of
'The Greatest Show On Earth.'"

—Tim Holst, VP of Ringling Bros. and
Barnum & Bailey Circus

I had a brief stint in 1995 as co-director of Ringling's Clown College. My actual title was Dean of Clown College, which enabled me to call my mom and declare, "Mom, rejoice! Your wayward son is the dean of a college!"

If I was to teach comedy to Ringling clowns, I wanted to know how it felt to run around an arena with an audience of eighteen thousand people, doing American-style group slapstick. So, I joined the Ringling Clown Alley for a couple of weeks and lived on the Ringling train.

Veteran clown Greg DeSanto was happy to welcome the new dean: he promptly threw me into their group routines in the show, without rehearsal. This included putting me at the back of the classic clown car gag, where eighteen clowns are stuffed like sardines into the shell of a little car.

Ringling Clown Alley was composed of mostly very young graduates, fresh out of Clown College, and was a veritable fraternity of practical jokers. Crammed into the bottom of the clown car—first one backstage and last one out in the ring—under eighteen smelly clowns, I flashed back to the Hoffman gang and Snorty George with the rotten fish under his caravan.

★

The Ringling experience rounded out my clowning education. But I was sure glad to get back to the intimacy of the Smirkus ring! In the early years of Smirkus, my goal had been to make sure there was a variety of clowning styles in our shows: classic European talking clown gags, partner and trio routines, knockabout group slapstick, male and female clowns, audience participation gags, parodies, and solo moments of gentle humor.

The comedy is strategically placed in a Smirkus show. There is an intentional pacing, which allows for a Quiet Moment of clowning near the end of the show before a dynamic whole-company finale. When I visited youth circus programs—which were beginning to pop up around the country—it became clear that good skills were being taught, but clown coaching was deficient. Clowning was at the heart of our Smirkus programming and set us apart from other programs. Smirkus clown graduates were gaining a reputation, winning awards at international circus festivals, and signing contracts with top companies around the world.

There were "Laws of Smirkus Clown Culture" serving as guidelines for our style. This document reads, in part:

> A circus clown in the ring does not think he or she is funny. The Smirkus clown doesn't find their situation humorous, though their very existence revolves around others laughing at how the situation is handled. The clown has a childlike curiosity about how the world works, together with a child's self-assured sense of how to do things—erroneously, of course. The Smirkus clown does not make others look funny on purpose; never embarrass an audience member. The clowns seem anarchic by nature, but really they just operate in a universe whose laws differ from ours. It is imperative that the Smirkus clown behaves without mockery, intentional malice, sarcasm, or cynicism, but instead with fullness of heart.

★

I directed the shows and performed in the ring with the Smirkus troupers for the first fifteen years of the company, 1987 to 2002. I had fun each year, designing new clown routines for myself in the show, to bring some gentle humor to balance the high energy of the young performers. Here are a few examples of my Robbo clown bits.

★

My source for the magic of Papillon, the Trained Butterfly Act, was Finn Jon, who inspired me back in the Benneweis days, with his innovative talent for animating objects. A butterfly landing on our arm in real life puts us into a kind of spontaneous spell, a Momentary Pause of Wonder, compelling us to hold our breath and step out of ordinary time. In my act, I get an audience volunteer to assist in the dance of a beautiful butterfly with pastel wings. She flutters across a tiny tightrope, up and around my arms, through a mini-hoop, and onto a flower in a small vase. Often after a show, a little kid would ask me how to train a butterfly. My response: "Well, first you need to find a very intelligent caterpillar."

★

Early in my career, I found a master of bubble science, a man named Eiffel Plasterer, who showed me amazing things with soap bubbles. In the circus ring, my Bubble Magic tricks were always cause for awe and delight. Huge, body-encasing bubbles; bubbles-inside-bubbles; smoke bubbles; carousel-revolving bubs—all added lyrical wonderment to a show.

I learned that as a performer, whenever I would play with an ordinary thing—a feather, a soap bubble—the way a child would, the ordinary becomes magical and my performance would connect instantly with kids and resonate with adults. Kids are in awe of the bubble performers, while grownups watch with childlike delight, having lived all their lives unaware that soap bubbles could do all these things.

★

The Feather Act was inspired by an event in my college years. I was visiting the home of one of my professors. His five-year-old child insisted on play-acting the whole story of Peter Pan. We sat on the couch and watched as he played all the parts, when suddenly through the open window, a fluffy, silky white, single milkweed seed floated into the room.

"Tinkerbell!" cried the delighted boy. With renewed purpose, he kept the little milkweed fairy flying above his head, talking to her, gesturing, gently blowing, totally absorbed. Time slowed down and hovered. He totally forgot us sitting mesmerized on the couch. In his playing, he was oblivious to the transfixed eyes of us grownups sneaking a forbidden glimpse into Neverland.

In the circus ring, Robbo plays a solo ballad on trumpet with the orchestra, and a feather floats out of the horn. As the clown continues to play, a child from the audience keeps the feather in the air by blowing it gently all around the ring, creating an improvised ballet between child, feather, and clown—as the audience watches, enchanted.

★

The Musical Chairs Act always got the loudest, longest laughter and was different each show. Robbo the clown is recruited by the teenage ringmaster to set up four chairs for audience members to play a game everyone knows. The winner, says the ringmaster with a wink toward the audience, will get a pie. He mimes getting a pie in the face.

Appalled, Robbo sets up the folding chairs and decides to play in the game with the volunteer kids. He cheats at every round of the game, hoping to avert the sight of a poor kid getting pied. Finally, it comes down to one kid against Robbo for the last chair.

Robbo pushes the kid out of the way. The kid rushes for the chair. Robbo carries him away by the seat of his pants to the other side of the ring. They both dash for the chair. The audience howls with laughter as the kid and the clown wrestle for the chair, falling, grabbing, crawling on the ground. This tussle goes on for several hilarious minutes. Kids in the audience scream with delight, encouraging the volunteer. Adults laugh with incredulity at what the well-meaning clown gets away with doing.

What fun we had doing that act! The two wrestlers ended up in a tie—and the ringmaster always ended up with the pie in his face.

★

The Rola Bola Act begins with Robbo assisting a young trouper in standing atop three stacked cylinders—difficult enough as it is—when Robbo inadvertently gets his hat stuck high up the safety wire. The only way he can retrieve it is to stack five metal cylinders on top of two milk crates and climb up the precarious seven-high rolling pyramid, behind the ringmaster's back.

I practiced this skill alone all winter in the cold barn at Smirkus headquarters. After my broken neck, I was determined to regain and hone my balance skills. When standing on a tightwire, or rolling cylinders, your focus must be brought down to be centered in the feet. Standing on one rola bola cylinder, you find the center of balance through subtle movements of toe and heel.

The addition of each new cylinder adds progressive difficulties, until cylinders roll in opposite directions, creating the problem of finding balance atop moving plumb lines in different dimensions. Circus uses the laws of physics to seem to defy those same laws.

If you stop and stand still on the rola bolas, you will fall, and the tumble is immediate. It becomes a matter of constant adjustments to realign. And that is the wonderful paradox: to find the center of balance, you must constantly leave it. Perfection in stillness is not attainable here: there is only moving meditation, a concentration in action and reaction, a constant striving for re-alignment.

This is an example of circus as metaphor. Physical skill represents emotional balance in life; our moral center is maintained only with effort. A fall is always imminent. Circus skills teach us to reach goals by overcoming mental and physical obstacles on the way to accomplishment. With a philosophical shift in perspective, every circus skill—flying, tumbling, balance, flexibility, juggling—becomes a metaphor for all the great personal explorations in life.

★

When I look back at all the fun I had in the Smirkus ring, I think of that little baby clown in the home movie, climbing the backyard picnic table and trying to roll the ball down the ladder. The little fellow was undaunted by that task alright, and just as persistent in his goal to start his own circus when he grew up.

It broke my heart that my dad and my sister Sheila did not live to see the founding of Smirkus. Illness took them both too early. I'm sure they would have eagerly gotten involved in the circus operation. My mother, Dorothy—intelligent, stoic, non-demonstrative—lived alone in Connecticut, a private person, content outside the family spotlight. Since her comment, "Circus, shmirkus! Go get a real job!" I had known it would take her some time to accept my path in life.

At the last show of the very first Smirkus season, she sat unobtrusively in the center bleachers with other members of the Mermin clan. When I took the microphone at the finale to thank the audience for coming, I announced there was a special guest in the house: "My mother!" The spotlight went to her and caught her by surprise. As the audience applauded politely, she sat there, mortified. I grinned happily.

The second year, mother came to the show and inconspicuously took her seat. At the end, I once again announced a special guest: "My mother!" She sat there quietly accepting the enthusiastic applause, gently nodding her head a few times, ill at ease with the whole thing.

The third year, I told the troupe to be ready to run out to where she sat, throwing confetti, surrounding her with hugs as the band played rousing music. But she got the jump on us! When I announced her, she promptly stood up, smiled broadly, and waved to the audience all around like a seasoned celebrity!

That's when I knew she'd finally accepted her son was in the circus business. In the following decade of cultural exchanges, in her quiet, competent way, she became the Smirkus matriarch. Dottie, Circus Mom, hosted groups of foreign kids and coaches in her tiny house in Connecticut, as a stopover on their way from the New York airport up to Smirkus headquarters in Vermont. She astonished me.

It made all the hardships getting to that point worthwhile to see her with guests who didn't speak English. She graciously received smiles from foreign professional coaches from around the world, and hugs from talented circus kids, who still remember "Mama" Mermin's banana pancakes and blueberry blintzes on their first morning in America.

Mime & Circus:
A Legacy

"Like you, dear friend, I live to enlighten dreams.
It is our common task to bring light to the art we love,
the silent language of the soul. I remain with all my
heart your friend in the battlefield of life,
your faithful Marcel Marceau."

—letter from Marceau to Mermin

Mime was my first love, before I ran off to join the circus. The art of mime remained popular in the 1980s, but it was hard for anyone to find places to learn it. I wanted to pass on my passion for the art of silence to those seeking a deeper knowledge of Marceau's legacy. For me, it was not so much the aspect of pantomime technique, but the silent communication that most influenced my philosophy of performance.

As Marceau often said: "Mime is the identification with the spirit and essence of all things in nature, and the portrayal of thoughts, emotions, and experiences of humanity through silent physical expression." Technique was important, but once acquired, it was secondary to what you expressed through the humanity of who you were.

Mime taught me how to move through the world with metaphor and grace. Mime taught techniques of physical articulation, projection of thought, a rhetoric of gesture and theatrical principles of silent resonance with an invisible world. Circus trained the body with athletic skills. Circus had shown me how to play with humor, having fun, in a very real world.

The legacy of Marcel Marceau—mime, artist, painter, teacher, mentor, and humanitarian—is an integral part of world cultural history. Marceau loved the circus, but he had never performed in a circus ring. In 1999, he agreed to perform a benefit show under the Circus Smirkus big top in Middlebury, Vermont. The Smirkus troupe would perform the first half, and Marceau would do solo numbers for the second half of the show. We had rented the largest RV trailer we could find for his dressing room.

His unease was palpable as I ushered him into the trailer. When showtime neared he was clearly nervous from all the bustle and noise of normal circus backyard preparations. Edgy, he paced behind the tent. I suggested he perform his "Tightrope Walker" act.

He was appalled: "Non!" he cried. "How can my invisible tight-rope walker compete with the real thing!"

Earlier in the day I had watched the maestro practice in the ring. He was already anxious about the soft ring carpet and the technical limitations of the tent. I had warned his technical director not to push the lights to their brightest level, as Marceau preferred, because it would blow out our system.

As the show began, the sold-out crowd was electric, the tent buzzing with anticipation. When Marceau appeared, the applause was thunderous. As he began his first number, I glanced nervously at the lights, which seemed to be turned up way too high. Sure enough, barely thirty seconds later the lights blew, and the tent plunged into silent blackness.

My heart stopped. This was an unspeakable disaster. That was it, I thought, no more—my career was over. Then I heard impressive cursing in French, and I ran out to escort the maestro backstage and bumped into him in the blackness. The crowd was silent.

After what seemed like years of backstage panic, really, maybe a minute, the lights miraculously came back on. Marceau came out to begin all over. It took all his virtuosity to overcome the situation before he relaxed into what was for him the awkwardness of the circus ring. It was a revelation to see him carefully adjust his performance to accommodate a full audience in the round. I realized then I had not taken a breath in ages. I exhaled slowly...

Sometimes calamity is the prelude to an experience of profound grace. A day that had begun fraught with anxiety ended in transcendent triumph. By the finale Marceau was beaming in a way I had never seen. The audience rose as one in standing ovation.

I was brought to tears at what followed. Marceau raised his finger to quiet the cheering audience, and he began to speak in his soft, wispy voice. The astonished crowd hushed. Never before, in all his fifty-year career had he spoken, in costume, in front of an audience.

Then, clearly deeply moved, he called all the young troupers to sit in the ring all around him and brought the coaches and me and Alla into the ring to stand with him. He spoke for fifteen minutes about the power of art for bringing people together, about his love of the art of mime, his emotions of the day, his pride in me—his "former student and now friend and colleague"—and art's power for bridging generations.

He said, "Circus is loved in the whole world. Like music, it explains nothing. Rather, it touches your heart, by the risks circus people take. Not only through physical movements, but by the poetry they give with their soul.

"Circus is both an entertainment and a profound human experience. People will understand the spirit of what you are doing in Circus Smirkus. The children of Smirkus will come to know that learning the mysteries of our being does not come from any specific nationality, religion, or technique, but comes from knowing the essence of what is humanity on this earth—what is love, what is giving to people the best of your life.

"The circus, and Smirkus in particular, is the essence of all children, from all backgrounds and cultures, united in one circus ring of spirit, struggling peacefully and artistically for a better world, while forever making us laugh and cry, with the silent language of the heart."

★

There was not a dry eye in the house. People saw three generations of mentors in the ring: Marceau and me; my former students, who were now Smirkus coaches; and their young trouper proteges, all standing together in a spirit of joy.

The culmination of my training with Marceau and my apprentice years in circus with Hoffman, Benneweis, and Kossmayer reached a peak with this event in 1999. I had done my best to pull it all together: mime, theater, circus, animals, clowns, kids, traditions. Future Smirkus directors, younger and contemporary, would not have the same background in circus traditions, nor a special focus on animal acts, or mime technique, or international relationships.

That's okay. New generations of Smirkus artistic directors— Jeff Jenkins, Jesse Dryden, and Troy Wunderle—have lent their unique talents and creative imaginations to Smirkus over the years. Interestingly, like me, they are former clowns.

I had fulfilled another long-held personal intention: having created a company that would last past my own term and, despite inevitable modern influences, pass on its legacy, a style of playfulness, kindness, and generosity of spirit that Smirkus still encompasses within its simple circle of sawdust.

After writing these many stories of life in circus, it feels like the last show of a long, long season. And so, I give a little wave of the hand, and say thanks for listening.

See you down the road!

Acknowledgments

The material in this book covers a period over six decades. To have reached this point of publication, the support I received from family and friends is enormous. I thank the staff at Rootstock Publishing: Samantha Kolber, owner, and Rickey Gard Diamond, editor, for patience in leading me through the book production process.

Kudos to Mason Singer and Laughing Bear Associates for book design, and Karen E. Gersch for delightful illustrations. I also am thankful to Dominique Jando for sharp observation and witty consultation on circus history.

I tip my oversize top hat to all the artists and companions—most of them no longer with us—on my early circus adventures with the Hoffman, Benneweis, and Scott circus companies, including the Mack family, the Kossmayer family, Bronett family, Peter Harrison, Antonio, Claus Jespersen, John Benesh, Niels Hovgaard, and my mentor Marcel Marceau. They are strong influences on my development as an artist, performer, producer, and director.

I raise my glass to those grand friends who helped shape the tone, mood, and spirit of early Smirkus, with a special nod to Stewart Lippe, Ozzie Henchel, Donny Osman, Karen E. Gersch, Jeff Jenkins, Troy Wunderle, and Alla Youdina.

Finally, I honor the hundreds of young people who stepped out of the bounds of conventional life to give themselves fully to the Smirkus vision, sharing their talents, idealism, energy, and laughter. They have made their mark, leaving a part of their hearts with everyone they encounter in the circus world of mud, myth, mirth, mayhem...and magic.

—RM

2024

Links and Bibliography

Internet sources

www.RobMermin.com
www.circopedia.org
https://circushistory.org/
www.Smirkus.org
https://www.youtube.com/@robmermin1339

Bibliography

Conklin, George. *The Ways of the Circus*. New York and London: Harper & Brothers, 1921

Coup, W. C. *Sawdust & Spangles, Stories & Secrets of the Circus*. Chicago: Herbert Stone and Co., 1901.

Cotes, Peter, and Rupert Croft-Cooke. *Circus, a World History*. New York: Macmillan Publishing, 1976

Croft-Cooke, Rupert. *The Circus Has No Home*. London: The Falcon Press, 1941.

Culhane, John. *The American Circus*. New York: Henry Holt & Co. 1990

Davis, Janet M. *The Circus Age, Culture & Society Under the American Big Top*. Chapel Hill: University of North Carolina Press, 2002.

Eipper, Paul. *Circus: Men, Beasts, and Joys of the Road*. New York: The Viking Press, 1931

Frost, Thomas. *Circus Life and Circus Celebrities*. London: Chatto and Windus, 1881.

Hoh, LaVahn G., and William H. Rough. *Step Right Up: The Adventure of Circus in America*. Virginia: Betterway Publications, 1990

Jamieson, David, and Sandy Davidson. *The Love of Circus*. London: Octopus Books Limited, 1980

Jando, Dominque, and Linda Grandfield. *The CIRCUS: 1870-1950*. Hong Kong; TASCHEN, 2008.

Lax, Robert. *Circus Days & Nights*. Woodstock, NY: The Overlook Press, 2000.

Madsen, Kurt Moller. *Markedsgogl og Cirkuslojer.* Copenhagen: Lademann Forlagsaktieselskab, 1970.

Mermin, Rob, and Rob Gurwitt. *Circus Smirkus, 25 Years of Running Home to the Circus.* Vermont: The Circus Barn, Inc., 2012

Mermin, Rob, *Circus Smirkus, A True Story of High Adventure & Low Comedy.* Vermont: The Circus Barn, Inc., 1997

Reynolds, Butch. *Broken Hearted Clown.* London: Arco Publications Limited, 1954.

Sanger, Lord George. *Seventy Years a Showman.* London: The Temple Press, 1910

Smith, Lady Eleanor. *British Circus Life.* London: George G. Harrap & Co. 1948.

Towsen, John H. *Clowns.* New York: Hawthorn Books, Inc.1976.

Credits

Illustrations throughout are by Karen E. Gersch (artbykarenegersch.com) unless otherwise credited.

The author has done his best to credit all the photographs. Unless noted below, the photographers are unknown.

p. 60 top and bottom left: Ellika Linden

p. 61 top: Benneweis publicity photo. Caroli family: AGIP - Rue des Archive /Granger, NYC

p. 65: photo of Marcel Marceau by Jean Lattès

p. 160-61: Joe Jackson, Jr. publicity photo. Kossmayer photos: Allan Karlsson,

courtesy Sjouke Dykstra and the Kossmayer family

p. 198 bottom right: Bill Thompson

p. 246 perch poles: Kate Russell

p. 247 bottom right: "Flying High" by Eric Workman

p. 248 top: Smirkus in Red Square by Jym Wilson

p. 249: Marceau photos courtesy of Kate Russell

p. 265: Illustration by Ed Koren, used with permission

p. 309: Self-portrait sketch by Marceau

p. 315: Melissa Mermin

About Rob Mermin

Rob ran off to the circus in 1969. He clowned with European circuses for a decade, including England's Circus Hoffman, Sweden's Cirkus Scott, Denmark's Circus Benneweis in the famous Circus Building by the Tivoli, the Hungarian Magyar State Cirkusz, and circus buildings throughout the former Soviet Union. He trained with mime masters Marcel Marceau and Etienne Decroux, and received an honors degree in Drama and Literature from Lake Forest College.

In 1987, Rob founded the award-winning international company Circus Smirkus, America's premier touring youth circus. Smirkus has initiated cultural exchanges with thirty-two countries, earning the title "The United Nations of the Youth Circus World."

Rob is former dean of Clown College for Ringling Bros.; president of Blackfriars Summer Youth Theater in Connecticut; artist-in-residence for the Vermont Arts Council; lecturer for the Vermont Humanities; and founder of the Parkinson's Pantomime Project, helping people with movement disorders manage symptoms through mime, magic, and circus techniques.

Rob's awards include Copenhagen's Gold Clown; Russia's Best Director Prize at the Black Sea Festival of Creativity; It Takes a Village Award; the Vermont Arts Council Award of Merit; and the 2008 Governor's Award for Excellence in the Arts. He has written two previous books on Circus Smirkus.

More Nonfiction from Rootstock Publishing:

A Judge's Odyssey by Dean B. Pineles

A Lawyer's Life to Live by Kimberly B. Cheney

A Peek Under the Hood: Heroin, Hope & Operation Tune-Up by Michael Pervarnik

All Who Believed: A Memoir of Life with the Twelve Tribes by Tamara Mathieu

Alzheimer's Canyon: One Couple's Reflections on Living with Dementia by Jane Dwinell & Sky Yardley

Attic of Dreams: A Memoir by Marilyn Webb Neagley

Catalysts for Change ed. by Doug Wilhelm

China in Another Time by Claire Malcolm Lintilhac

Collecting Courage: Anti-Black Racism in the Charitable Sector eds. Nneka Allen, Camila Vital Nunes Pereira, & Nicole Salmon

Cracked: My Life After a Skull Fracture by Jim Barry

I Could Hardly Keep From Laughing by Don Hooper & Bill Mares

It Was Her New York by C.O. Moed

Nobody Hitchhikes Anymore by Ed Griffin-Nolan

Notes from the Porch: Tiny True Stories to Make You Feel Better about the World by Thomas Christopher Greene

Pauli Murray's Revolutionary Life by Simki Kuznick

Preaching Happiness by Ginny Sassaman

Red Scare in the Green Mountains by Rick Winston

Save Me a Seat! A Life with Movies by Rick Winston

Snapshots of a Life: Essays by Ken Libertoff

Striding Rough Ice: Coaching College Hockey and Growing Up In the Game by Gary Wright

Tales of Bialystok: A Jewish Journey from Czarist Russia by Charles Zachariah Goldberg

The Atomic Bomb on My Back by Taniguchi Sumiteru

The Language of Liberty by Edwin C. Hagenstein

The Last Garden by Liza Ketchum

The Morse Code: Legacy of a Vermont Sportswriter by Brendan Buckley

Uncertain Fruit: A Memoir of Infertility, Loss, and Love by Rebecca & Sallyann Majoya

Walking Home: Trail Stories by Celia Ryker

You Have a Hammer: Building Grant Proposals for Social Change by Barbara Floersch

Learn about our Fiction, Poetry, and Children's titles at rootstockpublishing.com.

Printed in the USA
CPSIA information can be obtained
at www.ICGtesting.com
LVHW091511040624
782258LV00009B/120